# MOROCCO

The first edition of *Morocco* was published one year before the mass protests of the Arab Spring rocked the Moroccan state. Post-Arab Spring, the country has a new constitution and government, but the state remains uncompromising on any true reform of the monarchy's claims to power.

This new edition provides an introductory overview of the history, contemporary politics, economy, and international relations in Morocco and offers an examination of the challenges to tradition and modernity in the post-colonial state. It has been revised and updated to include analysis of the country's evolving politics in the years following the Arab Spring, and the consequences this has had for the country's traditional monarchy. It pays particular attention to the new constitution, the policies of the new Islamist-led government, and it includes an analysis of Morocco's foreign policy in the post-Arab Spring regional context.

Easily accessible to non-specialists, practitioners, and upper-level undergraduate students, the book will be essential reading for those working in the fields of North African studies, International Relations and Middle East studies.

**James N. Sater** is Associate Professor of Political Science at the International Studies Department of the American University of Sharjah in the United Arab Emirates. He spent more than four years in Morocco, where he worked and taught at Al Akhawayn University in Ifrane. He is the author of *Civil Society and Political Change in Morocco* (Routledge, 2007), and his research focuses on political transformation, elections, citizenship and migration.

# THE CONTEMPORARY MIDDLE EAST
Edited by Professor Anoushiravan Ehteshami
Institute for Middle Eastern and Islamic Studies, University of Durham

For well over a century now the Middle East and North Africa countries have formed a central plank of the international system. *The Contemporary Middle East Series* provides the first systematic attempt at studying the key actors of this dynamic, complex, and strategically important region. Using an innovative common format – which in each case study provides an easily-digestible analysis of the origins of the state, its contemporary politics, economics and international relations – prominent Middle East experts have been brought together to write definitive studies of the MENA region's key countries.

### Books in the series

**Jordan: A Hashemite legacy**
*Beverley Milton-Edwards and Peter Hinchcliffe*

**Syria: Revolution from above**
*Raymond Hinnebusch*

**Israel: Challenges to identity, democracy and the state**
*Clive Jones and Emma C. Murphy*

**Turkey: Challenges of continuity and change**
*Meliha Benli Altunışık and Özlem Tür Kavli*

**Sudan**
*Abdel Salam Sidahmed and Alsir Sidahmed*

**Saudi Arabia**
*Tim Niblock*

**Jordan: A Hashemite legacy 2nd Edition**
*Beverley Milton-Edwards and Peter Hinchcliffe*

**Morocco: Challenges to Tradition and Modernity**
*James N. Sater*

**Tunisia: Stability and Reform in the Modern Maghreb**
*Christopher Alexander*

**Libya: Continuity and Change**
*Ronald Bruce St John*

**Lebanon: The Politics of a Penetrated Society**
*Tom Najem*

**Libya: Continuity and Change 2nd Edition**
*Ronald Bruce St John*

**Morocco: Challenges to tradition and modernity 2nd Edition**
*James N. Sater*

**Tunisia: From stability to revolution in the Maghreb 2nd Edition**
*Christopher Alexander*

# MOROCCO

## Challenges to tradition and modernity

Second edition

*James N. Sater*

LONDON AND NEW YORK

Second edition published 2016
by Routledge
2 Park Square, Milton Park, Abingdon, Oxon OX14 4RN

and by Routledge
711 Third Avenue, New York, NY 10017

*Routledge is an imprint of the Taylor & Francis Group, an informa business*

© 2016 James N. Sater

The right of James N. Sater to be identified as author of this work has been asserted by him in accordance with sections 77 and 78 of the Copyright, Designs and Patents Act 1988.

All rights reserved. No part of this book may be reprinted or reproduced or utilised in any form or by any electronic, mechanical, or other means, now known or hereafter invented, including photocopying and recording, or in any information storage or retrieval system, without permission in writing from the publishers.

*Trademark notice:* Product or corporate names may be trademarks or registered trademarks, and are used only for identification and explanation without intent to infringe.

*British Library Cataloguing in Publication Data*
A catalogue record for this book is available from the British Library.

*Library of Congress Cataloging in Publication Data*
A catalog record for this book has been requested.

ISBN: 978-1-138-82826-1 (hbk)
ISBN: 978-1-138-82827-8 (pbk)
ISBN: 978-1-315-73852-9 (ebk)

Typeset in Bembo
by Taylor & Francis Books

**To my family**

# CONTENTS

*List of illustrations* ix
*Preface* x
*Chronology* xii
*Abbreviations* xv

1 Introduction 1

    *1.1 Historical roots: the Alawi monarchy 3*
    *1.2 Islam 5*
    *1.3 Political parties 7*
    *1.4 Elite politics 10*
    *1.5 Responding to challenges: regime strength and political liberalisation 12*
    *1.6 Plan of the book 14*

2 Combining modern with traditional state structures 17

    *2.1 The origins of the state in pre-colonial Morocco 17*
    *2.2 The colonial period and the rise of the nationalist movement 20*
    *2.3 Towards independence 26*
    *2.4 Independence and the struggle for power 29*
    *2.5 Summary 34*

3 The politics of exclusion and inclusion 37

    *3.1 Power struggles (1): the fragmentation of the state, 1961–73 38*
    *3.2 Power struggles (2): the re-establishment of the state, 1974–77 45*

3.3 The state's basis of power, 1956–77  51
3.4 Divide and rule: political parties and civil society, 1977–84  56
3.5 The rise of Islamism  60
3.6 From constitutional reform to alternance  68
3.7 NGOs and the rise of new agendas  75
3.8 Succession and new leadership: the early years of Mohamed VI  82
3.9 Democratisation  85
3.10 The Arab Spring and the 2011 constitutional reform  97
3.11 Summary  103

4  The challenge of economic development    113

4.1 Agriculture: from tentative reform to laissez-faire and perpetual crisis  114
4.2 From import substitution to debt crisis and structural adjustment  120
4.3 Economic changes and the development of a new ruling pact  125
4.4 The INDH, free trade and the future of Morocco's economic reform agenda  134
4.5 Summary  144

5  State legitimacy and foreign policy    150

5.1 Morocco's domestic, regional and international environment  152
5.2 The Western Sahara issue  157
5.3 The EU and foreign economic policy  165
5.4 The United States and the Middle East conflict  170
5.5 Moroccan foreign policy after the Arab Spring  173
5.6 Summary  174

6  Conclusion    179

*Glossary*    *182*
*Bibliography*    *184*
*Index*    *195*

# LIST OF ILLUSTRATIONS

## Figures

| | | |
|---|---|---|
| 1.1 | Political liberalisation and strength and weakness of the state | 13 |
| 4.1 | GDP growth and agricultural growth, 1961–2003 | 127 |

## Tables

| | | |
|---|---|---|
| 3.1 | Voter turnout in elections to the lower house, 1977–2011 | 101 |
| 4.1 | Illiteracy rates by gender and region (adults and children over ten years old), 1960–2004 (%) | 123 |
| 4.2 | Infant mortality rate, 1962–2004 (per thousand births) | 124 |
| 4.3 | Population living in poverty (%) | 126 |
| 4.4 | Remittances and balance of payments, 2003–14 (in million MAD) | 129 |
| 4.5 | Morocco's position in the corruption index, 2000–14 | 130 |
| 4.6 | Moroccan trade with Europe, France, Spain, 2001–14 (in million EUR) | 140 |

# PREFACE

The Arab Spring's impact on political and economic developments across the Middle East and North Africa (MENA) was profound and unprecedented. More than 9/11 and the 1991 Gulf War, it fundamentally challenged the balance of power in domestic politics in most MENA countries as well as in regional relations. In this revised and updated edition, I attempt to contribute to analysing these changes in Morocco in which the monarchy appeared to have emerged strengthened after a period of rapid reform in 2011.

In the last 20 years, academic interest in Morocco has significantly increased. For Western students of the Arab world, Morocco has been more accessible than many other Arab countries due to the prevalence of the French language in both oral and written conversation. It has also been more open to the West than many of its neighbours due to the importance of tourism as well as migration as a source of revenue, and Morocco has consequently dropped many of its restrictions on academic research. It has also become more dependent on foreign markets and transfers of capital, especially from the European Union, and it has campaigned extensively to attract foreign direct investment. Consequently, it has become a relatively open country, often considered stable compared to its neighbours in the MENA region, with which it shares a significant cultural heritage – most notably Islam and the Arabic language. More than many other states in the region, it has been involved in an extensive programme of political and economic reform, especially since Mohamed VI's accession to the throne in 1999, which even included sensitive questions of Islam in the area of women's rights. As these reforms have so far not touched upon the status of the traditional King, many students of Middle East politics remain intrigued as to how traditional rule in North Africa has been able to survive and reproduce itself.

Mostly due to its marginal status among the key players in MENA, far removed from oil and gas resources, violent Islamism, inter-state and civil wars, and also due to the traditional focus of French scholars on North Africa, English-language monographs on Morocco are still rare, even if their number is growing. This book aims to contribute to the growing volume of literature on Morocco by providing an historical, political, economic and foreign policy analysis of the key questions that the contemporary observer of Morocco faces.

The primary aims of this book are to link together the leading explanations provided for how the Moroccan state and nation have been constructed around the King following independence in 1956, and to produce an evaluation of the current political and economic situation. Many of these explanations have been introduced by Moroccan scholars in the last 30 years, and I attempt to do justice to the wealth of specialised literature that is available, while making it accessible to a broader readership. I believe that recent political and economic developments, which may be viewed as a continuation of long-term trends, justify this approach. In addition, I believe that the selection of themes adopted in this book renders justice to the current political and economic status and the corresponding policy options available to the country's political elite.

Much of the content of this book is based on my teaching of North African politics and international relations at Al Akhawayn University (AUI) in Morocco from 2005 to 2008. I was very fortunate to be able to learn from class discussions with Moroccan students in those years, which provided me as a foreigner with invaluable insights in addition to the lived experience itself. I also benefited from research material that Michael Willis prepared at AUI before my arrival, as well as from the many discussions that I had with colleagues. A conference co-sponsored by St Antony's College, Oxford, and the Moroccan-British Friendship Society in May 2008 at the University of Oxford on reforms in Morocco provided me with some key ideas that also form the background to this book. Another conference, organised by Roel Meijer and Nils Butenschon in Rabat in 2014, further encouraged me to reconsider questions of patronage and citizenship in Morocco post-Arab Spring. I am deeply indebted to Kevin Grey, Julie Egan, Birute Richardson, Tom Degeorges, Richard Gassan, as well as Mohamed Bouzidi, Michael Willis and Driss Maghraoui, for having reviewed parts of the manuscript at various stages. I am also grateful to the editors at Routledge as well as to the anonymous reviewers for their very helpful comments on earlier drafts. Of course, for all mistakes, factual or analytical, I alone bear full responsibility.

Finally, writing on North Africa where French and Arabic are equally often used poses a particular problem. Many of the Arabic terms and names have become anglicised or are otherwise widely used so that a translation into English seemed unnecessary or even confusing. On the other hand, many French words, names and acronyms have become so common in Morocco that it also makes sense to keep these in an English text. However, for the sake of clarity I have tried to keep these to a minimum, while I have used simplified Arabic transliteration to make Arabic terms as accessible as possible to an English-speaking readership. Unfortunately, the combination of Arabic transliteration, anglicised Arabic, French, and English translations comes at the price of inconsistency, even if I attempted to be as consistent as possible, especially with regard to names.

# CHRONOLOGY

| | |
|---|---|
| 788–791 | Idriss I, founder of the Idrissi dynasty |
| 789 | Foundation of the City of Fes |
| 1073–1147 | Almoravid dynasty |
| 1147–1269 | Almohad dynasty |
| 1195–1465 | Marinid dynasty |
| 1472–1550 | Wattasid dynasty |
| 1509–1627 | Saadi dynasty |
| 1631–present | Alawi dynasty |
| 1777 | Recognition of US independence |
| 1786 | US–Moroccan friendship agreement |
| 1830 | French occupation of Algiers |
| 1844 | Battle of Isly between French and Moroccan forces |
| 1856 | Anglo-Moroccan Treaty |
| 1859 | Moroccan–Spanish War |
| 1861 | Treaty of Madrid |
| 1884 | Spanish colonisation of Western Sahara |
| 1906 | Act of Algeciras |
| 1907–08 | 'Hafidhian' revolution |
| 1912 | Treaty of Fes establishing the French protectorate |
| 1922 | Declaration of the Rif republic by Abdelkrim |
| 1926 | Spanish defeat of Abdelkrim's tribal forces |
| 1927 | Mohamed V becomes Sultan of Morocco |
| 1933 | End of 'pacification'; the Ait Atta tribe surrenders to French forces |
| 1942 | Allied landing in Morocco and Algeria |
| 1943 | Churchill, Roosevelt and De Gaulle meet in Casablanca – Anfa |
| 1944 | Independence Manifesto (Istiqlal) |
| 1947 | Sultan Mohamed V visits Tangier in support of independence |

| | |
|---|---|
| 1953 | Forced abdication of Mohamed V |
| 1954 | Beginning of Algeria's War of Independence |
| 1955 | Return of Mohamed V |
| 1956 | Morocco gains independence |
| 1958 | French–Spanish Operation Ecouvillon in south of Morocco, defeating the Liberation Army of the South |
| 1958 | Rif rebellion |
| 1960 | Mohamed V and Crown Prince Hassan dismiss Socialist Ibrahim government |
| 1961 | Death of Mohamed V; accession to throne of Hassan II |
| 1962 | First constitution adopted by referendum |
| 1962 | Algeria obtains independence |
| 1963 | Moroccan–Algerian Sand War |
| 1965 | Riots in Casablanca and suspension of Moroccan parliament |
| 1965 | Mehdi Ben Barka disappears in Paris |
| 1970 | Second constitution adopted by referendum |
| 1971 | First coup attempt in Skhirat |
| 1972 | Second coup attempt |
| 1972 | Third constitution adopted by referendum |
| 1973 | Foundation of Polisario |
| 1974 | Spanish census for independence in Western Sahara |
| 1974 | Abdessalam Yassine publishes pamphlet *Islam ou la déluge* |
| 1975 | International Court of Justice (ICJ) Advisory Opinion on Western Sahara |
| 1975 | Green March; Spanish-Moroccan-Mauritanian Tripartite Agreement on Western Sahara |
| 1976 | War breaks out between Morocco and Polisario |
| 1977 | Parliamentary elections with participation of opposition parties |
| 1981 | Hassan II accepts referendum on self-determination in Western Sahara at Nairobi summit of the Organization of African Unity (OAU) |
| 1982 | Polisario is admitted to OAU; Morocco suspends its OAU membership |
| 1984 | Parliamentary elections |
| 1986 | Spain and Portugal join the European Community (EC) |
| 1987 | Hassan II applies for EC membership |
| 1987 | Morocco joins the General Agreement on Tariffs and Trade (GATT) |
| 1989 | Treaty establishing the Arab Maghreb Union (UMA) signed in Marrakech |
| 1990 | Creation of Human Rights Advisory Council |
| 1991 | Morocco participates in the US-led liberation of Kuwait |
| 1991 | UN supervised ceasefire between Morocco and Polisario; start of the UN referendum process |

| | |
|---|---|
| 1992 | Civil war in Algeria |
| 1992 | Fourth constitution adopted by referendum |
| 1992–93 | Parliamentary elections and first attempt at alternance |
| 1994 | Abderrahman Youssoufi goes into exile |
| 1994 | Morocco joins the World Trade Organization (WTO) |
| 1995 | Morocco signs Association Agreement with the European Union |
| 1996 | Fifth constitution adopted by referendum, creating lower and upper chambers |
| 1997 | Parliamentary elections and formation of alternance government under Abderrahman Youssoufi |
| 1999 | Hassan II dies; accession to the throne of Mohamed VI; dismissal of Minister of the Interior Driss Basri |
| 2000 | Mass rallies in Rabat and Casablanca in favour of and against a reform of the family code |
| 2000 | Abdessalam Yassine released from house arrest |
| 2001 | 11 September attacks and US war in Afghanistan |
| 2002 | Creation of 10 per cent women's list |
| 2002 | Parliamentary elections |
| 2002 | Appointment of Driss Jettou as prime minister |
| 2003 | US war in Iraq |
| 2003 | Islamist attacks in Casablanca |
| 2003 | Reform of the family code |
| 2004 | Signing of US–Moroccan free trade agreement |
| 2005 | Mohamed VI launches his *projet de règne*, the National Initiative for Human Development |
| 2005 | Justice and Reconciliation Commission organises public hearings on human rights violations under Hassan II |
| 2007 | Parliamentary elections |
| 2007 | Appointment of Abbas El Fassi as prime minister and Istiqlal-led government |
| 2008 | Creation of Authenticity and Modernity Party (PAM) |
| 2011 | Country-wide protests for constitutional reform |
| 2011 | Drafting and adoption by referendum of sixth constitution |
| 2011 | Parliamentary elections |
| 2011 | Appointment of Abdelilah Benkirane as prime minister and Justice and Development Party (PJD)-led government |
| 2014 | Morocco joins attacks on ISIS (Islamic State in Iraq and Syria) |
| 2015 | Morocco joins Saudi-led attacks on Houthi rebels in Yemen |

# ABBREVIATIONS

| | |
|---|---|
| AIU | Alliance Israélite Universelle |
| ALN | National Liberation Army (Algeria) |
| AMDF | Moroccan Association for Women's Rights |
| AMDH | Moroccan Association for Human Rights |
| BMCE | Banque Marocaine de Commerce Exterieur |
| CAP | Common Agricultural Policy |
| CCDH | Advisory Council for Human Rights |
| CDT | Democratic Labour Confederation |
| CGEM | General Confederation of Moroccan Enterprise |
| CIA | Central Intelligence Agency |
| CIH | Crédit Immobilier et Hôtelier |
| CMA | Global Amazigh Committee |
| CNSS | Caisse Nationale de Sécurité Sociale |
| CORCAS | Royal Advisory Council for Sahrawi Affairs |
| EC | European Community |
| EEC | European Economic Community |
| EMP | Euro-Mediterranean Partnership |
| ETU | twenty-foot equivalent |
| EU | European Union |
| FAR | Royal Armed Forces |
| FDI | foreign direct investment |
| FLN | National Liberation Front (Algeria) |
| FTA | free trade agreement |
| FVJ | Truth and Justice Forum |
| GATT | General Agreement on Tariffs and Trade |
| GCC | Gulf Cooperation Council |
| GDP | gross domestic product |

| | |
|---|---|
| GNP | gross national product |
| GSM | Global System for Mobile communication |
| GUP | Groupement Urbain de Securité |
| HACA | High Authority for Audiovisual Communication |
| HCP | High Planning Commission |
| IAM | Maroc Telecom |
| ICJ | International Court of Justice |
| IER | Justice and Reconciliation Commission |
| IMF | International Monetary Fund |
| INDH | National Initiative for Human Development |
| IRCAM | Royal Institute for Amazigh Culture |
| ISI | import substitution industrialisation |
| ISIS | Islamic State in Iraq and Syria |
| LMDH | Moroccan League for Human Rights |
| MAD | Moroccan dirham |
| MEDA | mésures d'ajustements |
| MENA | Middle East and North Africa |
| MEPI | Middle East Partnership Initiative |
| MINURSO | United Nations Mission for a Referendum in Western Sahara |
| MP | Popular Movement |
| MPDC | Democratic and Constitutional Popular Movement |
| NATO | North Atlantic Treaty Organization |
| NGO | non-governmental organisation |
| OAU | Organization of African Unity (now the African Union) |
| OCP | Office Chérifien des Phosphates |
| OCRS | Organisation Commune des Régions Sahariennes |
| OMDH | Moroccan Organization for Human Rights |
| ONA | Omnium Nord Africain (Western Sahara) |
| PADS | Party of Democratic Vanguard and Socialism |
| PAM | Authenticity and Modernity Party |
| PDS | Democratic and Socialist Party |
| PJD | Justice and Development Party |
| PLO | Palestine Liberation Organization |
| Polisario | Front for the Liberation of Saguia el Hamra y Rio de Oro (Western Sahara) |
| PPS | Party of Progress and Socialism |
| RAM | Royal Air Maroc |
| RNI | National Union of Independents |
| SADR | Saharan Arab Democratic Republic |
| SAP | Structural Adjustment Programme |
| SNI | Société Nationale d'Investissement |
| UAF | Feminine Action Union |
| UC | Constitutional Union |
| UMA | Arab Maghreb Union |

| | |
|---|---|
| UMT | Moroccan Labour Union |
| UN | United Nations |
| UNDP | United Nations Development Programme |
| UNEM | National Union of Moroccan Students |
| UNFM | National Union of Moroccan Women |
| UNFP | National Union of Popular Forces |
| USFP | Socialist Union of Popular Forces |
| WTO | World Trade Organization |

# 1
# INTRODUCTION

Less than a year after the Arab Spring rocked the Middle East and North Africa (MENA) region in January 2011, the Moroccan monarchy concluded an unprecedented process of political reform. Pressured by country-wide protests in which tens of thousands of Moroccans called for a constitutional monarchy and increased rule of law, King Mohamed VI engaged in a constitutional process that resulted in a new constitution. More than that, the monarch held parliamentary elections and formed a new, Islamist-dominated government, which reflected a significant parliamentary majority of the Justice and Development Party (PJD – *Hizb al 'Adala wal Tamniyya*), and even included Islamists in key positions, such as the premiership and the minister of justice.

There are several reasons why the events of 2011 marked such a radical change from Moroccan politics of less than a generation before. Not only did country-wide protests in favour of increased rule of law occur – protests that were unthinkable 15 years earlier – but even more radically, the protestors demanded constitutional reforms. Moreover, the events led to the election of a legal Islamist party into government, which continues to dominate. Until 2011, domestic protests had primarily focused on graduate unemployment, gender questions and, occasionally, large, country-wide public demonstrations focused on the various foreign wars in Iraq and Israel/Palestine. Clearly, the Morocco of the mid-2010s, both politically and socially, had changed radically from that of the mid-1990s, when, for example, Amazigh (Berber) rights militants were arrested in Goulmima and sentenced to one to two years' imprisonment for displaying pamphlets in their native language Tamazight.

Seen from the outside, the Moroccan political system remains one of stability and longevity. For six decades, the Moroccan political system based on the supremacy of the monarch has continued to exercise its hegemony over other political forces. It has done so because of its ability to adapt to social changes, identify challenges to its integrity, integrate these in the political scene through co-optation and alliance building, and create a multitude of allied classes.[1] This has caused apparently 'modern' political features and the establishment of quasi-modern societal characteristics. While the system thereby created seems well entrenched and stable on first sight, the absence of effective measures of inclusion of marginalised groups has created a fundamental dilemma and has continued to produce challengers to the status quo, culminating in the 2011 protests.

The central theme of this book concerns tradition and modernity as two core features in contemporary Moroccan politics. While traditional features of government have been omnipresent since independence was achieved in March 1956, the most remarkable characteristic has been their co-existence with seemingly 'modern' features such as parliaments, elections, referendums, inclusion of political parties, and constitutions, which gave the political system a cloak of modern institutional practice. Modernity as used in this book refers to a process that Max Weber called rationalisation, and it is closely connected to the rise of administrative institutions such as a modern bureaucracy that claim legal-rational legitimacy concerned with means-end efficiency and policy implementation.[2] Tradition, from a Weberian perspective, is the opposite realm – that of magic where the legitimacy of the ruler is based on primordial links, which may result in assumed leadership qualities or social and political privileges due to ancestry and blood ties. The combination of both realms and their intertwined character have had important repercussions on contemporary Moroccan politics. The monarchy and the political elite that it co-opts and controls has been in control of a modern state apparatus, which has resulted in the absence of any formal separation between the administration and the monarchical family including the network through which it rules.[3]

The peculiarity of Morocco lies in what Anderson calls key virtues that are embodied in monarchical traditional leadership styles and that make monarchs particularly adaptable to the early phases of state and nation building. This is because these phases are marked by exceptional uncertainty as to the continuing existence of old privileges and the ambiguous co-existence of new rights and procedures.[4] It can be argued that, in such times of exceptional uncertainty, personalised leadership qualities are more successful than bureaucratic ones in imposing themselves and in gaining acceptance. In contrast to nationalist movements, monarchs do not attempt to impose a particular vision of one nation that may be contentious. Instead, they create a larger definition of the nation that is inclusive and in which no particular feature gains prominence over others. This has been at the core of Morocco's post-independence political 'pluralism', in which competing political parties apparently justify and reinforce the King's role as an arbiter, in an otherwise unstable political field. This is despite the existence of a modernist current in Morocco's nationalist movement, which attempted to undermine the traditional basis of rule that did not correspond to its worldview and interests.

The Moroccan monarchy has undergone a vast political reform programme to give its traditional rule the cloak of legal-rational legitimacy and policies. After independence in 1956, political and economic reforms aimed at establishing the monarch's supremacy, often through political and economic patron–client relations, without, however, ignoring modern political institutions. Rising levels of education, a strong nationalist movement that used Mohamed V as a symbol for independence, and strong French influence well established in 44 years of French colonial rule, all supported the establishment of Western political institutions, such as a parliament or political parties. Nevertheless, the ruling family's claim to power is primarily based on a combination of tradition, lineage and religion: the Alawi family's traditional rule since the seventeenth century; the Alawis' claimed descent from the Prophet Mohamed; and the Moroccan monarch's supreme religious role as Commander of the Faithful, *Amir Al Mu'minin*. More than this, in a diverse linguistic and cultural society, this means that the monarchy embodies what Entelis called Morocco's Muslim consensus: Arabism, Islam and Moroccan nationalism.[5]

This book aims to analyse the inherent difficulties that have resulted from the political projects of tradition and modernity, of which the result has been a modernisation of traditional rule. Even if the Moroccan monarch has been a cautious moderniser, social mobility and the decreasing importance of traditional sources of identity have meant the development of both class-based and religious challengers to the regime. With economic development together with success in the Western Sahara becoming a priority throughout the state-building process, much of the regime's legitimacy has ceased to be exclusively based on religion and history, but rather on performance. To the extent that political structures and outcomes mutually depend on each other, it is the aim of this book to show that the political imperative of sustaining traditional authoritarianism has undermined the performance-related sources of legitimacy. This does not mean that the 'King's Dilemma', famously coined by Samuel Huntington in the 1960s, is being played out in full.[6] The purpose of this book is not simply to assert that modernisation undermines traditional rule, nor to view monarchies' tendencies to conserve the status quo and their adaptation to political pressure by liberalising the political field, as a simple survival strategy. Rather, the continuing ability of the state to use tradition has been a reflection of existing political ideologies, structures and social conflicts. This, however, has created inherent problems of state legitimacy as once hegemonic structures and ideologies are subject to conflicts and ultimately change. It is the purpose of this book to illustrate how these conflicts have evolved over the last 50 years.

## 1.1 Historical roots: the Alawi monarchy

Continuity is one of the kingdom's main political objectives due to the long legacy of its existence predating colonial rule by more than one millennium. The Moroccan monarchy is one of the oldest in the world, dating back to the eighth century when Moulay Idriss, a descendant from the Prophet Mohamed, found refuge in the hills around today's Meknes and founded what was to become the first Moroccan Muslim dynasty: the Idrissi dynasty. Ever since, Moroccan sultans' power has concentrated in the cities that were often used as capitals by new dynasties, such as Fes, Meknes and Marrakech. In turn, much of the mountainous countryside remained outside direct control. Here, mainly Amazigh tribes constituted what French ethnographers would later call *bled es siba*, unruly tribal society that the Sultan's power would not reach, with the implication of taxes not being collected. In areas under the Sultan's control, named *bled el makhzen*, taxes were paid. The Arabic word *makhzen*, which became synonymous for state, has a financial connotation and means 'treasurer'.

The current Alawi dynasty dates from the seventeenth century. The Alawi kinship group has its geographical roots in the Tafilalet oasis in the south-east of Morocco, near today's Algeria. After a period of civil strife after the Saadi dynasty with its capital Marrakech went into decline, the Alawis consolidated their grip on power in 1668 when Moulay Rachid destroyed a rival tribal formation, the *zawiyya* of el Dila. His successor, Ismail I, installed the first capital of the Alawis in Meknes and consolidated Alawi power through the use of a largely black slave army.

The consolidation of power of the early Alawi dynasty went hand in hand with growing external relations with France and Great Britain, commercial treaties allowing both powers freedom of movement and protection of their commercial goods and products. At the same time, Alawi consolidation of power meant increasing attempts at forcing back Portuguese and Spanish positions on the African continent (El Jadida, Sebta, Melilla, Peñon, Althusemas), which had been captured by the Europeans in the previous two centuries when dynasties were comparatively weak. However, power struggles within the Alawi family also led to periods of unrest (1727–57). Increased European firepower forced Morocco to accept France's colonial ambitions in neighbouring Algeria (1830), when France and Britain fought for control in the Mediterranean. It was under Moulay Abderrahman (1822–59), when the Sultan's army suffered a major defeat at Isly in 1844 against French forces, that France was able to affirm its control over Algeria. Spanish colonial ambitions resulted in the battle of Tetouan in 1860 under Moulay Abderrahman's son, Moulay Mohamed Ben Abderrahman (1859–73), forcing Morocco to give in to Spanish territorial demands around Ceuta and Melilla, and Sidi Ifni (Santa Cruz la Pequeña).[7] The military defeat also forced Moulay Mohamed to accept preferential commercial treaties with Spain, recognition of Spanish property rights, as well as granting Spain preferential fishing rights off the Moroccan coast.[8]

Clearly, the sultanate's increasing incapacity to resist colonial pressure undermined the Sultan's combination of traditional and religious legitimacy. When Moulay Abdelaziz found it impossible to resist the French occupation of Casablanca and Oujda, in addition to the Act of Algeciras of 1906, which confirmed the French presence in Morocco, parts of the Moroccan *'ulema* decided to impose a contractual relation between the Moroccan *'umma* and the Sultan. Consequently, Moulay Abdelaziz was deposed in a declaration of leading *'ulema* in Fes, and replaced by Moulay Hafidh, who was forced to vow to liberate the country from the French invaders. This vow became part of the *'ulema*'s act of allegiance to the new Sultan, *bay'a*, and it instituted a contractual relationship between the temporal powers of the Sultan and the *'ulema*, in the context of increasing commercial, territorial, religious and cultural threats to which Morocco was exposed.

Despite Hafidh's incapacity to resist French ambitions to impose a protectorate on the sultanate, the crown itself, combined with the Muslim faith, continued to be the symbol for national independence and resistance. A major challenge to the monarchy's role was Abdelkrim's declaration of an independent Rif *republic* in 1922, in the north with Oujda as its capital, indirectly rejecting the authority of the Sultan. The ultimate defeat of the tribal alliance of which Abdelkrim was the leader against French and Spanish forces in 1926 was as much in the interests of the monarchy as in those of the colonial powers: it challenged the monarchy's position as defender of both Islam and Morocco's territorial integrity based on the Sultan's religious and temporal authority over his subjects. Had Abdelkrim become the leader of a successful anti-French liberation movement, according to Riffians' own slogan 'from Oujda to Agadir', the clash with the monarchy would have been serious.

The colonial experience profoundly transformed the monarchy: security, foreign relations, economic policy were controlled by colonial administrators, the General Residency. In addition to cultural penetration of a large settler community, all of this meant that the monarchy was deprived of its vital functions to exercise power. Its close association with the colonial state, which officially aimed at 'protecting' the monarchy, was potentially threatening as a nationalist movement soon took root, first abroad and, from the early 1930s, inside the protectorate.[9] Conversely, seeking nationalist credentials potentially alienated the French military administration, and France had the means to impose a new sultan on the country. Moulay Yousouf was replaced shortly after the military administrator Hubert Lyautey arrived in 1912. At the same time, the French colonial practice in Morocco – especially under Lyautey – was based on the principle of not changing the traditional practices, working 'with, not against, native socio-political elites and respect[ing] pre-colonial customs and traditions'.[10] The ensuing alliance consisting of sultanate and Residency put the traditional sources of power and its administration at the disposal of the French. This had the potential to seriously de-legitimise the monarchy in the eyes of the nationalist movement and the Islamic reform movement (*salafiyya*) that it inspired. It was not until April 1947 that Sultan Mohamed publicly announced his favour for independence following his historic visit to Tangier, believing in US support for Moroccan independence.[11] This act, along with his increasing confrontation with the Residency, and the increasingly outspoken nationalist movement's choice to elevate Sultan Mohamed as a symbol of Moroccan sovereignty, enhanced his prestige as a sign of continuity of the Moroccan state.

## 1.2 Islam

Islam is the main source of legitimacy of the Moroccan monarch, who claims direct descent from the Prophet Mohamed. This confers sherifian status on the royal family, one of the bases for his calling himself *Amir Al Mu'minin* inscribed in the constitution. In fact, Mohamed V assumed the title of King, *malik*, in 1957 only to correspond to more Western notions of kingdoms, not because there had been a tradition in Morocco itself. Sherifian status alone, however, is quite common in Morocco, establishing a class of *ashraf* citizens with particular religious prestige. These sherifian families were often appointed in the bureaucracy and given local powers – traditionally constituting the 'agents of the Makhzen'.[12] The title itself, *Amir Al Mu'minin*, was introduced in the Almohad period (1145–1269), and competed with the title *Amir Al Muslimin* that was conferred by the caliphate in Baghdad. Even if only two preceding dynasties claimed sherifian credentials and used it to legitimise their rule, the Saadians and the Idrissis, 'sharifism [still] presented itself as a veritable catalyst for the legitimacy of all those who aspired power', as illustrated in the writings of Muslim jurists such as Qadi 'Iyad under the Almoravids.[13]

Islamic references therefore find their way into everyday political speeches and policies. The most important one is the act of allegiance, the *bay'a*, in which, traditionally, the *'ulema* and, since independence, political, military, tribal and technocratic establishment vow allegiance to the throne. Whereas it did not receive a lot of attention in the first 15 years of Hassan's rule, it gained importance from the *bay'a* of Layoune in 1979 in Western Sahara, when Sahrawi tribal notables performed this 'act' as a sign of their attachment to the Moroccan throne.

The importance of the *bay'a* relates to the legitimacy it confers on the King's title *Amir Al Mu'minin*, which makes the King effectively stand above constitutional constraints and the division of state powers into legislative, executive and judicial institutions. The official interpretation of the *bay'a* was published in the *Bulletin Officiel* of 20 September 1979. In short, it confers divine powers on the King: 'the holder of the legitimate authority is God's shadow on earth and his secular arm in the world.'[14]

In addition to these formal constitutional powers accorded to the King, popular Islam and its belief in symbolic and expressive forms of power are also associated with the King. The concept of *baraka* (blessing), with which sherifian families are endowed, forms a crucial aspect by which magic is transferred from one generation to another.[15] The King has been careful to be associated with these traditional Moroccan forms of Islam, for example by traditional dress codes (a white *jellaba* during the annual ceremony of *bay'a* and *La Fête du Trône*), or by wearing certain jewellery that is strongly associated to Moroccan sufism. On the other hand, another form of *baraka* is acquired, not inherited, and is based on purity (*tahara*) which is based on this-worldly conduct and can be lost.[16] This means that Moroccans' belief in *baraka* confers legitimacy on sherifian families to rule; however, it also scrutinises their conduct and public behaviour to the extent that the Moroccan monarch has been very careful to control public images of himself and of his family.

The monarch's Islamic credentials have imposed significant policy orientations in the conduct of state affairs. The *'ulema* have been given a privileged position in the policy-making process: the League of Moroccan *'Ulema* is regularly given the opportunity to advise the King on legislation. Morocco's conservative family laws, the privileged position of Islam and Arabic in school curricula, as well as the reference to political institutions in Islamic terms, are all important features. The parliament is a *shura* council – an Islamic advisory body. The links of ancestry to the Prophet Mohamed are frequently evoked, as for example during the opening of the parliament in October 1984, when the King addressed the deputies as receiving their political education in the school of Hassan II (the parliament), which is the same as the school of Mohamed V, his father, and that of the Prophet Mohamed.[17]

## 1.3 Political parties

Political parties in Morocco have a long history, as the nationalist movement was organised around the Istiqlal (independence) Party from the late 1930s. In the 1950s, trade unions and the Liberation Army formed part of a country-wide movement for independence. Despite strong ideological differences within the Istiqlal Party, ranging from conservative leader Allal El Fassi, pragmatist leader Abderrahim Bouabid, to leftist Mehdi Ben Barka, the Istiqlal made a clear bid to single-party status in the immediate post-independence period, posing a threat to the claims of the monarchy to absolute power. Educated in France and familiar with Western institutions, the Istiqlal leadership's relationship with the monarchy was ambivalent: on the one hand, the monarch's sovereign powers were used as a symbol of Moroccan sovereignty that the protectorate in its treaty of 1912 promised to guarantee and ultimately re-establish. On the other hand, visions of a constitutional monarchy meant that it was seeking power itself to govern the country, with the aim of delegating to the King a symbolic function only. The famous Independence Manifesto of 11 January 1944 reflected this ambivalent approach. It made four central demands: an independent Morocco under Mohamed V; Mohamed V should negotiate independence; Morocco should sign the Atlantic Charter and take part in the peace conference; as well as the establishment of a 'democratic government'.[18] The word 'constitutional monarchy' did not appear in the document itself. The document only required the King to establish a democratic regime 'similar to the form of government adopted in the Muslim countries of the Orient', and a 'consultative (*shura*)' regime in the Arabic version of the manifesto.[19]

Shortly after independence, the different currents that had been united within the Istiqlal Party split up. Probably the most important question that caused this break-up was the relationship that the Istiqlal wanted to establish with the monarchy. As the King had a guiding hand in promoting individual leaders to ministerial positions, he could promote particular political currents that leaders presented. Consequently, through frequent ministerial reshuffles shortly after independence, he could ensure that nationalist politicians would not accumulate too much power that would threaten the monarchy.[20]

In addition to playing on divisions in the nationalist movement, the monarchy managed to create new ones outside the movement's core reach that was limited to urban areas. This was due to the uneven nature of development and modernisation that had marked colonial rule. Essentially, as Camau points out, 'because of its configuration in terms of social stratification, [the nationalist movement] was not able to produce a project, which went beyond the aim of nationalising the colonial state'.[21] In addition, social fragmentation according to primordial tribal, regional, linguistic and ethnic links became the primary mode by which the national movement disintegrated into competing factions.

Consequently, in post-colonial Morocco the *makhzen* was kept in place and continued to be the main administrative structure of policy making and implementation. Despite the Sultan's association with colonial rule, he managed to become the symbol of *national* independence himself in an otherwise fragmented society. The Liberation Army, with a largely rural intake, had an opposite political orientation to the more modern elements within the Istiqlal Party. As mentioned, the Istiqlal Party itself was also divided between more radical and leftist leaders such as Abdallah Ibrahim and Mehdi Ben Barka, and its more conservative wing around Allal El Fassi and Ahmed Belafrej. In addition, the army and its officer class were alienated by the Istiqlal's repeated accusations that it had collaborated with the French – especially as key positions in the army were still filled by the French that were only slowly dismantled. The Istiqlal's attempts at centralising power to its own advantage – new appointments of Istiqlali judges, governors, key positions in the police and the Ministry of the Interior – were resisted by rural and more conservative elements that did not trust the urban-based Arab nationalist ideology of the party.[22] Mahjoubi Aherdane, a former leading Amazigh figure in the Liberation Army, strongly resisted Istiqlal's increasing power in the countryside and became the main intermediary when the Liberation Army staged an uprising against the Istiqlal. Consequently, King Mohamed V and Crown Prince Hassan encouraged the creation of an Amazigh rural party, the Popular Movement (MP), which gained numerous ministerial portfolios thanks to Aherdane's position of loyalty to the monarchy.[23]

It was not only the monarchy's position that encouraged the divisions within political parties and the creation of new ones, but also the elite's neo-patrimonial practices that structure Moroccan society. In a context in which Morocco was still in a process of nation building, primordial links and loyalties were more important than modern ones, based on ideologies or national myths. The result was that leaders of political parties became central figures that gave patronage to their fellowship in return for loyalty and political power. Aherdane's MP is a case in point. Established in the 1950s as a rural, conservative counter-movement to the urban-based Istiqlal, its sole ideology was the support of the King. In return, it was active in key policies such as the privileged position that agriculture obtained through preferential credits and state banks such as Crédit Agricole du Maroc or through government programmes such as the Office National des Irrigations and the Office de la Mise en Valeur Agricole. The distribution of former French land fulfilled a special role in the distribution of patronage. Some 600,000 acres were directly distributed to rank and file members of the MP, but more importantly 'collective lands' that belonged collectively to the tribes (15 million acres, of which 2.5 million are used in agriculture) were 'managed' by the Ministry of the Interior through turning them into a 'trusteeship'.[24] Control over these trusteeships was therefore achieved through party membership in the MP – the main incentive of joining the MP. Consequently, political parties increasingly appeared as interlinking organisations between local strongmen and economic opportunities. 'Recruitment drives by most parties consist not of public appeals to ordinary citizens but of the co-opting of notables and leaders from a local area or community into the party in the expectation that these figures will be able to "deliver" the support and votes of their local area or community.'[25]

This illustrates one central aspect among political parties in modern Morocco. Although a multi-party system was introduced by the monarchy as it fought Istiqlal's attempts at turning itself into a single party, and Morocco has a great quantity of new and old political parties, the majority is without ideological or political content despite apparent political names that indicate the contrary. A splinter party from the Istiqlal Party, the Socialist Union of Popular Forces (USFP) has little socialist content; the National Union of Independents (RNI) was founded by a relative of the royal family (King Hassan's brother-in-law, Ahmed Osman) and it is 'independent' only in its original meaning – from other political parties. The Authenticity and Modernity Party (PAM), created in 2009 by the King's closest friend and adviser, Fouad Ali El Himma, avoids any ideological references altogether. The above mentioned Popular Movement (MP) has been based on rural notables and their traditional capacity to make peasants vote for their strongmen. Neo-patrimonial practices are very strongly embedded in these political parties, which look for rapprochement with the centre of power, the monarchy, despite occasional repetition that it is democracy that is actually sought. This also applies to political parties that used to be in opposition to King Hassan. As it was rightly coined, these political parties (USFP, Istiqlal, the Party of Progress and Socialism – PPS) were, when in opposition, the opposition *of* His Majesty, and not *to* His Majesty. This is why they seem to adopt a language of change for greater participation and power sharing, while ultimately being a conservative force due to the existence of strong patron–client relations that make it easy for the monarch to co-opt their leaders. In return, leaders use their patronage to make sure that little dissent emanates from party congresses, which only rarely take place, with key positions being attributed by the party leadership to loyal elements.

At the same time, these political parties face increasing problems of legitimacy. One indicator has been the decreasing participation rate of the population in national and municipal elections; another is the difficulty of attracting younger generations in these political parties.[26] Change therefore has been on the agenda for a number of years – especially with the advent of Mohamed VI – to address these difficulties lest they are out-paced by a stronger and more dynamic Islamist party that established itself in the late 1990s, the Justice and Development Party

(PJD). Ironically, the foundation of the PAM, whilst expressing the system's dysfunctionality, also aimed to include the younger generations and political newcomers into the political system and counter the increasing hegemony of the ideologically powerful Islamist parties.

## 1.4 Elite politics

One under-analysed aspect of Moroccan politics is the relationship between wealth creation and politics, even if corruption itself has been the focus of much domestic attention. The dynamics of the relationship between wealthy classes and politics, however, is a very interesting one, especially as, unlike some of its neighbours in North Africa and the Middle East, Morocco never officially aspired to create a socialist economy based on state-led growth and development. This means that Morocco never tried to forcefully replace the private sector with state enterprises. 'Morocco has chosen the path of liberalism [and] ... we will serve as an example in this regard to all of Africa', announced Finance Minister Mamoun Tahiri at a conference sponsored by the World Bank in the late 1960s.[27] In addition, Morocco never broke with the colonial past concerning its agricultural developments: expensive plans to construct dams (*la politique des barrages*) in order to irrigate 1 million hectares of arable land by 2000 were French ideas that dated from 1938. A *laissez-faire* policy in the countryside was in effect the monarchy's response to opposition emanating from the urban-based Istiqlal Party in the late 1950s and 1960s.

The rural elite was not the only constituent of Morocco's political-economic elite. Economic development and increasing intervention of the state in the economy despite its allegedly *liberal* character resulted in some 700 state-owned enterprises by the late 1970s in which much of a state-dependent urban elite was employed. Privatisation processes that ensued often constituted another form of state patronage that the dependent elite enjoyed. In addition to being the country's largest landowner, King Hassan himself became the country's main businessman. His majority share in Morocco's most important financial holding, Omnium Nord Africain (ONA), which owned shares in more than 50 of Morocco's main private businesses, multiplied the many sources of patronage.

The result is a common trajectory of government ministers from state-owned or supposedly private enterprises to government positions, emanating from an economic elite that, even if apparently independent, owes its existence to royal patronage and opportunities that result from lucrative state contracts. This economic elite had its origin in Fassi families, originating from the city of Fes. Allal El Fassi, head of the independence movement, was also a member of one of these leading merchant families. The traditional combination of public office (*makhzen*), religious sherifian background and wealth creation was all illustrated in the background of Fassis: its administrative position and its membership in the *'ulema* of Fes had been inherited since the mid-seventeenth century.[28]

One of the Moroccan elite's major characteristics is that it has taken advantage of policies under Hassan II. Construction, transport, international trade, food processing, most of the post-colonial elite sprang up from the pre-colonial Fassi families, with names such as Tazi, Benslimane, Bensouda and Berrada dominating this post-colonial bourgeoisie. A survey of top businessmen in 1965 revealed that Fassis constituted almost two thirds of this group. In agriculture, French farmers left behind some 1 million acres (400,000 hectares) of prime agricultural land, which, along with buildings, were purchased at very cheap rates. Those rural notables already empowered both by the colonial power and then by the kingdom were those who were able to benefit from these lucrative deals – prominent families were the Nejjai, Bekkai, Gueddari and Kebbaj.[29]

Together with Moroccanisation in the 1970s, which empowered a new aspiring class of Soussi businessmen – originating from the south, especially from Agadir – these measures had the effect of increasing income and corresponding lifestyle disparities among Moroccans. In two household consumption surveys conducted in 1965 and 1971, respectively, the share of overall consumption of the wealthiest 10 per cent increased dramatically, whereas the share of others, and in particular the poor, declined.[30] Up to now, this disparity has increased sharply, creating an economically dependent and allied class to the state that has difficulties in emancipating itself from the centre, as it is alienated from its fellow citizens in terms of lifestyle, education, language and professional future.

This has had serious results for the development of a socio-economic opposition to the state and its allied classes. Excluded strata informed strong socialist groups up to the late 1970s, such as King Hassan's main rival in the 1960s, Mehdi Ben Barka, and more recently Islamic groups. Essentially, an 'alliance for profit' that is embodied by the state and wealthy strata has been challenged with reference to Islamic social justice.[31] Clearly, both Morocco's 'official' Islamic party – the PJD – *and* its 'unofficial' Islamic opposition party Justice and Benevolence (*Al 'Adl wal Ihssane*) have made the existing income disparities a central theme in their political programmes, as is already indicated in the names that they have chosen. The traumatising Islamist attacks of 16 May 2003 in Casablanca also targeted symbols of wealth, not power, and the origins of the actors – from one of Casablanca's most impoverished shanty towns – indicate the fragile political basis that income disparity creates.

Consequently, the balance between modernity and tradition on which the post-independence Moroccan monarchy has been founded is a fragile one. The increasing number of debates about principles of modern parliamentary institutions, political parties and constitutionalism weaken the traditional powers that the King enjoys. On the other hand, modern lifestyles and mass education not only challenge monarchical traditions, but also create expectations about levels of comfort and the potential for social mobility that only a small restricted minority enjoys. It is this experienced exclusion that has accompanied Morocco's post-independence development, which is the primary threat to liberal lifestyles that co-exist with conservative social and political practices.

## 1.5 Responding to challenges: regime strength and political liberalisation

With those structures in place Morocco had to adapt at times to substantial pressures and to adjust its mode of multi-party governance. The kingdom has promulgated six constitutions and major constitutional amendments during the past 60 years (1962, 1970, 1971, 1992, 1996, and 2011), sometimes making major concessions to political opponents, such as including them in government coalitions as well as the premiership. This has made Morocco appear more politically liberal in spite of the fact that the multi-party system's objective was not the establishment of a liberal system of checks and balances, nor was the monarchy's authority seriously questioned by any of the changes.

Nevertheless, Morocco's multi-party system performs a number of very important secondary functions irrespective of the fact that it has been co-opted by the country's political elite. One of these functions is to create a political sphere in which, at least in theory, contestation can be expressed.[32] It has been this potential for contestation and resulting appearance of political liberalism that has served as a source of legitimacy for Morocco's three post-colonial kings.[33]

Within this context, an analysis of the strengths and weaknesses of Morocco's political regime provides an interesting perspective for this book. Depending on its own relative strength, the regime has allowed or limited public criticism to develop. When it gained strength, it increasingly believed that it could clamp down on political opposition. Conversely, at times of relative weakness, the regime acted to reinforce the political consensus by integrating political parties, as long as they were not strong enough to seriously challenge royal authority, otherwise the regime would lose too much by engaging in necessary compromises.[34] The result was the creation of a zone of political liberalism in which the regime was neither too weak nor too strong in relation to other political contenders, establishing a balance between political liberalism 'granted' by the monarch, and the submission to authoritarian rule by political parties. This dynamic is expressed in Figure 1.1.

However, a balance between the appearance of political liberalism and submission to royal authority has not always been easy to achieve, and the primary objective of royal interventions in party politics in all three post-colonial kings' rule has been to ensure that no serious challenges arise. From this observation results the primary objective for analysing political liberalisation, political party activities and civil society in relation to economic and foreign policy matters. As I attempt to show, depending on particular contexts, royal interventions are indications of whether the regime feels either strong or weak. Similarly, the state may feel at times that it has to compromise with actors or, alternatively, that it is able to overlook the ambitions and ideas of potential rivals as expressed in civil and political society. An analysis of the system thus gives the observer an important way of assessing the stability and direction of the political system as a whole.

This book primarily argues that, towards the end of the 2000s, Morocco under Mohamed VI entered a period of increasingly open conflicts and tensions in which

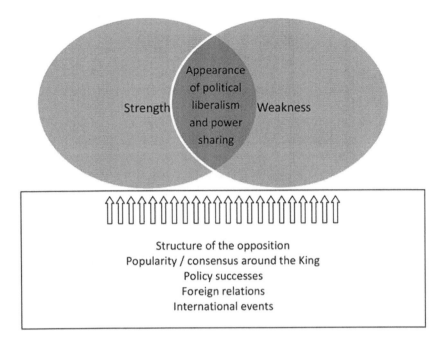

**FIGURE 1.1** Political liberalisation and strength and weakness of the state

power sharing and political liberalisation became less likely. In contrast to the regime consolidation period of the first half of his reign (1999–2005), the state felt increasingly strong with regard to regime legitimacy and the attraction of its citizens to the monarch. Although these tensions and conflicts were addressed at the state level by strategies similar to those used in the past, contemporary issues of contention are fundamentally different in structure and content from previous ones. They have shifted from a debate about the distribution of power, to a debate about moral values in a rapidly changing society. This means that old political manoeuvres of dealing with political parties have become recurrent, yet with a different political objective in mind. As I argued elsewhere, old bottles have increasingly been filled with new wine: the appearance of similar state strategies of dealing with political parties masks the changing content of political tensions. Yet, such a conclusion is by no means static as evidenced in the post-January 2011 era. The King's March 2011 promises of constitutional reform amidst the crisis and unrest across the MENA region brought the question of distribution of power back onto the agenda. Indeed, the ensuing constitutional change may be the most significant of all changes that occurred since his accession to the throne in July 1999. Consequently, the sudden and dramatic reappearance of potentially substantial political liberalisation occurred as a response to the systemic crisis and gridlock that the monopolisation of power by the monarch has produced over the last decade.[35]

## 1.6 Plan of the book

Chapter 2 outlines the origins of the contemporary Moroccan state, focusing on the immediate post-independence period that was marked by the power struggle between the nationalist movement and the monarchy for control of the state.

Chapter 3 deals with the basis of power and it understands Hassan II's and Mohamed VI's rule as a constant adaptation to domestic pressure and fields of power. The central focus of this chapter is the period since the mid-1970s, when King Hassan rode on a wave of nationalist fever with the Western Sahara issue dominating political debate. As I will argue in this book, it was at this time that the monarch's ability to engage in liberalisation and claim democratic legitimacy was for the first time revealed.

The fields of power have been evolving with economic processes and the kingdom's careful attempts to develop its economy, modernise and privatise key sectors whilst keeping a large traditional sector in place. This is analysed in Chapter 4, which emphasises the kingdom's agricultural policies and highlights the sectorial dualism of the country's industrialisation and modernisation efforts on one hand, and its traditional economic base on the other, in which political considerations remained paramount. For example, during the 1990s and the 2000s, the northern Rif region evolved into one of the world's most important hashish exporters as well as into a focal point for illegal departures to Spain, in large part due to the political animosity between Rifi tribal society and the political centre in Rabat. Increasing political pressure from the European Union (EU) to clamp down on hashish production and illegal emigration meant that the kingdom has looked into economic alternatives. Hence, the state developed a modern port facility in Tangier, Tanger-Med, as well as a specific tourism strategy for Tangier and the north.

Connected to economic imperatives, Morocco's foreign policy has had a dual nature, which will be analysed in Chapter 5: nominally a member of the non-alignment movement, Morocco's domestic situation has had a direct impact on foreign policy making. Finding financial, political and military support for its Western Sahara campaign has been the kingdom's main priority, as this issue proved crucial for the consolidation of King Hassan II's power, and the main diplomatic legacy that he left to his son, Mohamed VI. Starting from this priority, the successful establishment of friendly relations with European states, the United States, and other Arab states was contingent on their particular attitude towards this issue, with Algeria becoming a particular regional rival in this perspective. Given Morocco's resources in the context of the Cold War, Morocco negotiated its strategic position in return for support for its Saharan cause. Therefore, Morocco's moderate position towards the Arab–Israeli conflict, clouded in Islamic references since the late 1970s, guaranteed US support and weapons. More recently, its participation in Saudi-led military interventions both in Syria and Yemen, together with its expressed neutrality in questions of the Arab Spring and Egypt, further illustrate this point.

## Notes

1 I.W. Zartman, 'King Hassan's New Morocco' in I.W. Zartman (ed.) *The Political Economy of Morocco*, London and New York: Praeger Publishers, 1987, p. 1.
2 M. Weber, *Economy and Society*, Totawa, NJ: Bedminster, 1968, p. 24.
3 T. Desrues and E. Moyano, 'Social Change and Political Transition in Morocco' in *Mediterranean Politics*, Vol. 6, No. 1, Spring 2001, p. 28.
4 L. Anderson, 'Dynasts and Nationalists. Why Monarchies Survive' in J. Kostiner (ed.) *Middle East Monarchies: The Challenge of Modernity*, Boulder, CO: Lynne Rienner, 2000, p. 55.
5 J.P. Entelis, *Culture and Counterculture in Moroccan Politics*, Lanham, MD: University Press of America, 1996, p. 4.
6 S. Huntington, *Political Order in Changing Societies*, New Haven, CT: Yale University Press, 1968.
7 M.A. Alaoui, *Le Maroc Face aux Convoitises Européenne 1830–1912*, Salé: Beni Snassen, 2001, chapters 1 and 2.
8 Ibid., p. 69.
9 J.P. Halstead, *Rebirth of a Nation. Origins and Rise of Moroccan Nationalism. 1912–1944*, Cambridge MA: Harvard University Press, 1967; M. El Mansour, 'Salafis and Modernists in the Moroccan Nationalist Movement' in J. Ruby (ed.) *Islamism and Secularism in North Africa*, New York: St Martin's Press, 1999.
10 M. Gershovich, *French Military Rule in Morocco*, London: Frank Cass, 2000, p. 64.
11 Ibid., p. 66.
12 A. Claisse, 'Makhzen Traditions and Administrative Channels' in I.W. Zartman (ed.) *The Political Economy of Morocco*, London and New York: Praeger Publishers, 1987, p. 35.
13 M. Kably, 'Legitimacy of State Power and Socio-religious Variations in Medieval Morocco' in R. Bourqia and S. Gilson Miller (eds) *In the Shadow of the Sultan. Culture, Power, and Politics in Morocco*, Cambridge: Harvard Center for Middle Eastern Studies, 1999, pp. 21–22.
14 Cited in Claisse, op. cit., p. 38.
15 For a complete discussion of *baraka*, see H. Munson, Jr., *Religion and Power in Morocco*, New Haven, CT and London: Yale University Press, 1993, pp. 1–34.
16 Ibid., pp. 11–12.
17 D.F. Eickelman, 'Religion in Polity and Society' in I.W. Zartman (ed.) *The Political Economy of Morocco*, London and New York: Praeger Publishers, 1987, p. 87.
18 R. Pennel, *Morocco Since 1830*, New York: New York University Press, 2000, p. 265.
19 J. Waterbury, *The Commander of the Faithful. The Moroccan Political Elite – A Study in Segmented Politics*, London: Weidenfeld and Nicolson, 1970, p. 63.
20 R. El Mossadeq, 'Political Parties and Power Sharing' in I.W. Zartman (ed.) *The Political Economy of Morocco*, London and New York: Praeger Publishers, 1987, p. 62.
21 M. Camau, *Pouvoirs et Institutions au Maghreb*, Tunis: Cérès Productions, 1978, p. 200.
22 E. Hermassi, *Leadership and National Development in North Africa*, Berkeley, CA and London: University of California Press, 1972, p. 146.
23 See E. Gellner, 'Tribalism and Social Change in North Africa' in W.H. Lewis (ed.) *French Speaking Africa: The Search for Identity*, New York: Walker, 1965.
24 M. Bouzidi (under pseudonym A. Ben Kaddour), 'The Neo-Makhzen and the Berbers' in E. Gellner and C. Micaud (eds) *Arabs and Berbers*, London: Gerard Duckworth, 1972, p. 266.
25 M.J. Willis, 'Political Parties in the Maghrib: The Illusion of Significance' in *The Journal of North African Studies*, Vol. 7, No. 2, Summer 2002, p. 4.
26 Some political parties have therefore proposed a quota for young party members in national elections, similar to the women's quota that was established before the 2002 parliamentary elections.
27 J.F. Clément, 'Morocco's Bourgeoisie: Monarchy, State and Owning Class' in *Middle East Report*, No. 142, September–October 1986, p. 13.

28 A. Benhaddou, *Maroc: Les Elites du Royaume. Essai sur l'organisation du pouvoir au Maroc*, Paris: L'Harmattan, 1997, p. 21.
29 Clément, op. cit., p. 14.
30 Ibid., p. 16.
31 I borrow this expression from J. Waterbury, 'Democracy Without Democrats. The Potential for Political Liberalization in the Middle East' in G. Salamé (ed.) *Democracy Without Democrats. The Renewal of Politics in the Muslim World*, London and New York: I. B. Tauris, 1994, p. 27.
32 Michael J. Willis, 'Political Parties in the Maghrib: The Illusion of Significance' in *The Journal of North African Studies*, 7/2, Summer 2002, pp. 1–22.
33 A recent, thorough examination of legitimacy is found in Julie E. Pruzan-Jørgensen, 'Analyzing Authoritarian Regime Legitimation: Findings from Morocco' in *Middle East Critique*, 19/3, Fall 2010, pp. 269–286.
34 This idea was expressed by M. Rousset about the relative position of King Hassan and the *koutla wataniyya* (political opposition) in the early 1970s. See M. Rousset, 'Changements institutionnels et équilibre des forces politiques au Maroc: un essai d'interprétation' in J. Leca, *Développement Politique au Maghreb*, Paris: Centre National de la Recherche Scientifique, 1979, p. 194.
35 James N. Sater, 'New Wine in Old Bottles: Political Parties Under Mohammed VI' in Bruce Maddy-Weitzman and Daniel Zisenwine (eds) *Contemporary Morocco: State, Politics and Society Under Mohammed VI*, Abingdon and New York: Routledge, 2013, pp. 9–23.

# 2

# COMBINING MODERN WITH TRADITIONAL STATE STRUCTURES

The state of Morocco has its origin in an old institution, the *makhzen*, which is a synonym for royal power and traditions. This traditional identity of state – royal power and *makhzen* – is still very much enshrined in contemporary political practice and the constitution, diminishing the analytical distinction between government, regime and state. Another key aspect of the modern state is the duality of temporal and religious authority of the King, which has co-existed in an uneasy relationship since pre-colonial times. This chapter focuses on three distinctive periods: the pre-colonial state, the colonial period, and the state formation process in the period 1956–61 under Mohamed V. The objective is to illustrate the historical processes that inform contemporary notions of politics and state, as these notions led to the two modes of government based on tradition and modernity as briefly outlined in the introduction.

## 2.1 The origins of the state in pre-colonial Morocco

The nominal existence of the Islamic city-states in Morocco dates back to the eighth century, when Idriss I founded the Idrissi dynasty in the Roman town of Volubilis (788–91). He justified his political and military leadership by virtue of his descent from the family of the Prophet Mohamed (*shurfa*), thereby laying the ground for subsequent temporal-religious leadership claims. The different dynasties that follow each other were marked by periods of severe instability, the lack of clear state boundaries, international recognition and internal sovereignty. One constant in pre-colonial Morocco was the existence of a monarchical institution, the *makhzen*, whose power and sovereignty fluctuated. Its authority was interrelated with sovereignty and autonomous zones of power held by rival tribes in the north, in mountainous areas in the Middle and High Atlas regions, and even on the coastal strips such as around Rabat and Casablanca. As such, although royal power existed, it was limited to the main urban areas essentially around Meknes and Fes at the edges of the Middle Atlas and Marrakech in the south.

Waterbury defined the *makhzen* as a 'stable system of organised violence',[1] referring to the display of violence that marked much of pre-colonial Morocco, and that informed the King's relationship with some of his subjects in the post-colonial period, what Moroccans now refer to as years of lead. The *makhzen* was what Hammoudi refers to as the organisational structure of the abstract notion *dar al mulk*. 'Dar al-mulk presents itself as "the house of power," making a claim on a communal purpose whose guarantor is God.'[2] As such, Hammoudi asserts that it is in contrast to Western notions of a nation-state, based on 'an association of rational individuals or individuals made rational by the action of the state'.[3] The difference is an important one, as it explains the ambivalence of state power in the pre-colonial period. The transcendent reference to God and family (*shurfa*) created both a very large category of 'statehood' based on religion vis-à-vis limited authority that was based on lineage, whilst compounding a shared sense of belonging to an Islamic community of believers (*mu'minin*).

Temporal state power was based on a system of personal loyalty to the Sultan, which was exchanged for protection and partial autonomy. Taxes were paid by loyal groups but refused by those who did not accept the protection and the 'this-worldly' authority of the King. This meant that statehood was limited to the personal power that family and lineage could create. However, even if some groups did not accept the temporal authority, Friday sermons would still be held in the name of the Sultan. These groups accepted his religious authority, so that the wider, transcendent reference to God created a much larger notion of statehood.

Pre-colonial Morocco in the eighteenth and nineteenth centuries was therefore an ambiguous state. It consisted of an administration to which the expression *makhzen* referred, but with no clear state boundaries nor clear temporal subjects, due to tribes that refused the Sultan's authority and taxes in wide areas of today's Morocco. Increasing the strength of the administration or modernising it would have created tensions, as the basis on which tribes and towns paid taxes was a fragile one: increasing taxes was often resisted among the semi-autonomous tribes and towns, creating rebellions. When Morocco was faced with increasing foreign pressure after Algiers was occupied by France in 1830, it was not a modernising effort that made Morocco stop the threat and prevent French encroachment into Moroccan territory (in fact, the Sultan's army was defeated twice), but rather local tribal resistance against foreign armies. As they were already so capable of resisting and fighting the Sultan's army, they were even more capable of resisting attempts by the French, who did not know the terrain.

The monarchy's increasing inability to resist accelerated colonial pressure in the nineteenth century after Spanish and Portuguese conquest of coastal areas in the fifteenth and sixteenth centuries may be explained by its exposure. Trade with Europe and the trans-Saharan trade (especially in gold, spices and slaves) had been the origin of wealth for centuries, leading to the regional trading capitals from

Sijilmassa to Fes. In the nineteenth century, growing trade relations also benefited local, powerful merchants. Meantime, Moroccan ports such as Tangier and Essaouira became easy targets of French and other European warships in their quest to protect their commercial interests. This easily undermined the Sultan's protective relationship with his subjects. The Sultan was left to negotiate his way out of this pressure exerted on him from the inside, well aware of the military superiority of the foreigners. It is therefore no surprise that Moulay Abderrahman originally congratulated France on the capture of Algiers in 1830, even promising to provide supplies to French forces, not being aware that France would occupy the whole of Algeria, thereby exposing the eastern side of Morocco from Fes to Oujda and Marrakech. In addition, the French presence threatened Fassi commercial relations with towns in western Algeria, such as Tlemcen. The result was that the Fassi *'ulema* requested that the Sultan provide military aid and manpower to the people of Tlemcen against the French.[4]

To increase revenue of the state without raising taxes and upsetting the fragile basis of the Sultan's power, trade with Europeans was regarded as a viable alternative. Grain, wool, skins and wax were primarily exported from 1832 onwards, and export doubled from 1833 to 1834, with the Sultan taking a personal interest in these exchanges. As the purpose was to increase the government's coffers, the Sultan made sure that only selected people were controlling the trade, excluding European merchants.[5] Preferred intermediaries were the Jews, as Muslims were not allowed to deal with non-Muslim Europeans.[6] Famous *makhzen* families able to take advantage of this new source of wealth were the Benjellouns and the Bennises from Fes. Talib Benjelloun was a former state minister, *wazir*, and he was named by Edward Drummond Hay, the British consul in Tangier, as the richest merchant in the country. Both successful merchant families were heavily involved in trade with Gibraltar, re-exporting produce from the Saharan trade.[7]

Ironically, issues of trade were the reason for an increased foreign presence and confrontation between the *makhzen* and foreign interests, as the Sultan was not able to guarantee the security of merchant ships, often causing reprisals by France in Essaouira, Tangier, Salé, and by other European powers such as Austria, Britain and Spain. Lack of protection as well as limitations placed on the free choice of intermediaries and commercial representatives caused friction between foreign representation and the Sultan. These questions were crucial for the protection of local interests, tied as they were to *makhzen* families' interests and revenues. The result was that the various commercial treaties, the first one being the Anglo-Moroccan Treaty of 9 December 1856 under the threat of British military intervention, established the status of protégés under the protection of foreign commercial and consular authorities. It also stipulated that British nationals had the right to choose whom they wished to conduct their affairs with or employ as translators.[8] After the war of Tetouan against the Spanish, the treaty of Madrid of 20 November 1861 established what was to become the norm, and it indicates the imbalance that foreign relations had on the domestic political-economic *makhzen*: 'The chargé d'affairs of his Catholic Majesty to the King of Morocco can freely choose his translators, and servants among Muslim subjects ... These will be exempt from any personal or direct contributions, forced taxes, or any analogous payments.'[9]

Although trade with foreigners was to fill the *makhzen*'s official and the Sultan's private purse, making it capable of increasing its administrative strength, it also created domestic disturbances as it raised questions within conservative *'ulema* circles, resentful merchants and impoverished parts of the population, leading to banditry and general domestic insecurity. Exporting grain was politically risky when parts of the population were not well fed as a result of poor harvests. Attacks on foreign freight, foreign merchants and protégés, among them Moroccan Jews, remained frequent, creating embarrassment among the *makhzen* administration, and it raised fears concerning increased military protection as demanded by the foreign powers.

However, as long as access to the Moroccan market was subject to foreign rivalry, such as the British–French rivalry, the Sultan could guarantee Morocco's independence. The state's internal situation increasingly depended on foreign powers' geo-strategic and commercial interests, such as Britain's interest in having a weak southern shore at the straits of Gibraltar to control access. However, when British–French rivalry ceased due to Germany's increased colonial ambitions under Wilhelm II (1888–1918), Morocco's independence was far less secure, opening the way for French colonial ambitions in North-West Africa.

## 2.2 The colonial period and the rise of the nationalist movement

Whereas Hassan I (1873–94) was able to create relative calm among tribal elements due to his warrior ethos and frequent military campaigns (*harka*) in autonomous tribal areas (*bled es siba*),[10] his successor Moulay Abdelaziz (1894–1908) had neither the personal nor the traditional powers to keep rebelling tribesmen and their leaders under control. This was largely due to an increasing foreign presence in the court along with the presence of Western cultural goods such as bicycles and fireworks displays that the young Sultan frequently enjoyed, putting into question the new Sultan's religious and traditional authority as a defender of Muslim lands against Christians.[11] The Act of Algeciras of 1906 stipulated even more foreign economic presence in Morocco. This was then used for even more foreign military presence to protect commercial and strategic interests in Morocco (Casablanca and Oujda in 1907), contributing to the decreasing legitimacy of the ruler and his increasing reliance and dependence on foreign protection.

The result was the famous Hafidhian revolution of 1908, in which Sultan Abdelaziz was deposed, and replaced by Moulay Hafidh. Weakened control of the Sultan in the countryside meant that local groups could gain more power than before, due to autonomous trade relations or special arrangements with the French. Madani El Glaoui, one of the Berber tribal lords of the south, played an active role in promoting Hafidh as a new sultan. The protection El Glaoui granted to him when Abdelaziz tried to have Hafidh arrested is the most important example of the changed balance of power to the detriment of Sultan Abdelaziz.[12] After Moulay

Hafidh was proclaimed Sultan in Marrakech in the summer of 1907, a period of civil war until the end of the year ensued, reinforcing Abdelaziz's lack of control. The final blow to Abdelaziz's rule took place in January 1908 in Fes, when the 'ulema issued a new bey'a, the act of allegiance, in favour of Moulay Hafidh. Angry urban and rural rioters were motivated by new taxes that Abdelaziz had imposed (maks – a tax imposed on goods entering cities). Signs of wealth (the monopoly tobacco company) were attacked as well as symbols that were associated with foreigners, such as the Jewish quarter mellah.[13] As the Sultan had previously left Fes to be near French protection in Rabat, the rebellious Fassi crowd led by the influential 'alim Mohamed Kettani decided to ask the 'ulema to withdraw their allegiance to the Sultan as he was no longer capable of ensuring safety in Fes. The bey'a issued by the 'ulema was conditional, emphasising its contractual character, and it stipulated that Hafidh was required:

> (1) to abrogate the Algeciras Act; (2) do his utmost to restore Morocco's territorial integrity; (3) bring about the evacuation of French troops from Casablanca and Oujda; (4) undertake no agreements with foreigners except with the approval of the people; (5) abolish the maks; (6) restore and revivify the practice of Islam; (7) abolish foreign privileges and capitulations; (8) seek a closer cooperation with other Muslim powers, especially the Ottoman state; and (9) repudiate the debts which had been contracted by 'Abd al-'Aziz.[14]

Hafidh's mandate was clearly informed by contemporary notions of *jihad*, the Islamic struggle for religious purification and just rule, and nationwide support for this concept, reinforced through pragmatic self-interest as the taxation issue *maks* illustrates. Moulay Hafidh was an Islamic intellectual informed by Abu Shuayb al Dukkali, a Moroccan religious reformer (*salafiyya*) similar to the Egyptian Mohamed Abduh.[15] Historian Edmund Burke III reports that the Hafidhiyya – the process that pitted Moulay Hafidh against his brother Sultan Abdelaziz – was of major social political significance as it involved the population in support of either claimant:

> [It] was a truly national political event of major importance, perhaps the first in Moroccan history to affect so many people. At times, the lines of division pitted brother against brother. Years later old men still remembered, with a flickering of passion, who had been the 'Azizists and who the Hafizists. The Hafiziya therefore constituted a new phenomenon in Moroccan history.[16]

Ironically, the process that aimed at facing the Western challenge only accelerated the process in which the French protectorate was proclaimed in 1912. First, the new Sultan Hafidh needed the recognition of the French in order to act as an international actor and collect taxes on trade. France, however, would only recognise Moulay Hafidh if he recognised the Act of Algeciras. This, of course, only undermined his domestic support, based as it was on guaranteeing Moroccan independence. The *'alim* who became his greatest challenger, Mohamed Kettani, was also the person who had brought him to power.[17]

Second, customs and taxes did not provide Moulay Hafidh with the necessary financial means, and foreign borrowing meant increasing French control over the kingdom's finances. In exchange for a 90 million-franc loan, 'the Makhzan renounced to the French the remaining forty per cent of customs revenues that it still controlled, all indirect taxes, all receipts on state monopolies (tobacco and cannabis) and all receipts on Makhzan lands within 10 km of the coast',[18] putting a deadly end to the Sultan's sovereignty. These conditions were forced upon the Sultan, the constant threat being further foreign control of trade and custom revenues imposed by France's superior firepower.

Third, diminishing the Sultan's sovereignty only made matters worse. Rebellions became omnipresent, the surrounding of the city of Fes by 6,000 Middle Atlas tribesmen in 1911 prompted the French to seize military control over the city. Meantime, a German–French agreement of November 1911 de-internationalised the Moroccan question, making it a French question in return for French land near the Congo River. The Protectorate Agreement, signed on 30 March 1912, became unavoidable.

Article 1 of the Protectorate Agreement stipulated that the French government would 'institute a new system of rule in Morocco which will entail administrative, judicial, educational, economic, financial and military reforms that the French government would find useful to introduce in Morocco'.[19] The new regime would keep and protect religious aspects of life in Morocco as well as the traditional prestige of the Sultan. The sherifian *makhzen* was to be reformed. Spanish claims in the north and the international status of Tangier would not be affected by the treaty. Article 2 authorised the French army to occupy the territory as the French government deemed necessary to keep up public order.[20] In short, the treaty relegated a symbolic function to the sultanate whereas France was responsible for all domestic and international political decisions, including representing Morocco in international politics. The main centre of power became the institution of General Residency, the *makhzen* being stripped of the few powers it still formally enjoyed. However, the *makhzen* continued to exist as a reformed administrative institution. Morocco's longest and most important general resident, Hubert Lyautey (1912–25), strongly believed in indirect rule on the British model, which was a lot less expensive than France's experience in Algeria. This meant a reinforcement of traditional forms of rule complemented by a strong army and a tax system – ultimately 'pacification'. To achieve this, he relied on co-opted rural notables, such as the *grands caids* in the south including Thami El Glaoui who became pasha of Marrakech, local *caids* and pashas, controlled and appointed by the Grand Vizir Mohamed El Mokri. Militarily, Lyautey relied on a strong, locally recruited army.[21] In the Middle Atlas, leaders of brotherhoods, *tariqa*, such as Abdelhay Kettani, were incorporated into this system, in which they were protected by the French and thereby given unlimited power and consequently wealth in return for their loyalty – unconstrained by traditional systems of patronage and mediation.[22] Parallel to this system, the French built a 'modern' system of government, ministries of health, finance, education, justice and agriculture headed by French administrators. Traditional and modern sectors were kept separate, which is best illustrated in colonial city planning separating the ancient *medina* from the modern and French-populated *ville nouvelle*.

To pursue France's objective of making its Moroccan protectorate financially self-sustaining, formerly 'collective' land was nationalised and subsequently sold, filling the Residency's coffers. The land was distributed among French colonial settlers, who flocked to Morocco in large numbers. Modern equipment was thereby introduced, contributing to the Residency's plan of modernising the agricultural sector. By 1925, 500,000 hectares of prime agricultural land were under foreign ownership, increasing to 1 million hectares towards the end of the protectorate. As a result, trade with France increased tremendously, and when Morocco's phosphate industry started operating under the newly founded Office Sherifien des Phosphates, the protectorate continuously enjoyed a trade surplus with France. Most importantly, the tax system now became operational. The zone in which the agricultural tax, *tertib*, was collected increased steadily with the military campaigns that 'pacified' tribal areas. Locally empowered *caids* and sheikhs were charged with collecting the tax, and they were allowed a percentage of their collection, leading to massive corruption and exploitation. For the Residency, though, the income generated from the co-optation of local *caids* increased from 20 million francs in 1915 to 174 million francs in 1935. It should be noted that European settlers were often exempt from agricultural taxation, one of the means of encouraging investment in this area.[23]

Colonialism brought innovation and modernisation that also resonated favourably among the growing Islamic revivalist movement. It looked for Islamic renewal and reform on the basis of more modern institutions. Although the *salafiyya* movement was mostly alienated by French colonial rule, French administrative modernisation and centralisation also offered perspectives for a stronger Moroccan state. The movement took roots in the Free School movement, in which Arabic and Islam were taught outside the auspices of the French. In fact, education among Moroccans became an ideological battlefield. The protectorate's philosophy was based on conservatism and separation of Moroccans and European *colons*. The aim was to conserve *la belle hierarchie*: a handful of powerful Moroccan families had their offspring educated in special schools for 'sons of notables' (*écoles des fils de notables*), whereas urban artisans and Arab and Amazigh farmers had their children educated in urban and rural schools, respectively, with no perspective of further education and social mobility. Entry into secondary education was restricted for Moroccan Muslims, a policy that continued until the end of the protectorate. 'The fellah was to remain a fellah and go back to the soil, although a few sons of rural *caids* could climb out of this groove and pass on to the *écoles des fils de notables*.'[24]

In turn, French Jewish schools around the Alliance Israélite Universelle (AIU)[25] started challenging the Residency's policies. Present in Morocco since the late nineteenth century, the AIU encouraged Jewish co-education along French lines outside the auspices of the Residency, educating a French-speaking elite that looked to upward social mobility under the protectorate after centuries of Muslim control.[26] This was partly achieved as Jews, for example, increasingly moved out of the *mellahs*, Jewish quarters in Moroccan major towns, to which traditionally they had been confined. Of 154 lots placed for sale in the European quarter in Fes, 97 were allotted to Jews and 57 to Muslims – when the Jewish population of Fes only constituted a small percentage of the overall population. In 1948, only 738 Moroccan Muslims were enrolled in French *lycées*, compared to 928 Moroccan Jews, so French spread fastest among the latter.[27] This partly explains the ambiguous perspectives prevalent among Moroccan Jews towards the end of the protectorate period. It also explains many Moroccan Muslims' ambiguous relationship with Jews in this period, often accusing them of collaboration.[28] In addition, towards the end of the protectorate, Jewish schools became very politicised by Zionist organisations, whereas the Free Schools were the basis of the nationalist movement.

France's educational policies were among the most criticised, as they were rightfully regarded as keeping Moroccans, and especially Muslims, out of the segregated economy. Social progress was reserved for European *colons*, a few Moroccan Jews and some selected Moroccan *caids*, whereas large parts of the population remained backward, illiterate and disenfranchised. In the protectorate budget for 1921, 9,255,400 francs were reserved for the education of some 200,000 Europeans, compared to 2,970,390 francs for 6 million Moroccan Muslims. In 1931, the amounts changed to 41,712,348 francs and 14,863,385 francs, respectively.[29] Those who received Western-style education were those who challenged the educational system the most. As Halstead points out, rising education went hand in hand with rising expectations and finally frustration.[30] By the mid-1930s, after 'pacification' campaigns established a French-controlled army in the territory after 20 years of rural resistance, an urban-based nationalist movement increasingly took root.

The protectorate's Amazigh policy may be seen as the other side of its conservative policies. Influenced by colonial ethnographers such as Edouard Michaux-Belaire, France was seeking a 'natural' ally in Morocco among the population to pursue a divide and rule policy. *Assimiliationists* who came to infiltrate the Residency towards the end of Lyautey's reign believed that the Amazigh population, often coinciding with the *bled es siba*, was to be considered such an ally.[31] The empowerment of local tribal leaders, such as the *grands caids* in the south, was already part of its strategy of pacification. It was the Residency that strongly believed in what became an established policy in post-independence Morocco: whoever controls the (largely Amazigh-populated) countryside controls Morocco.[32] An Amazigh policy was already adopted on 14 September 1914 when Amazigh customary law, or *'urf*, was recognised by formal *dahir* (decree), in contrast to Islamic *shari'a* law that was to be applied by traditional religious courts in the towns. In 1915, tribes that submitted to the French army were organised in tribal assemblies, *jama'a*, and given judicial powers, in an effort to establish agencies of representation in tribal Morocco. Although this did not threaten the control of the *makhzen* as there had hardly been any *makhzen* control among these tribes in pre-colonial Morocco, by the 1920s there was widespread belief that the French would actively assimilate the Amazigh population into Frenchmen. The idea – expressed in various correspondence among *assimiliationists* – was that dividing Arabs and Amazighs was a means of preventing a united Morocco that would turn against its creator after pacification. Special schools for Amazighs were already established in 1923, in which the curriculum was wholly conducted in French. Here, Arabic and Islamic teachings were explicitly avoided.

A *dahir* of 16 May 1930 called 'Berber *dahir*' was to place under French jurisdiction all cases that arose in Amazigh territory, thus depriving Islamic *shari'a* courts judicial authority – already limited to cases that did not involve Europeans – over several million Moroccans with one single stroke. For the rising nationalist movement, it was only one small step to believe that the French would seek religious conversion as well, and corresponding rumours quickly informed the developing nationalist discourse. Rising protest against this *dahir* influenced the French withdrawal of the plan even after the Sultan had signed it. Protests focused on the argument that it infringed the protectorate treaty's stipulation that made Islam the Sultan's domain.[33]

The nationalist movement started in the Free Schools movement of the late 1920s, in which Islamic studies and Arabic were given more attention than in the primary schools run by the protectorate. It was run by a proto-nationalist group of men more influenced by *salafiyya* than by thoughts of independence. The curriculum stressed the history of the pre-colonial state in Morocco and engaged in myth making, for example, by claiming that Morocco in 1912 was a modern state guided by constitutional principles. A later group of proto-nationalists organised in the early 1930s in a secret society, named *Kutlat al Amal al Wattani* (National Action Bloc). It comprised people from a variety of backgrounds, ranging from those who received modern education in France, French schools in Morocco and traditional Islamic universities (Qarawiyyin in Fes or Al Azhar in Cairo). The 1930 Berber *dahir*, increasing suppression by the French and European–Moroccan segregation, strongly influenced this group, as did the perceived disempowerment of the Sultan, who seemed sympathetic to their grievances. Early demands did not include independence, but rather a more precise reading of the protectorate treaty, which should not lead to segregation or, worse, de-Islamisation, but rather modernisation.

The protectorate treaty, however, was based on a contradiction in Article 1 that was not to be resolved.[34] Although modernisation was its official goal, the principle of delegating traditional rule to the Sultan and preserving customs implied a dual policy of modernising segregated parts of European-controlled Morocco, whilst leaving traditional both the Sultan's authority and the countryside that remained outside the reach of European farmers. Therefore, 'traditional despotism' was reinforced and ultimately backed by French-style 'modern despotism'. Consequently, the nationalist movement used the Sultan as a symbol of traditional authority and created an alliance with him to challenge this contradiction.

Nationalists such as Allal El Fassi and Ouazzani organised petitions to the Sultan and asked for an audience. The Sultan listened to their grievances 'with tears in his eyes',[35] but he was unable to prevent the same group from being imprisoned by the French authorities only a short while later. After a visit to France, Allal El Fassi was refused entry into Moroccan territory in August 1933. His fiery speeches to his students at Qarawiyyin University troubled the French authorities.

Meantime, the nationalists, supported by elements of the *makhzen*, successfully published an Arabic newspaper, *Majallat al Maghrib*, in which articles were inspired by *salafiyya* ideas. Previous attempts at establishing more communist and nationalist newspapers had been refused. In 1932 *Majallat al Maghrib* came up with the idea of establishing a nationalist day to the glory of the Sultan, *La Fête du Trône*. As the Sultan's official protector, the French could not really refuse this demand. It became a public holiday in 1934, and during celebrations, expressions of 'long live the King' made clear that a modernist branch in Moroccan society was seeking modern sovereignty of the kingdom, and not a protectorate that was seeking to preserve the traditional, limited powers of an oriental 'sultan'.[36] A subsequent Reform Plan, published in Cairo and Paris, outlined the modernisation of Morocco with reforms in education and the economy. It called for an end to the segregation of the foreign and Moroccan populations. Co-education and equal rights of women and men should be pursued. It also demanded that the authority of the Sultan be maintained.[37]

## 2.3 Towards independence

Independence was achieved as a result of a variety of factors, the first being the increasing international trend towards full independence in colonies, mandates and protectorates after World War II. As Morocco was never officially colonised but was supposed to be 'protected' and 'reformed', the question of independence has been an ongoing feature of the protectorate's philosophy. A second factor was how French colonial rule was perceived in Morocco. The protectorate's philosophy was that a strong nation was protecting a weak one, but the reality of France's occupation by Germany and the need for Moroccan troops to liberate France illustrated that the international reality had fundamentally changed in the first half of the twentieth century. In addition, the establishment of a revolutionary movement in Algeria was paramount, but it is misleading to think that it was due to pressure in neighbouring French Algeria alone that independence was granted to Morocco.

It was fortunate for the Moroccan monarchy and one reason for its longevity that Mohamed V was associated with the independence movement, and not perceived as completely dependent on French protection. The Independence Manifesto of 11 January 1944 by the Istiqlal Party stressed that Morocco should be independent under the Sultan, and that the Sultan should negotiate independence on Morocco's behalf. The timing illustrates the influence of France's perceived weakness due to its occupation by German forces, as well as the presence in Morocco of US forces since November 1942 and supposed US pressure on the issue of self-determination and the Atlantic Charter. Ideas of democratic self-government were also indicated in the manifesto: Morocco should sign the Atlantic Charter, which calls for the principle of self-determination *and* the Sultan should establish a democratic government.[38]

Mohamed V, though careful, increasingly allied himself to these demands that went beyond the modernisation and reform in education, economy and legal authority. The means that were at his disposal were largely symbolic, such as his historic visit to Tangier on 10 April 1947, where he would affirm the inalienable and legitimate rights of the Moroccan people. He made it clear that his journey to Tangier and the speech itself had as its objective the re-establishment of an independent Moroccan state. In his words it should 'help Morocco to gain access to the community of states'.[39] The location of the Sultan's speech, the internationalised town of Tangier, was important in this regard, as it guaranteed international attention. It also emphasised that the international zone, the Spanish north and the French zone constituted one single nation. Much to the annoyance of the French, he did not pay tribute to France in his speech. Originally, he was supposed to make reference to France as 'the source of liberty that conducts the country towards prosperity and progress',[40] a phrase that General Resident Eric Labonne had included. According to a later comment by Hassan II, a massacre of Moroccans by Senegalese *tirailleurs* in Casablanca three days before on 7 April 1947 made this homage impossible.[41]

France blamed this failure to control the Sultan on Eric Labonne, and a new hard-line general resident, Alphonse Juin, was appointed. Labonne introduced reforms aimed at increasing the Residency's control over the Sultan *and* increasing Moroccan representation in the administration through elections. Administrative modernisation through elections aimed at weakening the independence movement, thereby influencing the Sultan's pro-independence opinions. Alphonse Juin also introduced the idea of co-sovereignty: French deputies would have an equally advisory function to their Moroccan counterparts. Due to their numerical inferiority, there was nothing democratic in these proposals, which was one of the reasons why the Sultan rejected them. The Istiqlal Party, although elected to the council, supported the Sultan. The idea of co-sovereignty and corresponding elections ultimately backfired.

The nationalist movement became increasingly well organised in the three main political parties: the Moroccan Communist Party, the National Independence Party, and the Istiqlal Party. Each party was informed by ideas of civil liberties that the French did not grant Moroccans, the principle of self-determination, inspired by the Atlantic Charter, and some unspecified form of constitutional monarchy. It reached out into modernised sectors, education, trade unions, women's movements, and sport clubs, but it was led by a wide mix of traditional, leftist, nationalist and Islamic-conservative leaders. In September 1948, the Istiqlal's newspaper *Al Alam* declared that trade unions should be led by notables, reasoning that mass action would be 'a danger for the mentality of the country, its traditions and its wholesome customs'.[42] This reflected the old Fassi bourgeoisie's fear of radicalised nationalists. It also announced the ensuing split in the nationalist movement between conservatives and leftists.

Meantime, the French continued to use force and threatened – without much success – to depose the Sultan should he align himself too closely with the nationalists. The Sultan used his remaining prerogative, that of signing *dahirs*, to paralyse the administration, which led to his deposition in 1953. This followed a well-orchestrated campaign and petitions in which the *grand caid* and pasha of Marrakech, Thami El Glaoui, assumed a prominent role. The campaign was portrayed by the French as an Amazigh uprising against a sultan who was regarded as too closely allied to the urbanised, educated and Westernised elites.[43] The first petition was signed by 20 *caids* on 20 March 1953 in Marrakech. Clearly, the reasoning was that, should Mohamed V and the nationalist movement be successful in obtaining independence, these *caids*' political and economic privileges and possibly their physical security would be at risk. After all, they largely owed their status to the French as they had been responsible for the administration of tax collection that constituted an important source of their income and power.

These men used religion and tradition, combined with the Sultan's contacts with modern parties that included communists, as reasons to ask for the deposition of Mohamed V. When asked by a French journalist why he no longer trusted Mohamed V, Thami El Glaoui showed a picture of the Sultan's sons and daughters wearing swimming suits on the beach.[44] The petition was sent to the French government in Paris on 30 May 1953, by which time more than 250 other pashas and *caids* had signed, of a total of approximately 400.[45] Clearly, they had been pressured by the most important pasha, Thami El Glaoui, but they also feared for the rise of an urban bourgeoisie that might put at risk their own rural identity.[46] When Sultan Mohamed refused, the southern rebels, joined by the powerful 15,000-strong Kettani *tariqa* from the Middle Atlas region, marched towards Rabat under the slogan 'Long live General Guillaume [the general resident], long live Franco-Moroccan cooperation, long live the brotherhoods'.[47] Its *tariqa* leader, Abdelhay Kettani, still wanted revenge against the Alawi family because Sultan Hafidh (1908–12) had brutally killed his brother and important *'alim* of the Kettani *tariqa*, Mohamed Kettani, in 1908.[48] Meantime, some pashas from the main cities, Sefrou, Fes, Meknes and Salé, joined by the *'ulema* of Fes, condemned the demands of the rebellious southern *caids*, but they remained a minority.

In another offensive by Thami El Glaoui, Moulay Mohamed Ben Arafa, a distant cousin of Mohamed V, was proclaimed the new Sultan on 15 August 1953. Increasing violence and riots in support of Mohamed V followed.[49] As a result, public disorder combined with the *caids*' rebellion was used as a pretext by the Residency to remove Mohamed V and his family officially on 20 August 1953, and to exile them first to Corsica and then to Madagascar. Mohamed V was given the opportunity to abdicate voluntarily, in which case he would have been taken to France and well provided for. He refused, saying that according to Hassan II's memory:

No deeds or words would ever justify me abandoning a mission, of which I am the only legitimate person in charge. If the French government considers the defense of a people's liberty a crime that merits punishment, I consider this defense a virtue that merits honor and glory ... I am the legitimate Sovereign of Morocco. Never would I betray the mission that my loyal people has charged me with. France is strong, it shall act the way it believes is just.[50]

Mohamed V's exile and Ben Arafa's accession to the throne only made matters worse. After all, Mohamed V represented the little sovereignty that Morocco still enjoyed. Ben Arafa, in contrast, was seen as a French puppet, and the nationalist movement became involved in the use of violence, urban terrorism, and was consequently subject to harsh police actions and French counter-terrorist activities.[51] It is probably because of Mohamed V's forced exile that he came to represent the struggle for independence, the *authentic* combination of traditional, religious and modern sovereignty. Consequently, it was his return that became the primary goal of the nationalist movement. This was effectively the smallest common denominator, as his expulsion was seen as the worst example of French colonial rule. This also made him stand above all other political factions, which is one of the reasons why he became the primary interlocutor when France allowed his return in November 1955 before granting full independence in March 1956. Increasing pressure resulting from Algerian and Tunisian national liberation movements, as well as the creation of the Maghreb Liberation Army, facilitated Morocco's relatively smooth accession to independence.

## 2.4 Independence and the struggle for power

During the transfer of authority, the crucial questions were what kind of 'constitutional' monarchy should be established, what relationship should exist between the monarchy and the nationalist movement, i.e. political parties, and, most importantly, what should be the relationship between the monarchy, the political parties, and the *ancien régime* based on rural notables, *caids* and pashas. The French tried to have Mohamed V accept the old *caids*, in order to guarantee a safe transfer of power. Mohamed V replied to this request in the following words:

Why should I reconfirm the appointment of Moroccan leaders that called for my abdication? Even if I wanted to, I could not do it. The Moroccan monarchy is now constitutional. It's a question that the government needs to deal with.[52]

The question was primordial, as there was only a minority of pashas and *caids* who had not signed the petition that asked for the removal of Mohamed V; consequently, the large majority of these pashas and *caids* were considered collaborators with the French. On the other hand, the countryside was very wary concerning the new, urban, Arabic-speaking and 'modern' *caids* appointed by the Istiqlal Party, since they lacked both prestige in the eyes of the rural population and knowledge of its social fabric they were meant to administer. At independence, more than 70 per cent of the population was living in rural areas controlled by rural notables. In the ensuing struggle for power between the monarchy and the Istiqlal, these rural notables would become the King's loyal political force. After all, the urban, educated bourgeoisie that was active in the Istiqlal was hostile to these rural notables as they had also formed the social basis of French colonialism. In the Istiqlal's eyes, they represented feudalism and backwardness, and they stood against its projects of modernisation. Consequently, political clashes followed a rural–urban rift to fill the power vacuum at the national and local levels, as pashas and *caids* had been disempowered. The ensuing alliance between the monarchy *and* rural notables was based on political expediency to fight a common rival, the Istiqlal Party.

To achieve this alliance, rural rebellions convulsed the country, targeting both the central government *and* the Istiqlal Party. It is indicative that, in these struggles against the Istiqlal-dominated government, their leaders expressed *their support* to the monarchy.[53] The first of these rebellions took place in 1957, in the stronghold of the Alawi family, the Tafilalet, in south-eastern Morocco near the Algerian border. Here, the governor, Addi Ou Bihi, considering himself loyal to the monarchy alone, resisted the imposition of new *caids* sent by the Istiqlal Party. 'He [Addi Ou Bihi] considered himself a delegate of the King in his region. Consequently, he alone was endowed with the legitimate right to appoint caids.'[54] King Mohamed V did not condemn Addi Ou Bihi's rebellion against the Istiqlal, and instead asked for a nationwide compromise. The compromise took the following form: after a first period in which approximately 400 colonial *caids* were disempowered, some of their family members succeeded in reintegrating the traditional rural administration. A number of these relatives of former *caids* had also been active in the resistance movement, and they successfully mobilised their local prestige, their superior education (through the French-sponsored school for 'sons of notables') and their economic wealth accumulated during the protectorate to re-establish their families' political and economic position.[55]

As pointed out earlier, although the idea of a constitutional monarchy was omnipresent in the nationalist discourse, its precise meaning was never clear, and it served not as a political project *per se* but rather as a convenient reference uniting the divergent views of the nationalists, leftists, Islamic conservatives, and monarchists. Istiqlalis, especially around the young charismatic leader of Istiqlal's leftist branch, Mehdi Ben Barka, frequently evoked the idea of constitutionalism connected to democracy. In the foreword written in Mohamed Lahbabi's *Le Gouvernement Marocain à l'Aube du 20ème Siècle*, Ben Barka affirms that the existence of constitutional ideas before 1912 showed that demanding a constitution after independence did not reflect foreign ideas. Instead, these were authentic, Moroccan thoughts based on continuity, and what he calls 'the expression of a profound national vocation'.[56] In his perspective and based on the 1908 *bay'a* that brought Moulay Hafidh to power, the *bay'a* is contractual and reversible, and constitutes an element of accountability and sovereignty that ultimately rests with the *'umma*, i.e. with the people.

Amidst these struggles at the level of social relations and political ideas, the appointment of Prime Minister Bekkai on 8 December 1955 was the first major blow to the Istiqlal Party. Bekkai was a former *caid* from Sefrou, and one of the few *caids* who had supported Mohamed V in August 1953. Although it was the Istiqlal Party that demanded the premiership, since it considered itself as representing the majority of the Moroccan people, it decided not to force its position on the Sultan, calculating that it was nevertheless the Sultan who enjoyed unrivalled popularity after his glorious return from exile in November 1955. Although it consequently claimed 50 per cent of government posts, it did not obstruct the government of national union when the Sultan only assigned nine of the 22 government portfolios to the Istiqlal. The problem was that the Istiqlal still had little political power in comparison with the palace, despite its relatively strong organisational base. As the Moroccan scholar Mostafa Bouaziz points out, '[t]he principal argument advanced was that one should not oppose the King. Who would have dared it at the time? Even Allal El Fassi, whose extended stay in Tangier was perceived as a sign of discontent against the King, was asked by the executive committee to present his allegiance to the King in Rabat'.[57] In an extraordinary congress, Abderrahim Bouabid declared that 'it [the congress] approves of the quota that the executive committee is obliged to accept, only because of some consideration. It insists that the executive committee makes sure that party representatives accede to the most important ministries'.[58] Clearly, this was the Ministry of the Interior, but, for precisely this reason, Mohamed V wanted an independent candidate for this ministry. Ben Barka suggested the compromise: the Istiqlal would appoint advisers and local positions in the Ministry of the Interior. In return, the minister would be an independent royal appointee, Lahcen Lyoussi, another former Amazigh *caid* and known for his hostility towards the Istiqlal.

French interests prior to granting full independence to Morocco also played into the hands of the monarchy. France was seeking a form of interdependence that would guarantee its economic and geo-strategic interests, especially as the situation in Algeria became increasingly confrontational. By granting full legislative power to the Sultan and not to another institution or elective body,[59] France chose the most reliable institution to achieve this goal. The King thereby being empowered, with an army and a police force at his disposal, gave the Istiqlal little choice but to accept his prerogatives, whereas rural rebellion weakened the grip on 'popular' power that the Istiqlal was claiming. In addition to banditry, rebellions were rocking the country, often in the name of the King. In the summer of 1956 Allal El Fassi was nearly assassinated in Boulemane, a rural Amazigh stronghold in the Middle Atlas.

One of the most important events was the formation of a new party in 1959, the Popular Movement (MP). It resulted from a rural uprising in the northern Rif area that remains anchored in popular Moroccan knowledge until today. In 1957, the struggle for power resulted in the Istiqlal's turning against a rival political party, the Democratic Independence Party. This ended in the assassination of Abbes Messaadi, one of the Liberation Army's leaders from the Rif, allegedly at the instigation of Mehdi Ben Barka. In 1958, after a governmental reshuffle, the Istiqlal dominated all ministerial positions including the premiership and the Ministry of the Interior. As a consequence, the Istiqlal sought to eliminate its political opponents and it had access to state institutions to pursue this aim. In particular, it inhibited the formation or legalisation of rival parties, such as the MP.[60]

Northern Morocco and the Rif had been economically negatively affected by independence, while Spain's more limited economic development efforts left the north marginalised vis-à-vis the rest of the country. Job opportunities in Algeria no longer existed because the border was closed, and trade was declining. There was no Spanish colonial army to enlist in anymore and the Istiqlal monopolised positions in the administration by bringing in outsiders who spoke Arabic and French, not Tamazight or Spanish.[61] The funeral of Abbes Messaadi added fuel to the fire, as Istiqlalis who occupied the posts in the Ministry of the Interior did not authorise a public transfer of Messaadi from Fes to Ajdar. When the funeral gathering commenced the procession, in spite of the absence of authorisation, the situation escalated. Auxiliary troops were called on to disperse the gathering. The leaders of the MP, who had called for the transfer, were arrested. Both Mahjoubi Aherdane and Abdelkrim Khattib, however, were heroes of the Liberation Army, and, while they were imprisoned, the Rifi rebellion spiralled out of control, culminating in December 1958 in the rebels' capture of the town of Al Hoceima.[62] This had a paradoxical effect: on one hand, in January 1959, then Crown Prince Hassan organised a brutal military campaign against the rebels from the base in Tetouan, resulting in casualties reaching more than 10,000 Riffians. During his time as King of Morocco, Hassan never visited the area again and the Rif chronically lacked state investment – resulting in more violence, riots and repression in the 1980s. On the other hand, the lack of control further undermined all of the Istiqlal's ambitions to single-party status. Aherdane became a privileged interlocutor between the monarchy and the Amazigh countryside, and the MP was recognised in 1959 as a political party composed of Amazigh rural notables.

During this time, the outlines of the modern state became increasingly clear. The Istiqlal broke into a leftist wing, the National Union of Popular Forces (UNFP), under the leadership of Mehdi Ben Barka, Abdallah Ibrahim, Abderrahim Bouabid and Abderrahman Youssoufi. The UNFP stressed the necessity of radical economic reforms and government accountability, in line with a socialist strategy to bring an end to Morocco's underdevelopment. In contrast, the more nationalist-conservative Istiqlal under Allal El Fassi stressed Islamic authenticity and 'territorial integrity', meaning a re-creation of historical Morocco. According to these ideas, Morocco's rightful borders stretched from the Senegal river in the south to the oasis of Tindouf in the east (in Algeria), including Mauritania and especially Western Sahara. In the words of El Fassi:

> If Morocco is independent, it is not completely unified. The Moroccans will continue the struggle until Tangier, the Sahara from Tindouf to Colomb-Bechar, Touat, Kenadza, Mauritania are liberated and unified. Our

independence will only be complete with the Sahara! The frontiers of Morocco end in the south at Saint-Louis du Sénégal.[63]

This strongly nationalist discourse was increasingly well pronounced and resulted in a series of articles published in the nationalist review *Perspectives Sahariennes* in the period of 1959–60. It influenced Morocco's post-independence foreign policy far beyond what had initially been believed by El Fassi himself, who admitted that 'originally, I was the only person to call for the liberation of the Sahara and I was greeted with laughter'.[64] Between both parties, the army, largely controlled by French 'advisers', had become allied to the monarchy, as were conservative rural notables. The remainder of the Liberation Army that may have caused a threat to the monarchy, as it was not under its immediate control, was crushed by the combined Franco-Hispanic operation *Ecouvillon* in February 1958. It fought against Spanish positions around Ifni and the Spanish Sahara.

In this national context, Crown Prince Hassan took an increasingly active role, competing with the older nationalist leaders and especially with Mehdi Ben Barka, his former mathematics tutor. As head of the armed forces, Crown Prince Hassan came to occupy the most important position in the struggle for power. In 1959, the UNFP's newspaper *Al Tahrir* was closed down for asking for a government that was responsible to the people. Only one year before, Lahbabi's book and Mehdi Ben Barka in its foreword argued likewise without being banned.

The crisis deepened with alleged plots against the state or the crown prince, and arrests made among prominent nationalists, such as Abderrahman Youssoufi, Mohamed Basri and Mehdi Ben Barka, despite the fact that some of their party colleagues were in government. Even amidst the crisis, Mohamed V continued to be popular, as Mehdi Ben Barka, for example, wrote to an American journalist in the spring of 1960: 'Solid democracy can be achieved through a union of the people with the king, if he could only free himself from the pernicious influence of an entourage of inefficient and corrupt adventurers.'[65]

The Istiqlal's increasing loss of control, and the UNFP's more outspoken critique, led Mohamed V to assume an ever more outspoken position. He assumed the premiership in May 1960, dissolved the government of Abdallah Ibrahim, which represented the leftist wing of the Istiqlal, and named Crown Prince Hassan his vice prime minister, less than a year before Mohamed V's sudden death in 1961. In this new government, the Istiqlal kept its marginal role, but Bouabid and Ibrahim joined the UNFP under Ben Barka and accused the monarchy of absolutist-style rule, cementing the rift between the left and the palace. However, with no election and no constitution in these first five years of independence, forms of political power were based on support from popular constituencies, which the Istiqlal and the UNFP could count on less and less, nor mobilise at a national level. The monarchy successfully prevented such a political unity around the Istiqlal. It is important to stress the difficulty of the Istiqlal's project, due to strong rural–urban divisions compounded by the legacy of how the French had empowered the rural elite. As a result, the monarchy struck an alliance with rural elements, establishing patron–client relationships from these early days of independence.

## 2.5 Summary

All these events showed quite clearly that, although the lack of control over the countryside provided a security challenge for the King too, he was more capable of achieving loyalty due to his combination of traditional and religious legitimacy rather than the urban-based nationalist Istiqlal. The concept of nationalism itself was still developing in Morocco, and up until then was only based on a common front against French colonial rule. Tribal and family-based alliances were primordial, reflected in political loyalty and even business relations,[66] and the Istiqlal's incapacity to impose itself on the countryside and its rural elite was also a reflection of primary, lineage-based rivalry that came to dominate the new political arena – reinforced by educational and linguistic differences. The Arab–Amazigh difference may have been less important in Morocco's traditional political system, but through the establishment of a national project in which an urban-based, largely Arabic-speaking educated elite attempted to impose itself on the countryside, the ethnic-linguistic overtone of such an attempt could be easily exploited. Aherdane's MP was just such a political formation, as was, arguably, the Istiqlal itself. After all, based on notions of Arab-Islamic culture, the Istiqlal represented the culture of established Fassi families, where intermarriage, and economic and political power were closely associated.

Hence, the origins of the state need to be understood as resulting from a very differentiated political field, marked by regional, ethnic, linguistic and cultural rivalries. The monarchy was empowered by the French and continued to draw on military support, but it was the symbolic loyalty it could count on, combined with its control over the security apparatus, that gave it pre-eminence. This gave the state the dual nature that has prevailed ever since. On one hand, a neo-patrimonial monarchical state controls the means of coercion and is legitimised by its central role in the national movement (Mohamed V became *Le Libérateur*). It is supported by patron–client relations that structured the Moroccan political elite towards its centre. Ideologically, the monarchy's role in the liberation from French colonial rule drew on the religious prestige that the Sultan enjoys as *Amir Al Mu'minin*. Together, this largely accounted for Mohamed V's personal charisma portrayed as being solely capable of keeping the country together against the centrifugal forces at work in the immediate post-independence period. On the other hand, a modern, urban-based, political current existed, even if weakened by clan-based loyalties. It remained attached to a symbolic role of the monarchy; however, proto-democratic institutions such as constitutionalism informed their political action, to the extent that Mohamed V's taking over of the premiership in April 1960 was called a palace *coup d'état*. Ideas of government accountability have been very influential since, and they also had an impact on Hassan II's thinking, who sought constitutionalism and elections as a means not to be associated with sultanic despotism, even if real power was increasingly located in informal royal networks and shadow ministries consisting of appointed advisers.

## Notes

1 J. Waterbury, *The Commander of the Faithful*, New York: Columbia University Press, 1970, p. 15, cited in C.R. Pennel, *Morocco Since 1830*, London: Hurst and Company, 2000, p. 37.
2 A. Hammoudi, 'The Reinvention of *Dar al-mulk*. The Moroccan Political System and its Legitimation' in R. Bourqia and S. Gilson Miller (eds) *In the Shadow of the Sultan. Culture, Power and Politics in Morocco*, Cambridge, MA: Harvard University Press, 1999, p. 130.
3 Ibid.
4 Pennel, op. cit., pp. 41–42.
5 Ibid., pp. 43–44.
6 D.J. Schroeter, 'Royal Power and the Economy in Precolonial Morocco: Jews and the Legitimation of Foreign Trade' in Bourqia and Gilson Miller, op. cit., pp. 74–102.
7 Pennel, op. cit. p. 44.
8 M.A. Alaoui, *Le Maroc face aux convoitises européenne 1830–1912*, Salé: Beni Snassen, 2001, p. 87.
9 Cited in ibid., p. 87.
10 For a vivid account, see G. Maxwell, *Lords of the Atlas*, London: Cassel and Co., 2000, chapter 2.
11 Ibid., chapter 3.
12 E. Burke III, *Prelude to Protectorate in Morocco*, Chicago, IL: The University of Chicago Press, 1976, pp. 102–104.
13 Ibid., p. 114.
14 Ibid., p. 116.
15 Ibid., p. 101.
16 Ibid., p. 124.
17 For an interesting account of the multifaceted nature of religious and temporal power associated with the Kettani *zawiyya* of Fes, see S. Bazzaz, 'Reading Reform Beyond the State: Salwat al-Anfas, Islamic Revival and Moroccan National History' in *The Journal of North African Studies*, Vol. 13, No. 1, March 2008.
18 Pennel, op. cit., p. 147.
19 Alaoui, op. cit., p. 228.
20 Alaoui, op. cit., p. 228.
21 D. Maghraoui, 'Moroccan Soldiers: Between Selective Memory and Collective Memory' in *Arab Studies Quarterly*, Vol. 20, No. 2, 1998, pp. 21–42.
22 Pennel, op. cit., pp. 160–164.
23 M. Salahdine, *Maroc: Tribus, Makhzen et Colons. Essai d'histoire economique et sociale*, Paris: L'Harmattan, 1986, pp. 149–152.
24 J.P. Halstead, *Rebirth of a Nation. The Origins and Rise of Moroccan Nationalism. 1912–1944*, Cambridge, MA: Harvard University Press, 1969, p. 108.
25 M. Laskier, *The Alliance Israelite Universelle and the Jewish Communities of Morocco, 1862–1862*, Albany, NY: State University of New York Press, 1983.
26 For a discussion of the status of Jews, see Norman A. Stillmann, *The Jews of Arab Lands*, Philadelphia: The Jewish Publication Society of America, 1979; M. Laskier, op. cit., pp. 10–24.
27 M. Laskier, op. cit., p. 306.
28 As found in the majority of Istiqlalis, as reported by Laskier, op. cit., p. 313.
29 Halstead, op. cit., p. 111.
30 Halstead, op. cit., p. 109.

31 Halstead, op. cit., p. 70.
32 See R. Leveau, *Le Fellah Marocain: Défenseur du Trône*, Paris: Fondation Nationale de Sciences Politiques, 1985.
33 J.P. Halstead, op. cit., pp. 72–73. Prominent examples of actual conversion included the brother of a very well-known nationalist, Omar Abdeljalil.
34 'Traité pour l'organisation du Protectorat français dans l'Empire Chérifien', 30 March 1912, www.ambafrance-ma.org/EfMaroc/cea/hg/dosh1.pdf (accessed 12 March 2007).
35 Pennel, op. cit., p. 213.
36 M.A. Alaoui, *Maroc: Du Traité de Fes à la libération 1912–1956*, Rabat: La Porte, 1994, p. 73.
37 Pennel, op. cit., pp. 227–233.
38 Alaoui, 1994, op. cit., pp. 263–264.
39 Ibid., p. 106.
40 Ibid., p. 109.
41 Hassan II, *Le Defis*, Paris: Albin Michel, 1976, pp. 40–41.
42 Cited in Pennel, op. cit., p. 275.
43 Alaoui, 1994, op. cit., p. 136.
44 Ibid., p. 130.
45 Figures mentioned by Leveau, op. cit., p. 24.
46 Leveau, op. cit., p. 8.
47 Pennel, op. cit., p. 281.
48 Alaoui, 1994, op. cit., pp. 138–139.
49 Ibid., p. 149.
50 Hassan II, op. cit., pp. 54–55.
51 For a vivid account, see S.O. Hughes, *Morocco Under King Hassan*, Reading: Ithaca, NY, 2001, pp. 57–66.
52 Cited in Leveau, op. cit., p. 20.
53 E. Gellner, 'Patterns of Tribal Rebellion in Morocco' in P.J. Vatitiokis (ed.) *Revolution in the Middle East and Other Case Studies*, London: Allen and Unwin, 1972, pp. 120–145.
54 Leveau, op. cit., p. 24.
55 Ibid., pp. 24–25.
56 Mehdi Ben Barka in M. Lahbabi, *Le Gouvernement Marocain à l'Aube du 20ème siècle*, Rabat: Editions Techniques Nord-Africaines, 1958, p. 3.
57 M. Bouaziz, *Aux Origines de la Koutla Démocratique*, Casablanca: Editions de la Faculté des Lettres Aïn-Chock, 1998, p. 99.
58 Ibid.
59 Article 1 of the 'Protocole Annexe', cited in Alaoui, 1994, op. cit., p. 237.
60 Pennel, op. cit., p. 304.
61 Ibid.
62 Waterbury, op. cit., pp. 240–244.
63 Allal El Fassi, 19 June 1956, cited in T. Hodges, *Western Sahara: The Roots of a Desert War*, Westport: Lawrence Hill and Co., 1983, p. 85.
64 Ibid., p. 86.
65 Cited in M. Howe, *Morocco. The Islamist Awakening and Other Challenges*, Oxford: Oxford University Press, 2005, p. 101.
66 Leveau, op. cit., pp. 86–89.

# 3
# THE POLITICS OF EXCLUSION AND INCLUSION

As outlined in the previous chapter, contemporary Moroccan politics owes many of its characteristics to the way that the state's primary institution, the monarchy, interacted with plural political forces. One basic feature of this interaction has been alliance building against a common, domestic rival, while offering to selected groups opportunities to be included in the distribution of societal power and wealth. While these alliances tended to follow clannish and tribal logics until the mid-1970s, it has increasingly become based on socio-economic characteristics and political ideologies. Effectively, the rise of political Islam since the early 1980s, as well as the mass arrival of countryside dwellers to the main cities, created strong incentives for former opposition parties to ally with the regime. After 1992, tragic events in neighbouring Algeria compounded the political elite's willingness to make concessions to the monarch, a trajectory that some Islamists followed in the late 1990s. Concessions did not just emanate from opposition groups, however, as the monarch also attempted to include groups and create alliances depending on internal or external events challenges. Military coups, economic crisis and more recently the Arab Spring were all such important catalysts that triggered political reforms – from constitutional changes over human rights protection to participation in government – which corresponded to some of the political aspirations of these groups.

The aim of this chapter is to analyse the contemporary politics through the prism of inclusion and exclusion, as well as support and opposition (with its corresponding characteristics of regime strength and weakness) that have been constant binaries in Morocco's post-colonial state and nation-building process. Neo-patrimonialism[1] has been central to the process of inclusion and exclusion, and it led to what Mohamed Tozy called Morocco's defused political game: selected inclusion gave individuals and their political parties the possibility of participating in governments. Consequently, even if formal elections were held to give popular legitimacy to inclusion, political power was first of all conceived of as a royal gift. In turn, this gave rise to a changed meaning of politics, as it ceased to be associated with a struggle for power. Instead, the monarchy successfully associated politics with consultation legitimised, *inter alia*, by Islamic concepts such as *shura*.[2]

Once accepted and imposed by the modern coercive apparatus of the state, this accounted for much of what is perceived as political flexibility that came to characterise monarchical rule since the early 1990s. As Anderson has convincingly argued, it has been flexibility that accounts for the regime's longevity and even survival.[3] As I will show, the monarchy's method of dealing with the mass protests following the revolution in Tunisia is illustrative of this point. However, as I argue in this chapter, strong challenges to the status quo continue due to the apparent mismatch between the promises of efficient government, accountability and social justice at the level of political discourse, and the perception of corruption, electoral manipulation and extreme income disparities on the ground. Consequently, anti-systemic criticism has been expressed by Islamist groups that display an ideological hostility towards both the Western-inspired practice of electoral democracy and the re-traditionalisation of politics under the monarch. From this structural feature, Morocco under Mohamed VI was able to dominate over the political sphere before and after 2011, by engaging in a largely uncontested reform drive that significantly strengthened his authority. In spite of prevalent contradictions between electoral accountability and multi-party institutions on the one hand, and monarchical authoritarianism on the other, the events leading up to and following the 2011 Arab Spring indicate that these contradictions in themselves do not account for many of the political changes that observers witness in Morocco. Instead, reforms and concessions to opposing groups reflect both the relative strength and legitimacy of the monarch, as well as the support that he can rely on from well-entrenched and politically significant patron–client networks.

## 3.1 Power struggles (1): the fragmentation of the state, 1961–73

When Mohamed V unexpectedly died in August 1961 and Hassan II succeeded to the throne, the new independent state had already achieved a core that was crucial for the continuation of Morocco's efforts at state and nation building. By 1961, state building relied on pre-colonial forms of alliances that had been reinforced by the colonial period. This was based on the delegation of power to rural elites in exchange for their loyalty to the throne. On the other hand, an alliance with the urban elite began to take shape and was based on ideologies such as nationalism, Arabism and Islam, which were reinforced by the spoils that the King could distribute through patron–client relations.

From the very beginning, the alliance with the urban elite included proto-democratic legitimacy, even if legitimised primarily in Islamic terms. As Allal El Fassi declared to the journal *Al Istiqlal* on 11 June 1960, in preparation for Morocco's first communal election held in the same month: 'You know that our country is a Muslim state, and that Islam has always promoted the consultation of the people by its rulers in all aspects of public life. In our tradition we see that the Prophet and Islamic rulers have continued on this path, each one according to his own temperament and according to the requirements of the moment.'[4] El Fassi continues affirming that 'in Morocco, this consultation and even elections have always been characteristic of this country's democratic institutions, from the tribal jama'a to the bay'a, which is something of a referendum for the Sovereign, as the spiritual and temporal head of state'.[5]

Allusions to traditional democratic practices notwithstanding, the Istiqlal Party, together with the UNFP as the main inheritors of the nationalist movement, continued their power struggle with the monarchy. For El Fassi, elections seemed a viable strategy as it 'constitutes a political test that will clearly delineate the country's geopolitical map as well as define the balance of power between the different political currents'.[6] This illustrates that in 1960, after the dismissal of the left-wing Ibrahim government, Istiqlali attempts at power sharing with the monarchy gave way to an attempt at strengthening its own position vis-à-vis the monarchy through electoral support. At around this time, the monarchy adopted a similar strategy: it no longer focused on power sharing with the nationalist movement – however limited this was. Rather it focused on increasing its own power and ability to manoeuvre. First, it encouraged splits within the nationalist movement. Second, it took over the government itself shortly before the organisation of municipal elections in June 1960. Finally, it entered the electoral game by supporting and organising an increasing number of independent pro-monarchical candidates. In the end, the organisation of a referendum on the constitution, drawn up in 1962 largely by the new monarch, Hassan II himself, fulfilled the same purpose: the monarch succeeded in contesting the electoral base of the nationalist movement by drawing on people's overwhelming support and popular legitimacy.

Interestingly, whereas Hassan II sought to undermine the nationalists' more secular basis of power, the conservative branch of the Istiqlal continued to seek an alliance with the monarchy based on religion. Although the intention seemed to render more powerful the traditional-orthodox current of Islam expressed in the traditional Fes-based *'ulema*, it also increased the monarch's religious registry of legitimacy and rallied this important segment of Moroccan society in support of the King. Hence, it was El Fassi's ascension to Ministry of Habous and Islamic Affairs in 1961–62 that introduced in the 1962 constitution the title Commander of the Faithful, thereby 'illustrating that power was of divine origin, and could not simply result from referenda or party struggle'.[7] Emphasising the religious dimension of the state also had the effect of outlawing the Moroccan Communist Party on 9 February 1960 by a Rabat court – 'because *the Moroccan state is a theocratic monarchy*', in the words of the Moroccan judges.[8] The foundation of the League of Moroccan *'Ulema* in 1961 in Tangier, headed by Minister of Habous and Islamic Affairs Allal El Fassi, also aimed at establishing a conservative Islamic doctrine as the basis for the Moroccan state and society. As a result of the increasing influence of Islamic orthodox currents within the state, Moroccan converts to *Baha'i* faith were sentenced to death in 1962. This shocked not only the Moroccan left but also the general director of the royal cabinet, Ahmed Reda Guedira, prompting the King to issue a general amnesty on their behalf. Clearly, the monarchy's alliance with the *'ulema* expressed through the Istiqlal was important; however, it should not challenge the modern and secular basis of the state and its alliance with the increasingly secularised elite, nor should it limit the state's margins of manoeuvre internally or externally.[9]

The first parliamentary elections of 1963, after the adoption of the first constitution of 1962 by referendum, served the purpose of increasing the state's and the monarchy's margins of manoeuvre vis-à-vis the political parties that resulted from the nationalist movement. The design of electoral districts favoured the rural countryside – home to more than 70 per cent of the population that was led by pro-monarchical independents. Hence, the results guaranteed the King's hegemony and limited the urban-based nationalists' claim to represent the people. Coming after the 1962 landslide victory of the constitutional referendum, the parliamentary elections further increased the political weight of the King, who claimed a direct link between himself and the Moroccan nation. As the King put it when he dismissed the holding of a constitutional assembly: 'why should I accept intermediaries, whatever their number or qualities, between My people and Myself? Why should I imagine that three hundred or four hundred, or two hundred and fifty people could be representatives of three and one-half or four and one-half million electors?'[10]

This attitude caused immense frictions between parts of the nationalist movement that had split from the Istiqlal, the UNFP and the monarchy. King Hassan constantly referred to assassination attempts, culminating in an alleged plot in July 1963. The ensuing trials consummated the rift and served to chastise the more radical opposition around Mehdi Ben Barka with 11 death sentences being pronounced, seven in absentia. The break between Morocco's left and the monarchy dated from shortly before the municipal elections of 1961 still under Mohamed V. The government headed by the more leftist Ibrahim was dissolved and Mohamed V took over the premiership himself, with Crown Prince Hassan as his vice-premier. According to the memoirs of Hassan II, the power of the UNFP became more and more threatening. The left had used the government not to form an alliance as Mohamed V intended, but rather to prepare for a *coup d'état*. In his words:

> Attempts at assassination, plunderings and sporadic riots succeeding one another. 'Delegations' came to Rabat to threaten the sovereign, jostling him even within the palace precincts. A section of the press adopted a provoking and insulting attitude ... Preparations had been made not for a general election or for establishing a true democracy, but for a nihilist revolution.[11]

After Mohamed V and Crown Prince Hassan had taken over the government, the UNFP increasingly adopted a hostile attitude towards the monarchy. This started with an unpublished document called *'option révolutionnaire'* that Ben Barka presented in June 1962 to the UNFP congress, and it culminated in a joint declaration in *Jeune Afrique* on 8–14 April 1963 in which Ben Barka and Abderrahim Bouabid declared:

> Our real adversary is the person, who refuses to fulfill his task that was his, that of arbitrage ... We want to talk about the king ... We want to create a constitutional monarchy in which the king is the symbol of institutional continuity, and in which a government accountable to the people exercises power ... Considering the recent attempts at stifling the people by the administration, we are forced to riposte and we can no longer exist as a legal party ... The national movement's options have changed, and it will start a new phase of its combat.[12]

A few days before the 1963 elections, on 5 May 1963, the UNFP published a manifesto in which it declared itself 'the adversary of a feudal and personal regime. One of our objectives is to end this regime ... which means to abolish it. No collaboration with this regime, no national union around it!'[13] The fundamental problem for the young monarch in the period up to the dissolution of the parliament in 1965 was his incapacity to rely on either the Istiqlal or the UNFP to form an alliance on his terms. This left the rural countryside and independent King's men as the only alternative. Although their number in the unicameral parliament was relatively high, the parliament still provided for an arena in which the monarchy could be criticised and challenged. Despite the fact that the UNFP and the Istiqlal only had a minority of seats, accounting for less than 30 per cent of the total, together both parties were able to gain almost 50 per cent in direct elections, which constituted about 50 per cent of the parliament.[14] This enabled both parties to claim popular democratic legitimacy, which was used to challenge the government, rather than accepting their marginal status. The landscape of the opposition, however, was far from monolithic: the Istiqlal Party in parliament claimed a balanced distribution of power inside the government, as did the UNFP parliamentarians. This was not shared by politicised groups outside the parliamentary confines: at one end of the opposition, the National Union of Moroccan Students (UNEM) adopted a policy of complete resistance against the system; at the other, the Moroccan Labour Union (UMT) asked for a compromise. In turn, UNFP leaders in exile such as Mehdi Ben Barka believed in 'the likelihood of toppling royal power, by a coup d'état or by armed action of partisan groups'.[15]

When riots broke out in Casablanca in March 1965, even the appearance of an alliance with the parties of the nationalist movement in parliament vanished, and the King dissolved the parliament. He justified his decision in the following terms:

> Unable to find either a government of national union or a parliamentary majority, We faced two options: to remain faithful to the virtues of democracy that We have always considered the best and most efficient way, or to resign Ourselves to maintaining a parliamentary system that has only given rise to

> fruitless discussions and that, if it continued, would injure the very democracy, Our moral values, Our dignity, and Our creative genius. We are convinced that the paralysis caused by futile parliamentary debates would result in nothing but the disappointment and condemnation of democracy.[16]

His reference to 'futile parliamentary debates' was due to a parliamentary inquiry into the repression of the Casablanca riots by the trusted General Oufkir, an investigation that meant to include overall governmental policies. In this atmosphere of generalised tension, the government confirmed and executed the death sentence of 14 detainees on 27 March 1965. These prisoners had been stopped the previous year at the Algerian border and had been charged with plotting against the monarchy.[17] In turn, Hassan publicly acknowledged problems such as unemployment and even warned that 'the future will not be brilliant'.[18] However, in his speech on 29 March 1965, he severely criticised the deputies for their encouragement of the protests.

> Why did they not take to the streets themselves instead of sending their students? ... Let me tell you that there is no danger more serious for the state as that of a self-proclaimed intellectual. It would have been better if you were all illiterate. I doubt your commitment to democracy ... enough of these hollow discourses and arrogant speeches ... Enough of these slogans of this or that reform, as you are all, or at least a good part of you, completely ignorant of what you are talking about.[19]

In the name of democracy, the parliament was dissolved on 7 June 1965. The King promised a new constitution that would prevent the threatening effects of a parliament that the King did not control. This meant that, although political parties continued to be legal, limitations were placed on their activities through emergency laws. The army being called on 23 March 1965 to quell the Casablanca riots, it started to play a more significant role in politics. As a result, direct patron–client relations based on personal favouritism replaced political institutions such as political parties or the parliament. This created the appearance of severe corruption at all echelons of Moroccan society in a time of severe economic difficulties typical of transitional economic systems. Morocco was marked by high rates of urban unemployment, rural exodus, inadequate housing and the spread of shanty towns.

Nevertheless, it would be misleading to understand this period as one in which the monarch believed he could do without political parties. By indicating that a new constitution would be elaborated, Hassan II would leave the door open for 'constructive' – i.e. more docile – participation of individuals and political parties and renewed alliance. Rather, a process of neo-tribalism and segmented politics needed to confirm the position of the King as 'supreme arbiter' in which different social factions vied not for power but for the King's favour. To establish this, a system of sticks and carrots punished those who continued to oppose the regime – first and foremost Mehdi Ben Barka. In October 1965 Ben Barka was kidnapped in

Paris and allegedly murdered by the Moroccan secret service. On the other hand, the traditional system of *makhzen*, based on *shurfa* families, tribal chiefs and selected *'ulema*, continued to provide for stable administrative authority through *caids*, *walis* (regional governors) and the neighbourhood *mouqqadem* (a low-level functionary of the Ministry of the Interior). Political, administrative and economic resources were all tied to favours that the centre-*makhzen* distributed in the newly independent state. However, the individualisation of these traditional relations, hence the expression neo-tribalism, had the negative effect of not granting the King widespread organisational, institutional support that would comfort his uncontested position. The newly drafted constitution of 1970 and the subsequent referendum were meant to provide an opportunity out of the impasse.

Unfortunately for Hassan II, the opposition parties, despite their ideological heterogeneity, refused the terms of the contract that he offered, and thereby the alliance that the King sought. Both the Istiqlal and UNFP had no input in the drafting of the new 1970 constitution, and consequently the constitution reflected the domination of the monarchy. It diminished the powers of both the parliament and the government vis-à-vis the monarchy. Article 19 of the constitution added to the King's title *Amir Al Mu'minin* (Commander of the Faithful) that of the 'supreme representative of the nation', to be kept in all subsequent constitutions.[20] As a response to their political marginalisation, the parties of the former nationalist movement (UNFP and Istiqlal) formed the alliance *koutla wataniyya* (National Bloc) in 1970, and rejected the King's offer of participating in subsequent parliamentary elections. Ironically, whereas the King aimed at isolating the opposition parties and neutralising their violent discourse in the aftermath of the March 1965 riots, he ended up isolating himself. He thereby increased his reliance upon the army, but also his vulnerability to military coups.

## The two attempted military coups

Along with the Western Sahara campaign that started in 1975, the two attempted military coups that succeeded each other in the summers of 1971 and 1972 were turning points in Moroccan political history as they illustrated the fragility of an isolated system based on patronage and little political support outside the military. They were such turning points that the subsequent construction of a new political system can safely be regarded as Hassan's 'new Morocco'.[21]

The first coup attempt, often called the palace coup, took place on 10 July 1971, when 1,400 young cadets from the military school Ahermoumou in the Middle Atlas stormed the King's birthday party in his beach palace in Skhirat, some 20 km south of Rabat. The course of events is not completely established; however, an important account by one of the surviving participants explains that the cadets were told by their superiors, Colonial M'hamed Ababou and Colonel Larbi Chelouati, as well as General Mohamed Medbouh, that they were on a military mission in Skhirat that aimed at *protecting* the King against insurgents who had allegedly penetrated the palace grounds.[22] Once the cadets entered the palace, however, it seemed that their mission went out of control as they targeted the political nomenclature that was present and the symbols of conspicuous wealth that the King's birthday party illustrated in abundance. Despite being politically sidelined by the palace, many leaders of the independence attended the party, including Allal El Fassi who was among the hundreds of injured during the events. About 60 guests were killed.[23] The coup failed when a leadership struggle broke out, Mohamed Medbouh was shot by the commander of the 1,400 cadets, M'hamed Ababou *before* control was actually seized. Essentially because of the uncontrollable character of the cadets' military conduct, the situation was thereafter controlled by General Oufkir, the interior minister. In popular wisdom, however, it was the King's recourse to his *baraka* that saved his life: when one of the soldiers found him hidden in the bathroom, he knelt down to the King. King Hassan had been reciting the first *sura* of the Koran, the *fatiha*.

The following year, on 16 August 1972, another coup attempt, allegedly masterminded by General Oufkir, weakened the monarchy even further. On a return trip from France, the King's personal aircraft, a Boeing 747, was attacked by a Moroccan fighter plane, but again the King miraculously survived. The Moroccan fighter plane was armed with the wrong ammunition – air-to-surface missiles instead of air-to-air missiles. He even survived a second air attack on his palace in Rabat, which killed ten people and injured 45. The principal organiser of the attack, Mohamed Amoukrane, was probably motivated by incidents of corruption associated with four government ministers that became public in this year, and for which very mild sentences had been given. Amoukrane, at 34 years old, was the oldest of the commanders who had ordered the attack. In contrast to the Skhirat attempt, the organisers of the Boeing attack were supported by a faction of the UNFP, and one of its leaders, Fqih Basri, went into exile in Algeria. This group no longer believed in a negotiated settlement of the conflict between the UNFP and the monarchy. From their perspective, this was confirmed by the two constitutional referendums of 1970 and 1972, which gained an approval rate of 99 per cent despite *koutla wataniyya*'s calling for a boycott.

At this moment, the monarchy faced such severe resistance that even King Hassan's sole support base, the military and the Ministry of Defence, had turned against him. Although never explicitly stated as a threat, the two coup attempts also indicated that an Amazigh numerical majority in security institutions might cause a problem. In this situation, repression alone was no longer feasible due to the monarch's vulnerability to, and dependence upon, trusted individuals with questionable motivations. This system of governance created a critical mass of dissatisfied members of the security forces – often from rural backgrounds – who had the means to change the status quo. In other words, a new equilibrium needed to be found based on consensus and participation of the nationalist movement, including the UNFP. In addition, the authority of the King needed to be re-established and the military controlled to prevent subversive currents from instrumentalising widespread dissatisfaction and social upheavals that were so characteristic of this period.

In turn, the nationalist movement was also threatened by the possible advent of a military ruler. Had a military regime been installed and led by General Oufkir, then the domestic political situation would have fundamentally deteriorated. Hence, the disappearance of Oufkir,[24] and the official blame he received for having masterminded the Boeing attack was used by political parties to attempt reintegration into the monarchical order. This was done by attributing political oppression, not to the King but rather to the minister of the interior, thereby creating space for reconciliation between the monarchy and the nationalist movement. For example, in the following passage the foundation of Istiqlal's Moroccan League for Human Rights (LMDH), shortly after the second coup, is explained and motivated by the repression associated with an 'Oufkiran' order from which the monarch seems dissociated.

> Our action was a historical necessity in order to face the dark Oufkiran order ... He [Oufkir] ruled as an absolute ruler over Morocco ... It was a question of dignity ... the Istiqlaliens and all active forces of our nation, which had fought colonialism and who had sacrificed a lot so that Moroccans could live as free citizens in a free country, could not tolerate this ... The will of our people was ridiculed, and our freedom was tied up. We lived under terror, although we had conquered our independence long before.[25]

As a result, momentum was achieved for launching a new process aimed at finding a consensus and including the nationalist movement in the King's system. The Rabat branch of the UNFP rallied around Abderrahim Bouabid and created the Socialist Union of Popular Forces (USFP) in 1974. Bouabid now dismissed the 'revolutionary option' espoused ten years earlier by Mehdi Ben Barka and Bouabid himself.[26] On the other hand, the more radical Casablanca branch continued to espouse more revolutionary means and supported an ill-fated uprising in the first months of 1973.[27]

In turn, the monarchical state reacted in the following period by adopting typically nationalist policies. Moroccanisation of the economy, Arabisation in education, and especially the primarily nationalist Western Sahara claim all served the purpose of re-establishing and reinvigorating consensus. Constitutional questions based on the exact extent of power sharing were temporarily shelved.

## 3.2 Power struggles (2): the re-establishment of the state, 1974–77

Above all, it was the King's successful Western Sahara campaign and the pre-eminence that this nationalist issue had in domestic political discourse that triggered the nationalist movement's ultimate acceptance of the constitutional status quo. The ensuing re-establishment of the state's authority came as a result of the need to increase domestic support. This was achieved by changing the King's role from that of the 'Great Creator' in Zartman's terminology, to that of the leading player among other actors whose autonomy was guaranteed by their acceptance of the rules of the game as defined by the King. In Zartman's words, '[i]t is a fundamental characteristic of the new system that it is not a play with puppets, but with real actors, and the royal author has written the roles, but not the script or even the plot'.[28] The August 1972 coup interfered with a process with which the King aimed to defuse the former nationalists' (Istiqlal and UNFP) opposition: a new constitution in March 1972, to be followed by elections planned for the latter half of the year. However, the immediate consequence of the second coup was to delay the King's renewed attempt at power sharing. First, he had to bolster his own position, which was challenged by poor economic performance and the coup attempts.

Hence, in November 1972 the King broke off negotiations with the Istiqlal and UNFP, engaged in a massive economic and bureaucratic expansion programme that was fuelled by rising phosphate prices, started nationalisation of colonial lands, and the Moroccanisation of the industrial and service sectors. All of this constituted formidable resources for the re-establishment of economic patron–client relations with both the urban *and* the rural elite, both military and civilian. At the same time, the last leftist attempts to plot against the regime, in 1973, triggered draconian security measures, such as the suspension of the student organisation UNEM and the UNFP, and the trial of subversives in Casablanca and Kenitra. The radical leftist opposition chastised, the strengthened King could revive the alliance with the nationalist movement based on a new opportunity – the decolonisation process of the Spanish Sahara in 1974.[29] Within this general context, the following three elements strengthened the state:

(1) *Re-adjustment of the alliance with the military*: The King needed to find a new occupation for high-ranking military officers without, however, adding to the corruption that was already prevalent. Immediately after the 1972 coup, he gathered high-ranking officers in his palace in Skhirat and announced that 'this means some work for me but I will take you by the hand. You need to be involved in politics'.[30] In reality, recruitment practices into the army and its higher echelons changed to de-emphasise its Amazigh character. The King himself asked the Fassi bourgeoisie to make it more attractive to their offspring to pursue a military career.[31] To better control the army, the position of minister of national defence was abolished, and its responsibilities were taken over by the King.[32] In addition to its involvement in the Western Sahara campaign following the Green March of November 1975, military missions abroad became an important aspect of the army's preoccupations: Moroccan troops participated in the 1973 October War against Israel, and later a military involvement in Zaire followed.

(2) *The Western Sahara issue*: By 1974, the Western Sahara issue became the most important national concern, rallying the fragmented opposition around the nationalist cause of which the supreme coordinator became the King. The integrating role of the issue is best illustrated by the reaction of Ali Yata, one of the historical leaders of the Moroccan Communist Party. The party was outlawed in 1963 and readmitted in 1974 under the name Party of Progress and Socialism (PPS). In 1976 Yata declared to the Italian journalist Attilio Gaudio:

For the Moroccan Left, ... and in particular for us, the avant-garde party of the working class, the problem of the Sahara is a problem of national liberation. The Sahara, occupied by Spanish colonialism, has always been Moroccan soil, culturally, historically, and ethnically. For us, the combat for its liberation signifies a continuation of the anti-colonialist struggle. The Party of Progress and Socialism could not remain outside of this struggle, and in my knowledge no other communist party has ever refused to join forces with the resistance.[33]

(3) *Reconciliation process with political parties*: A key component of the state's renewed strength was the successful integration of formerly excluded political parties. The success of this process following the coups depended on each side's perspective on the other,[34] and not simply on the emergence of a nationalist issue. Before 1974, a new restrictive modification of the law on public liberties in April 1973, in addition to the Kenitra and Casablanca trials of political opponents, meant that the King's oral affirmations of his intentions at political opening lacked credibility. The result of this was that both the UNFP and Istiqlal rejected repeated invitations to form a 'national union government'.[35] In addition, the monarch and both Istiqlal and UNFP were relatively weak. The coup attempts weakened the King; his recourse to strong authoritarian measures including the new constitutions that elevated him to the position of 'supreme representative of the nation' (Article 19 of the 1970 constitution) weakened political parties. As Rousset comments: 'Weakness is not normally conducive for compromise, neither on the part of those who dominate, nor on the part of those who are dominated. The latter prefer to wait until the situation has improved, so to increase their bargaining power.'[36]

Consequently, both the King and the opposition worked on strengthening their respective positions. In March 1973, the state's nationalisation of French-owned agricultural lands, and the 'Moroccanisation' of industry and the service sector, meant that the King adopted a core nationalist demand. In the eyes of the nationalists, he therefore proved to be the defender of the nation's interests. The King's Western Sahara policy, which was triggered by Spain's 1974 intention to grant independence to the territory, had the same effect. It was his lack of nationalist credentials that had previously weakened his position. However, instead of completely monopolising the Western Sahara issue, he sent opposition party leaders to defend Morocco's claims abroad. This meant that he strengthened the nationalists' position, which remained until that point marginalised. It is important to note that this happened in the second phase, starting in 1974, which preceded the re-establishment of electoral politics in 1976–77. All leaders except for Abdallah Ibrahim of the UNFP accepted the King's invitation: Ali Yata from the now reformed and formerly communist PPS and the USFP's Abderrahim Bouabid went to the Eastern bloc and East Asia; Istiqlal's Allal El Fassi, M'hamed Boucetta and Boubkir Al Qadiri went, among others, to other Arab states.[37] The Istiqlal, the newly founded USFP and the PPS were able to hold their national congresses in 1974–75 without hindrance, increasing the credibility of the King's attempts at limited political opening.[38] The indirect effect of this was both to strengthen these parties on the national scene and to make the King's gestures towards renewing parliamentary politics more credible than in the previous period (1971–74). Finally, the King's appointment of M'hamed Boucetta (Istiqlal) and Abderrahim Bouabid (USFP) in 1976 to an electoral supervisory committee added to the political atmosphere of appeasement and trust in the King's proposal. The result was the political parties' participation first in municipal elections (1976), and then in national elections (1977), with the Istiqlal even participating in government after 15 years of formal absence. This marked the beginning of a period of reconciliation between the nationalist movement and the monarchy based on electoral politics.

Nationalism and acceptance of the King's prerogatives, though, were the acid test in this reconciliation process. Internal repression continued and targeted those who did not accept the nationalist agenda, such as the Marxist-Leninist organisation *Ilal Amam* led by Abraham Serfaty. It is therefore interesting to note that this reconciliation process was also characterised by the absence of increasing pressure on the King in terms of human rights and protection of individual liberties: the Istiqlal's LMDH, founded in the early 1970s, seemed subservient to the party's interest not to threaten the reconciliation process and the party's increasing alliance with the monarchy.[39] It entered a dormant phase of its history, from which it never recovered. Being a member of the 1977 government, the Istiqlal could finally realise its most important ideological demand next to the integration of Western Sahara: Arabisation of national education.

## *The new political formula as electoral process*

The basis on which this reconciliation process was founded remained fragile. It consisted of the re-establishment of limited electoral participation, hence popular legitimacy *and* the acceptance of the King's constitutional priorities that are derived from divine legitimacy. This explains the short longevity of this experiment that ended with the absence from government of both the Istiqlal and the USFP in 1984 after the elections for another 14 years until 1998. Nevertheless, managed electoral processes became the centre stage of political conflicts that, depending on the circumstances, allowed for inclusion or exclusion of the various political currents.

The success of this electoral process partly depended on the consensus about the primary nationalist mission, the integration of Western Sahara and the defence of what is considered Moroccan territorial integrity. In one stroke, critics of the King could be chastised on the grounds not only that it violated the constitution, but also that it jeopardised the sacred Sahara mission. This is why the process of re-adjustment that started in 1974 was paralleled by a process of severe political repression evidenced in mass trials of the radical left or *gauchistes* in its various formations such as *Ilal Amam* and *Frontistes*. Some of these groups argued not only for a republican model, but also in favour of Sahrawi's right to self-determination in Western Sahara. This clampdown even included extra-judicial killings such as that of the leftist leader Omar Benjelloun – even if officially the Islamist group *Shabiba Islamiyya* was held responsible for his murder. In France, the best-known examples of this repression became Abraham Serfaty of *Ilal Amam* and the family of General Oufkir.

By participating in the 1977 parliamentary election, the nationalist elites temporarily accepted the status quo in exchange for royal favours, contributing to what Mohamed Tozy later called 'defused politics'.[40] The PPS leader Ali Yata was 'elected' in Casablanca thanks to the sudden retreat of the main candidate, the former 'independent' government minister A. Lasky.[41] The Istiqlal's M'hamed Boucetta, together with the USFP's secretary-general Abderrahim Bouabid, accepted a position as minister without portfolio *before* the parliamentary elections of June 1977, apparently to supervise the fairness of the electoral process. After the election, the Istiqlal participated with eight government ministers in the government, resulting from its relatively strong electoral performance: it gained 49 seats out of a total of 263. While the Istiqlal was relatively strong, its achievement was far below what it might have expected as the leader of Morocco's independence movement. For the Istiqlal, the 1970s resembled its failed 1950s attempts at rallying the countryside behind the party. Strong rural–urban differences based on kinship, regionalism and linguistic differences were still paramount. Almost 15 years after the previous elections of 1963, in which the nationalist parties participated, the rural base of politics continued to be important. The fact that the rural party MP now also won seats in urban areas[42] even illustrated how rural categories based on kinship groups started to be exported to urban settings, a side effect of Morocco's massive post-independence rural exodus.

A last observation of this new formula concerns the continuing importance of indirect elections by municipal advisers, chambers of agriculture and of commerce, as well as by trade unions. It is here outside the direct control of the electorate – as minimal it may be given the importance of election rigging – that patron–client relations were greatest. This translated into the diminishing importance of political parties with little royal support that have, as a result, also little patronage to dispense – i.e. parties that are officially based on opposition to the monarch. This explains the predominance of two candidate types in indirect elections: either independent, or members of explicitly pro-monarchical parties with links to the Ministry of the Interior and special access to sources of wealth. In addition to rural exodus, this eroded the long-term sustainability of the Istiqlal's and the USFP's opposition. In the long run, continuing opposition to the regime would potentially translate into complete electoral insignificance.

## *Effects of the new political formula*

The effect of this electoral political process temporarily weakened a united opposition, as the USFP and the Istiqlal competed not only for votes, but also for monarchical patronage. It is worth pointing out that it was not the Western Sahara issue *per se*, but rather its combination with the electoral process that provisionally shelved the tensions between the monarchy and the opposition parties. This explains why the conflict resurfaced in the early 1980s, despite the escalation of war between Polisario and the Moroccan army in Western Sahara. This means that, largely unrelated to the Western Sahara issue, underlying tensions concerning constitutional issues and power sharing reappeared as soon as the power-sharing formula lost its credibility in the early 1980s.

First, the elections had the result of splitting the *koutla wataniyya* that was formed as a united 'National Bloc' in protest against the King's monopolisation of power after his writing of the 1970 constitution. Strong personal and political rivalries between USFP and Istiqlal leaders emerged as soon as their united opposition to the monarch no longer held them together. In 1977, the USFP accused the Istiqlal and the Ministry of the Interior of vote rigging against its candidates. Its leader, Abderrahim Bouabid, was unable to secure a seat from his Agadir constituency. From the USFP's point of view, the Istiqlal had formed an alliance with the monarchy and the administration, as the Istiqlal had made clear its intentions to participate in the government, regardless of the electoral outcome.[43] On the other hand, the Istiqlal's claim to single-party status and its claim to be the sole holder of the nation's patriotism continued to inspire its leadership's thinking: after the Istiqlal had lost the Taza by-election on 16 April 1978, it accused the government of election rigging on the grounds that 'citizens who have ousted the colonialists and who have fought against feudalism could not have voted for anyone except for the candidate of the Istiqlal Party'.[44]

Second, the USFP opted for a 'constructive opposition' and supported the government in foreign policy decisions as they related to the now predominant Western Sahara conflict. The country's military budget was approved without any opposition. However, its primary aim was to increase its political weight through an improved performance in the next round of elections. Its marginalised status due to only 14.6 per cent of votes and 8.6 per cent of seats in direct elections, accounting for only two thirds of the parliament, was further eroded by indirect elections of the remaining third.[45] Here independent, pro-monarchical candidates scored even better. This is why it chose to continue its semi-opposition, in order to rally more support from critical voters, without, however, being branded as an opposition with the negative consequences of such a stigma. Hence, the USFP's acceptance of the status quo appeared tactical in nature.

Third, from the King's point of view, the electoral process and the formation of the 1977 government that included the Istiqlal meant an acceptance of the King's constitutional supremacy. The provision of the 1970 and 1972 constitutions did not guarantee the political parties basic political liberties such as parliamentary immunity (see for example Article 37 of 1972 constitution). Whereas the 1962 constitution conceived of the government as an 'intermediary' between the King and parliament, this changed in the post-1972 constitutional order. First, the King had wide regulatory powers that need not be countersigned by the prime minister. Second, the prime minister was accountable to the King alone. This effectively diminished the power-sharing formula to which the King, in rhetoric, was alluding: the King repeatedly said that the government was to be a critical force in the policy-making process, affirming that 'We do not want in any way to impose Our opinion nor manage State affairs according to Our own personal point of view' (10 October 1977), claiming, 'I never wanted to monopolize power and alone ensure all responsibilities' (17 February 1972).[46] Later attempts to include USFP politicians in the government were meant to ensure that the USFP could also be part of the national 'consensus'.

## 3.3 The state's basis of power, 1956–77

After having reviewed Morocco's immediate post-colonial political history, it is the purpose of this section to analyse the foundations of the state's power that was created in the first 20 years of independence. These years were the most crucial, as the socio-political fabric was created that, with minor modifications, continues to be prevalent in contemporary Moroccan politics.

### Divisions in the nationalist movement

The main 'official' players were the nationalist movement on one hand, and the monarchy on the other. Underlying this binary opposition was a whole set of institutions that provided for the hegemony of the monarchy as they served to weaken and divide the homogeneity of the nationalist movement. The first was Islam, which attracted conservative elements to the nationalists, who were inspired by the Islamic reformist *salafiyya* movement.[47] These 'official' or 'orthodox' Islamic scholars aimed at creating an alliance with the monarchy against rural, popular, mystical Islam that had evolved in folkloric (or maraboutic) and tribal forms as brotherhoods in North Africa – the *zuwaya* and *tariqa*. As these brotherhoods frequently centred on a Sufi sheikh who tended to claim a direct link to God, they were often regarded as heretic by orthodox Islamic scholars of the learned institutions such as the Qarawiyyin. Both Islamic currents pre-dated the colonial period, but their division was reinforced by the colonial administrator as some *tariqa* were often seen as cooperating with the French. This was one of the reasons why, in the first five years after Morocco's independence, a clear constitutional process was not initiated by the nationalist movement. It was important to establish with the help of the monarchy the party's, i.e. the Istiqlal's and 'orthodox' Islam's, hegemony over other socio-political and religious currents, including the *zuwaya*. This illustrated the Istiqlal's ambiguous understanding of the concept of democracy as much as it conflicted with its own view of the importance of the monarchy and 'official Islam'.[48]

Whereas this created a certain unity in the nationalist movement, and it led to its association with the monarchy to promote itself and its position, it also limited its ability to challenge the monarch. The Istiqlal's glorification of the monarchy made it difficult to oppose the religious legitimacy of the King once the power struggle erupted.[49] This is especially relevant in a society in which its own orthodox religious reference was not the prevailing one, but competed with the equally (if not more) important *zawiyya*-based, maraboutic forms of Islam. It is important to remember that it was the predominantly rural *zuwaya*, and not the urban *'ulema*, that 'have determined the outcomes of power struggles in all Moroccan history'.[50]

Ultimately, this means that it was the nationalist movement's use of religious and monarchical references to broaden its appeal, its reliance on salafism and Arabism to create internal cohesion that provided for internal contradictions about its position on constitutionalism, monarchism and Islam. These were exacerbated by the monarchy and the rural–urban, tribal, Arab–Amazigh distinctions that overlapped with that of the urban Istiqlal and the rural Liberation Army. As a result, as was pointed out by Hermassi,[51] the Moroccan nationalist movement's weakness, as well as the rise of the monarchy, was a result of how the traditional bourgeoisie was structured after independence. It was fragmented and weak, pre-colonial in its roots, partly the result of the French attempt at safeguarding traditional society, partly the result of the relatively short period of colonial rule (44 years) compared with its neighbours. From this perspective, the nationalist movement's apparent 'unity' only lasted as long as French colonialism provided for a common purpose. Traditional divisions based on language, regions and tribal categories were compounded by divisions between a modernist, secular wing and a more traditional, Islamic current. All this meant that the democratic credibility of politicians from Allal El Fassi, Abdallah Ibrahim to Mehdi Ben Barka was limited. It also meant that the political struggle that developed after independence was about the specific content of Moroccan society that each of these protagonists represented. It was not about the development of democratic processes, practices and values that would effectively challenge the monarchy's dominance. In this context, it is important to note that by the early 1970s, when the nationalist movement was not only fragmented but also reduced to insignificance, the *koutla* (bloc) that was formed by the UNFP and Istiqlal was nationalist, *watani*, and not yet 'democratic', as the *koutla* would call itself in the 1990s (*koutla dimukratiyya*).

## Controlling Islam and 'ulema

Perhaps the most important aspect of the construction of the post-colonial state relates to the institutionalisation of Islam. After all, the Sultan-King was legitimised with explicit religious references, both in constitutional theory and in political practice. More importantly, religion together with references to what Hammoudi calls *dar al mulk*[52] provided for an important source of symbolic power that was mobilised to claim the monarchy's hegemony over the political field.[53] Due to the fragmented nature of Islamic belief systems in Morocco, and their underlying political character as mentioned above, it was important not to emphasise one particular current too much and to represent both currents more or less equally. Equally important was to grant a certain degree of protection to the traditional, often more rural maraboutic forms of Islam that orthodox currents frequently attacked as heretic (especially salafi *'ulema* such as Bochaib Doukali, Allal El Fassi and Al Makki Naciri).[54] The maraboutic idea of *baraka* was such a traditional feature that the monarchy was able to blend with what Clifford Geertz conceptualised as Morocco's form of legitimacy based on charisma.[55] However, as pointed out in Chapter 1, it conferred not only legitimacy but also policy constraints on the monarch, due to *tahara* (purity) that is publicly scrutinised.

A second traditional, kinship, quasi-tribal and religious feature has been the emphasis placed on the male lineage from the Prophet Mohamed via his daughter Fatima and his cousin Ali. As elaborated by Hassan II, the Prophet's sherifian successors via their genealogy are endowed with the right to rule. Genealogy is being politically exploited, and the 'purity' of it emphasised, especially as rival groups claim a similar genealogy. In the words of Hassan II:

> God, with his high wisdom, decided to confer to caliphs and to emirs of Muslims the responsibility to assure his reign on earth, to protect the shari'a, to protect faith and to protect Muslim society against all deviations. Morocco, as part of the Muslim world, is characterized by a lineage of Kings that are particularly upright and honest ... Among its sovereigns have been the renowned and blessed descendants of the prophet such as our ancestors of the Alawi dynasty.[56]

However, it would be misleading to consider lineage and ancestry as a sufficient variable that explains the Alawis' control over religion. As Hart explains concerning the Alawis' genealogy in comparison with the purity and prestige of that of the Idrissi *shurfa*:

> Before their conquests of the late seventeenth century, by which time the tomb of Mawlay Idris II in Fes had long been a nationally revered shrine, the 'Alawids had absolutely nothing to resemble the status of the Idrisid *shurfa'*, descended as they were from Morocco's very first two sultans, Mawlay Idris I and II. *Shurfa'* they are indeed, but they emerged considerably later than the Idrisids did, and there are 24 generations between the Prophet's daughter and 'Ali ibn Abi Talib and their point of fission, Mawlay 'Ali ash-Sharif.[57]

Hence, equally important for the Alawi dynasty's longevity has been statecraft and specific state-building features that are mobilised to legitimise the King's hold over power, as well as controlling potentially threatening Islamic claims as they may arise from traditional, rival groups to the Alawis. The state under the Sultan-King endeavoured to monopolise the symbolic representation of Islam: first by institutionalising the concept of *Amir Al Mu'minin* in the 1962 constitution; second by making the *'ulema* as producers of Islamic ideology an integral part of the state by employing them in the Ministry of the Interior; third by attempting to control their expression in the newly created League of Moroccan *'Ulema* (1961). Mohamed Tozy explains the changes of *'ulema* integration in the public sector in the following words: 'Ulema have become state bureaucrats that manage the Islamic patrimony. Their hierarchy no longer exclusively follows the degree of religious knowledge accumulated, nor the number of followers among non-ulema.

Instead, their status has become based on ranks used by the administration.'[58] Through this integration into the administration, the Moroccan *'ulema*'s socio-cultural-political body lost its autonomy.[59]

This loss of autonomy, however, was not the result of the state's simple appropriation of religion. The loss of autonomy was more reciprocal. *'Ulema* themselves sought articulation with the religious basis of the state rather than integration in what may have been perceived as a main threat to its existence – the more secular Ministry of Education. This was exemplified in what was called the 'Qarawiyyin crisis' of 1957–60, at Morocco's most prestigious religious institution in Fes. When the Qarawiyyin University was celebrating a millennial anniversary since its foundation in 957, the festivities were delayed by six months due to resistance by its *'ulema*: a modernist faction of Morocco's political elite had organised the festivities and the *'ulema* resented this interference on what was regarded their turf. In a similar vein, the Qarawiyyin University resisted integration with Mohamed V University under a secular director, and the League of Moroccan *'Ulema* led the protest that would eventually lead to Hassan II declaring Qarawiyyin an independent institution by royal decree.[60] This illustrates how Morocco's *'ulema* felt threatened by a secular, modernist branch of the political elite that aimed to control it. As a result, the King could easily appropriate their movement and use the ideological split to become the political arm of traditional *'ulema* to protect their interests against those of the modernists. This reinforced the alliance that the conservative Istiqlali Fassi bourgeoisie and its *'ulema* – two partially overlapping categories in this post-independence period – sought with the monarchy, an alliance that was already noted above. In exchange, though, its independence was sacrificed and the monarch assumed a sacred character to which an acquiescent *'ulema* consented.

As Mohamed Tozy illustrates, this accounts for the establishment of a religious countermovement that does not receive its legitimacy from the 'learned' and the sherifian successors of the Prophet (king-caliph). Instead, this countermovement remained outside administrative channels, claiming through the sufi brotherhoods a direct link to God, based on Islamic mysticism.[61] Interestingly, this countermovement, even if not directly political in nature, corresponds to tribal-regional traditional practices that characterised the Moroccan countryside, especially in mountainous areas. Here, sufi brotherhoods and traditional maraboutic practices continued to exist, and many towns too had important sufi shrines. Since the 1970s, though, with rural exodus came an increasing articulation of brotherhoods with different, urban lifestyles. It is within this articulation together with increasing co-optation of the political elite that Islamist movements emerged. Especially Abdessalam Yassine from the sufi brotherhood Bouchichiyya came to represent the most outspoken political-religious movement that called for political transformation.

## *Centralisation of power and constitutionalism*

The post-independence monarchical state attempted to create alliances with partially conflicting groups that are on the one hand modern-bureaucratic and secular in nature, and on the other Islamic, conservative and traditional. The idea would be that the King is the expression of unity in an otherwise fragmented polity. Although this proved a relatively stable formula, it also engendered substantial conflicts as a modernist, developmentalist faction was disillusioned with the weak institutional capacity of the state to promote social progress adequately, hence the importance of leftist opposition groups. In turn, one central aspect of the state-building process was the King's monopolisation of power through violence and control over the public expression of dissent. Nationalism around the monarch as illustrated by the Sand War with Algeria in 1963 only partially provided for unity, even if the 1975 Western Sahara mission was more successful. Consequently, Moroccan authoritarianism was based on perceived and actual divisions and conflicts, centrifugal tendencies based on primordial links and alliances that needed a supreme referee to remain unified.[62] When Hassan II was criticised in 1962 because the constitution granted him too many powers, his response on 13 December 1962 was indicative of his own perception that his role needed to be constitutionally protected:

> The constitution makes of Us an arbiter ... I am certain that many have said 'The powers of the King are enormous' ... I would say to them, to take a very simple example: 'Imagine two football teams on a field, take away from the referee the power to whistle out and expulse a player, and then gentlemen, play.' The problem is very simple, and thus is it posed.[63]

Despite the King's overwhelming constitutional powers to dissolve the parliament and to appoint the government without consultation, the monarch abstained from abolishing party politics on the grounds of the existence of one single Moroccan people, as much as the 1962 constitution ruled out the possibility of a single-party system (Article 3). Instead, pluralism was used as a means not only of divide and rule, but also to emphasise cultural, regional and religious differences − Morocco also being home to the largest Jewish minority in the Arab world until the mass exodus after 1967 − which only the 'supreme representative of the nation and the symbol of unity thereof' (Article 19 of the 1970 constitution) was able to overcome. The role of the political parties was reduced by granting them *next to* trade unions, district councils and chambers of commerce the right to participate in the organisation and representation of the citizens (Article 3).

In addition, starting at independence, the press laws were used to prevent public criticism, such as the decree of 1 June 1959, which gave the minister of the interior the right to seize newspapers that had defamed any public employee or government official. The first more comprehensive decree, from 28 May 1960, entitled 'Preventive Repression', defined acts that were punishable as 'attacks on the institutional, political, or religious basis of the Kingdom'.[64] As Bennani comments:

> Because of its general and vague character, and because the constituting facts for the intervention are not clearly determined, this new text would give rise

to serious impairments of the freedom of press. This is because this text justified suspensions and interdictions that were not motivated by legal judgment, nor were they submitted to any kind of legal control.[65]

A major revision took place on 10 April 1973. The decree, which also reduced the liberty of association, increased the punishment for all offences that were included in the press code and criminalised all declarations that were suspected to 'pose a threat to public order'. Moreover, in order to seize a publication, it was no longer necessary for the courts or for the minister of the interior to prove that a journalist wrote something with 'bad intentions'.[66] Constitutionally, as the King became the supreme 'representative of the nation' with the 1970 constitution, it put critics outside the confines of the national community. Consequently, individuals would ultimately no longer enjoy the protection of the King as Article 19 stipulates. This 'secular' dimension of constitutional authoritarianism was reinforced by introducing in Article 24 the 'sacredness' of the person of the King, rendering criticism of him both unconstitutional *and* a sacrilege.

These powers, though, were not used to crush all opposition. Even if opponents were punished according to the constitutional and legal provisions as laid out above, they could count on the King's clemency and integration after they 'repented' in order to reintegrate the 'national community'. As King Hassan said on the occasion of the religious holiday Eid El Kebir in April 1965, with reference to recently pardoned prisoners:

> I offer those whom I have pardoned a precious opportunity that they may reintegrate themselves into the national family and that they may work in the context of its constitutional institutions and political organisations. If they miss this opportunity, if they persist in error and believe that clemency is a door open widely to them at all moments, I warn them against the unfortunate consequences of their poor intentions and manoeuvres, and I call their attention to the fact that Our clemency is equalled only by Our firmness.[67]

## 3.4 Divide and rule: political parties and civil society, 1977–84

The political reality after 1977 meant that the King's religious and constitutional powers – as well as his claim to be beyond constitutional constraints – were increasingly accepted. The fact that religion and constitution were blended has given the King what Claisse calls a 'double status', inside and outside the institutions. The constitution of 1972 gave the King specific administrative powers, such as the appointment of a government and presiding over the council of ministers. In addition, the King's direct legislation through decrees (*dahirs*) has been ruled beyond constitutional control due to the King's status as Commander of the Faithful. In numerous constitutional court rulings, any appeals in courts against these decrees have been ruled illegal.[68] This was made even more explicit in the

1979 act of allegiance, the *bay'a*, of the inhabitants of Dakhla and the tribes of Oued ed-Dahab in Western Sahara. The *bay'a* was published in the *Bulletin Officiel* of 20 September 1979, blending this worldly authority with the prophetic: 'the holder of the legitimate authority is God's shadow on earth and his secular arm in the world.' As a result:

> The Moroccan legal system seems to be based on a hierarchy of rationalities. The religious rationality that is interpreted by King Hassan II through the act of allegiance sets the king at the top of any command. Constitutional and administrative laws have only a subordinate position because they are both temporary and residual. The bureaucracy, successor to the Makhzen, is in the service of the king to confirm and implement this hierarchy of commands.[69]

This hierarchy of commands was not unanimously accepted, though. The issue of accepting to wear a white *jellaba* during the King's addresses to parliament after 1977 became an important symbol in this respect. According to USFP and PPS parliamentarians, wearing the white *jellaba* in parliament replicates codes of submission and the submissive connotations of the *bay'a*,[70] and they argued that this was incompatible with the institution of parliament that represents the people. Consequently, the majority of parliament simply passed a law in June 1979 making the dress code obligatory during royal addresses, which was confirmed by the constitutional court on 19 July 1979. Subsequently, the 'right' dress was worn by all deputies and, as Claisse remarks, 'the King had dictated his will through the instrumentality of law'.[71]

This increasing acceptance resulted in what has been called since 1977 a democratisation process. In 1977, the US State Department's *Country Reports on Human Rights Practices* wrote that there was a noticeable 'strengthening of democratic institutions'.[72] The effect of this 'strengthening' was a new phase in the state's divide-and-rule policy. Marginalised and excluded political currents faced severe repression whereas mainstream political parties sought a place in the state's constitutional 'consensus'. Amnesty International's 1977 briefing reported on the arrest of 300 *Frontistes* as prisoners of opinion. Although these leftist currents were very prominent in the 1970s, this period also saw the development of an Islamist current led by Sheikh Abdessalam Yassine, who published a pamphlet in 1974 called *Islam ou la déluge*, which earned him two years of forced 'hospitalisation' in a mental health hospital – without trial. A 1978 Middle East Research and Information Project (MERIP) report adamantly describes how these political currents lacked an important national support network that previous prisoners had when they were subject to political violence, due to the co-optation of *koutla wataniyya* parties into the government:

> In the past, when opponents of the regime were arrested, tortured – or, like el Mehdi Ben Barka, assassinated – the opposition parties had internal and external networks of supporters to highlight their plight and succeeded in

making international opinion aware of their condition. Those now under attack do not have a comparable support network at their disposal and therefore the authorities have dealt with them brutally. Recently Information Minister Muhammad Larbi Khattabi admitted that arrests of the *Frontistes* should be seen as preventive acts: 'It was necessary to imprison them *before* they undertook any criminal or terrorist activities.'[73]

Despite its 'constructive opposition', the USFP also faced repression. In 1981, this divide-and-rule strategy was applied to the USFP, when it considered that the 1980 referendum that extended the legislative period to six years could not apply to the current legislative period. Consequently, USFP deputies decided not to attend parliamentary sessions anymore, and sent their resignation to the parliamentary president. The King decided that 'these people have excluded themselves from the Muslim community'. When the Sahrawi liberation movement Polisario attacked the village of Guelta Zemmour, USFP parliamentarians were put under house arrest. They had not attended the parliamentary meeting that condemned these attacks. According to an official statement, this was to protect them 'against a possible violent reaction of Moroccan citizens who might have badly appreciated their anti-national attitude'.[74]

Similarly, royal attempts to include a silenced plurality of political actors in *his* government failed when a major turn took place in his Sahara policy. At the Nairobi summit of the Organization of African Unity (OAU) in 1981, he accepted holding a referendum on independence in Western Sahara. Consequently, Abderrahim Bouabid (USFP) openly criticised this decision, saying that this should have been approved by a referendum prior to being suggested by the King, which suggested that national sovereignty did not belong to the King, but to the people. Together with Mohamed El Yazghi, he was sentenced to one year's imprisonment for criticising the King.

Given the threat of declining electoral support, it proved difficult for the USFP to sustain this opposition. If the USFP's marginalisation was to continue, it might very well follow its sister party's fate (UNFP) and lose all of its remaining political significance. Hence, as Michael Willis observes, 'parties in Morocco that had initially been denied access to the political system were afforded entry once they were able to demonstrate [...] that they had changed certain aspects of their platforms and discourse'.[75] This forced appeasement, however, only underscored intra-party conflicts and splits that the early 1980s witnessed. Major political events such as the 1981 Casablanca bread riots, the 1983 International Monetary Fund (IMF) standby agreement, as well as Hassan II's Western Sahara policy, affected the political positions of political parties, human rights groups and trade unions towards each other.

This policy of controlled pluralism and co-optation of individual leaders caused splits not only inside political parties, but also in unions and associations that were heavily interrelated with political parties. The Moroccan Association for Human Rights (AMDH) was created in 1979 by the USFP when in opposition. The Istiqlal's LMDH, referred to above, was dormant with the Istiqlal participating in the post-1977 government. When in June 1981 two trade unions, the UMT and the Democratic Labour Confederation (CDT), called for strikes that turned violent, the suppression of the riots in Casablanca by the military created an internal split within the USFP. Radicals under Benamor no longer advocated a dialogue with the palace. A splinter group – the Party of Democratic Vanguard and Socialism (PADS) – formed when the USFP decided for the first time to be part of the government on 30 November 1983. The USFP secretary-general Abderrahim Bouabid accepted a post as minister without portfolio, and Abdelwahad Radi as minister of cooperation.[76] The King asked Bouabid and the successor of Allal El Fassi as the head of the Istiqlal, M'hamed Boucetta, to participate in the government. The goal of this gesture was to find a stronger support base for increasing IMF-imposed austerity measures after the experience of the Casablanca riots of 1981. This was at a time when 150 militant radical leftists including Benamor were tried and persecuted.[77] Despite Bouabid's prior imprisonment, he accepted, but controlled elections of 1984 illustrated a change in the King's strategy: instead of simply taming the opposition parties to transform them into ruling allies, he created his own parties with which he could achieve the government coalition without incurring any political cost in terms of potential resistance that especially the USFP still represented.

After 1984, the domestic political situation reached a stalemate. The domestic political scene was marked by what Mohamed Tozy called defused politics.[78] Through the attribution of neutral, defused, i.e. 'unchallenging' characteristics to institutions in which, in theory, power is located – parliament, political parties, elections – the King traditionalised the meaning of politics. Representation and parliament were successfully de-linked from questions of sovereignty and came to mean 'intercession' and '*shura*', a right that is granted to individuals by the King. As it is granted, the traditionalised political field emphasises the 'submissive' and 'supportive' aspect of political behaviour – to the extent that in 1985 the King declared to parliamentarians that 'the King of Morocco is probably the only one in the world who has at his disposal more than 300 ministers'.[79]

In addition to this, the King's power continued to increase through the support he could mobilise from loyal technocrats and co-opted traditional religious groups. Still, his control over the security forces after the 1971–72 coups remained shaky. His army was fighting the Western Sahara war and, although it struggled until the early 1980s, the Royal Armed Forces (FAR) started to prevail on the battlefield afterwards. The delegation of power to the *colonel-major* Ahmed Dlimi, who successfully coordinated all six Moroccan battle units, also increased his potential threat. According to some sources, Ahmed Dlimi planned another attempt on the King's life. On 23 January 1983 he was killed in what appeared a man-made car accident, and eight days before a number of superior officers had disappeared too. According to rumours, the monarchy was tipped off by the US Central Intelligence Agency (CIA).[80]

This illustrates that, for King Hassan, by the mid-1980s the army still remained an unknown factor and a potential threat that needed to be checked. The most loyal institution that could fulfil this function was the Ministry of the Interior and its head, Driss Basri. The ministry became a 'super' ministry, managing all political and security affairs that guaranteed the King's uncontested position. Diplomacy, war strategies, referendum, censorship, imprisonment, electoral engineering and dealings with political parties – all of this became Basri's responsibility as the right hand of the King.

## 3.5 The rise of Islamism

Amidst this stalemate between the monarchy and *his* majesty's opposition, and what has been coined the demise of the Moroccan left all through the 1970s, Islamism quickly developed as a force promising a political alternative to the tame power struggle within the political elite. Its rise was encouraged by a social process of state-imposed 'retraditionalisation' that was already taking place in the *social* realm, distinctive from the *political* retraditionalisation described before. Originally observed by Abdallah Laroui,[81] Zakya Daoud describes this social process of the 1970s:

> This is a systematic return to the sources. There are arrests during Ramadan for not fasting. 570 people are condemned to one month in jail on bail for having publicly broken the fast. The parliament discusses the role of religion and the reinforcement of the patriarchal family, a law is presented to ban the sale of wine and alcohol. Masjids (Koranic schools) are encouraged. Everything is done to stop the progressive liberalisation of morals and customs, visible especially in Casablanca, of which we would say later on that we lived through its cosmopolitan period, which wasn't bad at all! … In this decisive turn, the 'ulema raises its head and demands the dismissal of non-Muslims from the administration, an Islamic party and a strict observation of religious practice. Morocco isolates itself, lives as it did a hundred years before, in an isolation that is again magnified.[82]

It is tempting to view the rise of political Islam and Islamist ideologies in Morocco as replacing leftist ideologies in the 1970s, best illustrated by the take-over of the UNEM by Islamic groups in the 1980s.

The Islamist groups *Al Islah wal Tajdid*, *Al 'Adl wal Ihssane* and *Jama'at Shabiba Islamiyya* were all gaining ground when the Moroccan regime was containing the leftist challenge in the 1970s and 1980s. However, the roots of Islamism are to be found not so much in a failed socialist project or ideologies, but rather in the registries of political power in Morocco itself, which will be reviewed below. Although it is reasonable to assume, along with other authors, that the relative weakness of Islamist groups in Morocco is due to the King's occupation of the religious space,[83] it is worth recalling that this religious monopoly was multifaceted: in Morocco central religiously legitimated power and local forms of Islam had a long history that alternated between resistance and partial co-optation.

## Historical roots

On one hand, orthodox, official Islam of the learned institutions, especially the Qarawiyyin University in Fes, extended legitimacy to rulers by stressing the duty of obedience and the notion of submission, *'abudiyya*. In the anti-colonialist struggle it was the Sultan's sovereignty that was stressed by the Salafi, Islamic renewal current within the Istiqlal that first and foremost Allal El Fassi represented.[84] The longest-serving Moroccan official *'alim*, Abdallah Guenoun (1956–92), expressed the principle of *'abudiyya* in the following words: 'Clerics will be the last one to renounce this duty of obedience to authority, regardless of its illegitimacy.'[85]

On the other hand, the Moroccan pre-colonial state was more dependent on support from *zuwaya*, sufi sheikhs and their intermingling with tribal networks as a source of power – the *tariqa*. Here, temporal allegiance to a higher authority was regularly contested and widespread rebellions (*siba*) were the norm rather than the exception. This is because ultimately, these were the social, political and economic organisations where spiritual power and organisational strength were intrinsic. As they were based on a tribe and a spiritual chief (*marabout*), central government interference could be resisted.

Subsequently, although *tariqa* and *zuwaya*, as well as tribes (*qabila*), were crucial as the brokers of state power, with colonial interference they were ultimately coerced into acknowledging the state's secular interference and power. First the colonial French army (1912–32), then the Royal Armed Forces (1957–58) crushed resistance against the central state. In order for these social structures to accept central state power, though, both the French and later the monarchy gave a privileged position to their continued independence and existence, repeatedly kings have visited shrines of venerated founders of sufi brotherhoods, such as Moulay Idriss. The monarchy's political power was even legitimised as a compromise between these two currents: the sacred nature of the personality of the King that is enshrined in the constitution is a non-orthodox means of justifying royal authoritarianism. In other words, the King becomes the chief *marabout*. Unique to Morocco, royal sacredness is being regularly repeated and displayed all around the country in public rituals such as marriage, the Prophet's birthday, and especially the Great Sacrifice at Eid El Kebir.[86] This does not mean that orthodox Islam was neglected. On the contrary, *'ulema* and graduates from religious *madrasa* were given privileged access to the state, the Ministry of the Interior, and education, in order to guarantee their cultural hegemony in the post-independence state, including Arabisation and the imposition of public morals. As a result, the modern state appropriated existing religious currents whilst giving it its own particular temporal meaning by stressing servitude. This is what Mohamed Tozy called *dar el makhzen* and *qa'ida*, a social and cultural *habitus* that legitimises the monarchy's appropriation of modern state power.[87]

This, however, is inherently contradictory: while controlling Islam and *'ulema*, as outlined before, was partially achieved, the social basis of this control itself was changing and subject to unequal development, urbanisation, social and geographical mobility, and ultimately education. Although the registry of *dar el makhzen* and *qa'ida* remained crucial for state power, its usefulness was limited to incorporating the tamed elite.[88] In turn, this registry was unable to incorporate historical reference to *siba* inherent in the social and religious structures of *qabila* and *zuwaya*. With the demise of *zuwaya*'s social, political and economic importance since independence especially as a result of urbanisation, what remained of *siba* is its rebellious *ethos*, without, however, the traditional centres of Islamic learning *zuwaya* being able to give it its particular meaning based on social autonomy and sufi spirituality.

In this context, the post-colonial state and nation-building process undermined the very same mode of legitimacy and even empowered Islamic ideology to turn against its master. This is because reference to Islamic doctrine and tradition has been emphasised in a new, modern, but now uncomfortable setting marked by social uncertainties and anomy that accompany modernisation in late developing countries.[89] In other words, although Islam provided for a source to claim obedience to pursue a project of modernity that the post-colonial state represented, so could Islamic doctrines based on justice, morality and social order be used to claim a different type of modernity and state.[90] Hence, the disenfranchised and excluded, especially the younger, relatively well-educated generations that aspired but failed to achieve meaningful social mobility, easily turned to radical Islamic discourse, provoked by failed economic development that increasingly came to mark Morocco. This new discourse of resistance is fundamentally different from that expressed in pre-colonial times. It addresses the modern state and it uses modern texts from other contemporary Islamist thinkers such as Rachid Ghanoushi, Hassan Tourabi and Abdessalam Yassine.[91] These are what Tozy calls 'freelance imams' as they are not part of official Islam and not on the government payroll, and even express their hostility towards co-opted and state-controlled *'ulema*. Other examples in Morocco include Ahmed Raissouni, Abdelkrim Motii and Abdelbari Zemzemi.

While political Islam has its roots in Moroccan social and political traditions, evidenced by its leaders' frequent membership in traditional *zuwaya*, these roots are now articulated with a different political and social urban setting. Islamist groups call into question the Islamic nature of the Moroccan state, and therefore the Moroccan King's position of *Amir Al Mu'minin*. In this sense, Islamism is revolutionary, although not all movements fall into this category.

## *Islamic groups*

Entelis distinguishes between religious, reformist and radical Islamist movements.[92] The religious is best represented by al-Fiqh Zemzemi's Sunni Movement, which advocated spiritual renewal and purity 'from the bottom up' without explicit political action. Zemzemi abandoned his sufi background from the Darqawiyya in northern Morocco, although he kept part of his charisma in the sense that he is regarded by some as a saint in the north. His criticism of unequal distribution of wealth and power appealed to the disenfranchised yet somewhat included the class of 'small shopkeepers, blue collar workers and labourers'.[93] Upon his death in 1989, the movement that numbered some 10,000 to 20,000 members disintegrated, and it is no longer recognised as an organised movement. Still, more recently, one of his sons, Abdelbari Zemzemi, has taken on a more political role as radical, outspoken imam and elected parliamentarian from the district of Casablanca – Anfa.

In comparison, Abdelkrim Motii's Islamic Youth, *Shabiba Islamiyya*, has been the most radical of all Islamic movements. It is also Morocco's oldest organised Islamist group, founded in 1969. The authorities recognised it in 1972, which led many domestic observers to conclude that it benefited from support of the state in its attempt to diminish the appeal of the leftist groups.[94] Even though it was outlawed and exiled in 1975 after the assassination of the leftist figure Omar Benjelloun on 18 December 1975 (of which the movement was accused), the political current that Motii represented continued to exist. As late as 2008, it was charged with terrorist attacks and plans. Abdelkrim Motii, like some of his supporters, such as Mustapha El Mouatassim, had a background in leftist activism before changing ideological direction. Motii was a militant in the UNFP, whereas El Mouatassim was active in the underground movements *23 Mars* and *Ilal Amam*, led by Abraham Serfaty. In his early career, Motii was an inspector in education, but originally he was born into the *zawiyya* Taghia.[95] The *Shabiba Islamiyya* under Motii's exiled leadership underwent further radicalisation, and was consequently accused by the state of stirring up violence. Since the Iranian revolution of 1979, Morocco's authorities increasingly believed in anti-monarchical Iranian influence inside the country. When the authorities found pro-Khomeini tracts after the January 1984 riots, triggered by another round of structural adjustment, which forced the government to increase the price of basic staples, Motii was sentenced to death in absentia.[96] Hassan II went as far as publicly showing pro-Khomeini pamphlets on Moroccan TV, apparently distributed by *Shabiba* activists, clearly intending to blame foreign influence for the outbreak of violence.[97]

Since the mid-1980s the movement has undergone important transformations. Four of Motii's colleagues, Abdallah Benkirane, Mohamed Yatim, Abdallah Baha and Saadeddine El Othmani, formed the *Jama'a Islamiyya*, the Islamic Association. This association increasingly emphasised non-violent means as well as its acceptance of the monarchy. In a 1992 declaration, Mohamed Yatim emphasised the Islamic nature of the Moroccan state, and that the movement's aim was to support it:

> The objective of the moment is to confirm the pacific and legal character of the movement in order not to be penalized for former references. We believed wrongly that the problem would be to change the state from above. However, the problem in Morocco does not consist in the construction of an Islamic state. An Islamic state exists constitutionally and in terms of doctrine. The problem is not that of a secular political party which tries to get rid of all religious aspects of the social and political life, but to give this religious legitimacy, recognized socially and politically, the means to be really present …[98]

The Islamic Association was renamed *Al Islah wal Tajdid*, Reform and Renewal, and the regime increasingly tolerated the group. Other Islamists accused the group around Benkirane of complicity with the regime, compounded by rumours that he received a stipend from the government so that he could spread his message of non-revolutionary revivalism.[99] While *Al Islah wal Tajdid* later participated in mainstream politics by forming the Justice and Development Party, a splinter group from the *Shabiba* was more marginal and only had limited appeal. It organised around Mustapha El Mouatassim, Mohamed Marouani and Mohamed Al Amine Regala, who founded the *Al Ikhtyiar al Islami*, the Islamic Choice, in 1981. Ideas expressed here have a leftist and secular appeal. The Moroccan authorities seemed more reluctant to recognise this movement, as the difficulties of later foundation of the political groups *Hizb al 'Umma* and *Al Badil Al Hadari* in 2002–06 illustrated.[100] One of the reasons may be that these groups attempted to create a type of leftist Islamism together with other leftist groups, with more reference to opposition.

While these groups remained either too radical, intellectual or co-opted, it has been Abdessalam Yassine's particular oppositional and spiritual actions that have given Morocco's most important and popular Islamist group, *Al 'Adl wal Ihssane*, its appeal. In contrast to the splinter groups of *Shabiba*, it has not become an official political party due to its more radical stance towards the monarchy. In this sense, it is more revolutionary than any other Islamic group, even if it has never espoused violence as a means to achieve its political goals.

## *Islam or deluge? 1974–90*

*Al 'Adl wal Ihssane*'s spiritual leader, Abdessalam Yassine (1928–2012), was a prolific writer, producing more than 20 books in the course of more than 30 years. He started his career as a public employee for the Ministry of Education in charge of Arabic programmes. Born in 1928, his CV includes frequent travel to Europe and to the United States prior to his famous 1974 letter, which earned him three and a half years' imprisonment, of which he spent two in a mental hospital. In 1965 he entered the sufi brotherhood Bouchichiyya and he remained there until 1973. He was very close to its spiritual leader, Sidi Abbas Ben Moukhtar Bouchich. Upon Ben Moukhtar Bouchich's death, he left the *tariqa* due to differences with his successor related to political activism.

At the time largely unknown inside Morocco, his pamphlet *Islam or the deluge* is according to Yassine within the Moroccan tradition of independent *'ulema* who have given advice to sultans on a variety of social, economic and political issues. In his letter, he justified his religious authority with reference to his own sherifian background, introducing himself as an Idrissi sherif, a noble lineage that in the past had claims to the Moroccan throne. Claiming his equal religious authority, he criticised King Hassan for *jahiliyya* that his rule has brought to Morocco, *jahiliyya* being a religious reference to the age of ignorance prior to the arrival of Islam.[101] He refused all kingly protocol by saying 'announce redemption, return to God, reconcile yourself with God'.[102] The title of his pamphlet that includes deluge indicates the importance of sufi *mehdism* in Yassine's thinking – apocalyptic prophecies – although its importance is limited in Morocco and more common in Shi'ism and in West African sufism. He is particularly concerned with the relationship between Islam and modernity, believing that, under Western/modern/secular influence (all three concepts are intertwined), Islam cannot exist.[103] Clearly, this is related to Morocco's political system, and while he does not yet claim a different system *per se*, he urged the King in his 1974 pamphlet to restore 'to the Moroccan people the wealth he had amassed through plundering the country's rich resources' – a request repeated in an open letter to Mohamed VI after his accession to the throne.[104]

After being released from the mental hospital in the late 1970s, he founded the movement *'Usrat al Jama'a*. His leadership was based on his spiritual charisma and the intermingling of intellectualism with political activity: in interviews of the early 1980s in his home town Marrakech, he would discuss ideas of post-modernism and Western philosophy with his visitors, with the aim of creating a new framework for Islamist thinking. Starting in 1979 his thinking changes and includes more nuanced criticism. He no longer employs *jahiliyya* as a concept to describe social anomy in Morocco, preferring *fitna* (social disorder). Instead of calling for a revolution, *thawra*, he predicts an uprising, *qawma*. Official *'ulema* as well as Morocco's Westernised elites are rejected as credible actors under a political system that controls and co-opts them, and under Western influence that results in cultural alienation. His criticism of Western influence included the secular basis of nationalism based on ethnicity and language – secularism that does not give Islam a central role in government practice. He specifically criticised Western influence in Morocco's education system, which reproduces Morocco's Francophile, secularised elite. In his analysis, these issues are at the heart of underdevelopment in Morocco.[105]

On the other hand, founding the association *'Usrat al Jama'a* illustrates that intellectualism alone is not enough to unite the rising tide of Islamists. On the contrary, his own mystical past that was associated with his Islamic project may even have isolated him from other Islamists, hence the necessity to be involved in organisational activism that he borrowed from the Egyptian Muslim Brotherhood.[106] While he was again imprisoned for two years in December 1983 for articles that criticised the King, his organisation *'Usrat al Jama'a*, which later changed its name to *Jama'at Al 'Adl wal Ihssane*, was gaining ground, especially among a new, socially mobilising class of university students, teachers and educated professionals.

## *Ideological roots and Morocco's education system*

Yassine's increasing success was related to his ability to unite traditional thought, sufism, intellectualism, charity and welfare programmes with a tinge of populism in search of Islamic authenticity. Political Islam's increasing ideological appeal was also related to Morocco's changing educational programmes in the 1970s, specifically with regards to Islamic education.

First, Morocco's 1,000-year-old Qarawiyyin University lost its monopoly over granting the religious title of *'alim* through its degree *'alimiyya*. Graduates from the Qarawiyyin were joined by competitors from Rabat's Institut Dar al Hadith. This meant an end to Qarawiyyin graduates' virtual monopoly over jobs in the religious field. Second, religious education was further fragmented by introducing Islamic studies to humanities faculties of public universities in 1979. The official purpose was to give more importance to Morocco's Arabisation in a government that now included the nationalist Istiqlali Minister of Education Azzedine Laraki.[107] Clearly, though, the undeclared purpose included – along with the official support for English literature degrees – the marginalisation of philosophy and other social sciences (sociology, political sciences) as a result of the Marxist-inspired student contestation of the early 1970s (*23 Mars* and *Ilal Amam*). Hence, student numbers in Islamic studies rose from 2,223 in 1982–83 to 11,834 in 1993, of whom only about one fifth finished with a diploma.[108]

This increasing fragmentation and broadening of religious education meant that only a fraction of its graduates was able to find employment in traditional state services as imams or in the Ministry of the Interior. Even at Qarawiyyin University, a notable rise in student numbers was registered from 1983 to 1987, from 3,184 to 6,530 students. Of these numbers, the proportion that was already employed in the public sector decreased from about two thirds to about one quarter, from 2,033 to 1,813.[109] This illustrates decreasing opportunities for Qarawiyyin graduates in the public sector. In addition to high drop-out rates at Morocco's public universities, this indicates that a growing proportion of Morocco's young population received religious education, but was unable to work in the religious sector. Instead, Arabic-language instruction in Morocco's Arabisation campaign, which succeeded in having the secondary education system entirely Arabised by 1989,[110] was a common employment possibility.

With increasingly Islamic educated graduates entering the education system as teachers, Morocco's education system entered a period of linguistic contradiction, which contributed to the appeal of Islamist groups. While all *public* schools were completely Arabised up to high school level, university education was not. Elite branches (engineering, medical school, economics and business, natural sciences, Morocco's *Grandes Ecoles* and *Instituts Techniques de Formation des Cadres*) were conducted in French, whereas only social sciences and humanities were Arabised.[111] As a result, it was mainly Morocco's francophone elite who was able to enter these branches. This is because they were able to receive its education in a well-established *private* school system (*missions françaises*) where studying was not only relatively expensive but also competitive from a very early age. In the mid-1990s, only about one tenth of all applicants to Rabat's French schools (*missions*) were admitted. Vermeren concludes that the meaning of French education became more and more elitist from the mid-1950s to the mid-1980s: 'Social elitism, which has been since the early years of the protectorate, one of the characteristics of the *mission* in its treatment of the Moroccan public, has become more and more rigorous.'[112] The consequences are clear: since the 1980s, only the elite have had access to promising subject areas, study abroad or expensive tuition-based universities. A recently Arabised generation has had only limited access to higher education and it ultimately remained excluded from upward mobility and job opportunities. This is because opportunities have been confined to those that have obtained complete fluency in French and access to Morocco's well-funded and -organised elite university system.[113] In Vermeren's words:

> The duality of this education system means its division, in two unequal parts. On one hand, there are branches that result in qualifying diplomas and in high income-generating careers (not to mention the positive symbolic power). On the other, there are branches that only give access to secondary professions, or that even result in the impasse of graduate unemployment, which has become in the last years mass unemployment. The dividing line between these two ensembles is not fixed, nor easy to determine, as they are also inside the educational branches that seem to be homogeneous.[114]

Other important socio-economic developments during this period include rural exodus. While, at independence, Morocco's rural population was over 70 per cent, by 1992 less than 50 per cent continued to live in rural areas.[115] It must be pointed out that what is classified as rural had undergone significant change in the same period, so that the percentage of 'rural' is actually lower. To provide for new integration of rural society in urban areas, mass education aimed at achieving social integration from traditional, segmented society into an urban setting. The number of first-year entries into higher education increased from 5,000 in 1964–65 to 198,000 in 1990,[116] while the total number of students enrolled in primary and secondary schools increased from 10,490 in 1956 to 797,110 in 1980.[117] While clearly university education was originally perceived as a means towards social mobility, a survey of a sample of 500 fourth-year students at Mohamed V University in Rabat in 1991–92 indicates a high percentage of general dissatisfaction. Some 67.6 per cent were dissatisfied with the humanities, 59.5 per cent with sciences, 55.6 per cent with law and 56.9 per cent with medical studies, while a high proportion ranging from 17 to 30 per cent did not express an opinion. At the same time, only a small fraction of this sample expressed some amount of trust in 'modern' institutions such as political parties, state and university, achieving 1.8 per cent, 2.2 per cent and 3.8 per cent, respectively.[118]

This leads to a socio-economic dilemma that renders the religious status of the state fundamentally fragile. In addition to Morocco's specific problems related to its class structure and education system as mentioned above, education as the primary means towards social integration and inclusion quickly becomes illusionary. As Pierre Bourdieu pointed out, the multiplication of diplomas has a particular effect:

> The effect of the inflation of diplomas is more complicated than it is normally believed. From the fact that a title is only worth as much as its holder, it follows that a title that becomes more frequent becomes devalued. But it loses

even more of its value because it becomes accessible to people who have 'no social value'.[119]

In addition to rural exodus and geographical mobility, it is primarily mass education that destroys the bases of segmented society as it creates expectations of selection by merit. These expectations based on individual merit and educational achievements decreased the integrative importance of vertical solidarity groups based on kinship in the modern sector, including lineage claims advanced by the King. In contrast, though, the decreasing value of diplomas means that the younger, better-educated generation quickly falls back to kinship groups as the only way to achieve a minimum of economic integration, with urban unemployment rates hovering somewhere between 20 and 40 per cent.[120] For those without a network, it remains that: 'This is not serious. We study but we know very well that we will not find a job.'[121] Instead, the prevailing mechanism of professional integration becomes informal. In a modern setting marked by particular uncertainty, those who do not work do not eat or find shelter either. Hence, the importance of semi-illegal/tolerated means, such as drug trafficking, *faux guides* for tourists, entering patron–client groups if available, or paying for jobs in the administration. All of this leads to 'deculturalisation': questions of identity are not resolved in this particular, uncertain 'modern' setting. Instead, identity questions can more easily be resolved with recourse to readily available, decentralised and authentic Islamic practices that take a political overtone.[122]

## 3.6 From constitutional reform to *alternance*

After the 1984 bread riots King Hassan asserted that he could listen to the Moroccan people like a medical doctor examines the heart of a patient with a stethoscope. He could hear every palpitation.[123] In the 1990s, he warned of an imminent heart attack, and asserted that Morocco required urgent reform including renewed participation of the political parties in government. While the sustained economic crisis, austerity measures, rural exodus, limitations on migration to Europe, as well as droughts were all important socio-economic factors, the main catalyst in this process was the December 1990 riots in Fes against the US-led intervention against Iraq. This was the third violent mobilisation in a decade, which triggered the massive intervention by the security forces leading to scores of deaths. In addition, the US-led intervention resulted in the open opposition of political parties to the King's decision to send Moroccan troops in support of the US-led coalition, compounding the threat of the monarch's political isolation. Although the King often warned that he would declare a state of emergency,[124] this would have isolated him even further and was therefore not a policy option at the time. Also, in 1991 the conflict in Western Sahara entered a diplomatic period. This reduced the importance of the army but it increased the threat that it might again turn against him and the project of referendum that he had agreed to. Consequently, the need for national consensus became more important than in the 1980s, and with it the willingness of the King to make concessions.

Political changes primarily responded to this need of more closely allying the King to Morocco's political elite through renewed consensus. In the late 1980s this occurred in areas where it was easiest established and on which attention focused the most: international criticism with regard to Morocco's badly tarnished human rights record. Amnesty International took the lead and it was followed by the 1990–91 French–Moroccan crisis about human rights, triggered by the publication of a book. Gilles Perrault's *Notre Ami Le Roi* listed many human rights violations and criticised France's policy of turning a blind eye to such abuse.[125] In this respect, probably the most fundamental keystone for renewed electoral politics that brought the prospect of the participation of opposition parties in government was the foundation of the Advisory Council for Human Rights (CCDH) on 8 May 1990. Prior to this, the Moroccan Ministry of Foreign Affairs established a department explicitly to deal with Amnesty International reports on the long list of Moroccan political prisoners and other continuous human rights abuses. The creation of the CCDH established a dialogue with Morocco's own independent human rights organisation, the Moroccan Organization for Human Rights (OMDH), as well as with 'opposition' political parties. Both were integrated into the CCDH's decision-making body. The need for compromise and concessions was fully established in the King's first address to this quasi-governmental body, in which he asserts that 'we are tired ... of hearing that there are people imprisoned for political reasons in Morocco'.[126] Although he clearly stated that in *his understanding* there were no human rights issues in Morocco, his statement that 'I do not wish to influence you'[127] with regard to his opinion shows that there well existed margins of manoeuvre of which the human rights organisation within the CCDH could take advantage. This was significant as he could re-establish political consensus by giving this institution enough domestic credibility for the reintegration of some part of Morocco's political elite.

The creation of institutions was followed by individual decisions that showed his willingness to embark on important changes. The closure of an infamous prison, Tazmamart, where prisoners were kept in inhumane conditions,[128] was probably the most important of these symbols. Another change was the explicit confirmation in the 1992 constitution's preamble of Morocco's 'attachment to human rights as they are universally recognised'. A state-controlled human rights campaign led to the creation of a human rights ministry and almost reached absurdity when in 1994 Driss Basri, minister of the interior, edited a volume entitled *Morocco and Human Rights*, to which members of the 'opposition' such as Abdallah Saaf, Thami El Khyari, Habib El Malki and Boubker Kadiri contributed essentially technocratic/legalistic essays.[129]

The goal was to break up opposition by showing the King's willingness to integrate political newcomers (the carrot) while continuing with a policy of selective punishment of opponents (the stick), such as Noubir Amaoui, trade union leader and USFP militant, as well as Abdessalam Yassine. In 1992, Amaoui was sentenced to two years' imprisonment for alleging and not withdrawing a statement that some government officials were involved in corruption.[130] Yassine was again put under surveillance and house arrest without trial. The carrot included constitutional reforms and renewed electoral politics in 1993. General elections had repeatedly been postponed due to the Western Sahara and Gulf crisis. The King increasingly clarified that he did not only wish the participation of opposition parties in the election, he wanted them to form *his majesty's* government. Hence, the parliamentary election of 1993 became a means through which elite integration and renewed consensus were again attempted.

In order to strengthen their own position, the Istiqlal, USFP, together with the communist PPS, started another electoral alliance, this time called the 'democratic bloc' (*koutla dimukratiyya*) also better to distinguish themselves from an increasing number of 'administrative parties', those created by the palace and Minister of the Interior Driss Basri. In turn, Hassan II defined the substance of the electoral process as a limited 'delegation of power'. As he explained in 1992 to a French TV station, 'I can delegate my powers but I do not have the right to renounce my prerogatives on my own initiative because they are also religious'.[131] More importantly, for Hassan II the key to the content of democracy became changing governments, *alternance*. This meant that divisions between more right-wing and more left-wing governments were now accepted, placing less emphasis on national union. In a royal speech of 14 October 1994 he explained: 'I said that my wish was to install *alternance* in this country, because without *alternance*, democracy would be void of sense.'[132] As a consequence, by linking *change* through election to the core meaning of *alternance*, the issue arose that elections needed to be more meaningful, transparent and fair.

As the Ministry of the Interior had organised all previous elections, and had consequently been charged with election rigging, its 1993 involvement became the acid test for the opposition to see whether or not the state was serious about its commitment to *alternance*. Involuntarily, though, fairness and transparency of elections received so much attention that the question of whether or not the King should renounce any of his prerogatives was marginalised in political debate. Clearly, this reflected political parties' marginal status, of which they were continually reminded by the government. In early 1992, three legislative propositions by opposition parties to change the electoral code were not even put on the agenda of the parliament, leaving as their ultimate recourse an appeal (*arbitrage*) to the King himself.[133] This, however, strengthened rather than weakened his authority as that of supreme arbiter: his *arbitrage* on 29 April 1992, which introduced the use of ballot boxes made out of glass, comforted the King's position as that of a guarantor of the election's fairness and transparency.

### What type of alternance?

The path to alternance started with the constitutional changes of 1992 prior to the legislative elections of 1993. The new constitution not only included the human rights clause in its preamble, but more importantly made a concession concerning the role of the prime minister in choosing a government. One recurrent criticism of the King had been that the government ministers were not accountable to the parliament, nor to the prime minister, but to the King alone. This top-down authority was reflected in how government ministers were selected: they were directly appointed by the King. In the new 1992 constitution, the King responded to this criticism and introduced in Article 24 that the King appoints the prime minister, and that '[a]fter the proposition of the Prime Minister, He nominates the other members of the government'. This seemed to strengthen the institution of the premiership by making government ministers more accountable to him. Clearly, though, this accountability is relative only, as, ultimately, the King continued to preside over cabinet meetings (Article 25), and through his appointment of the premier, ultimate control remained in his hands. To avoid all ambiguities with regard to ministers' accountability to the King, Article 24 stipulates that 'He [the King] can dismiss them from their functions'. As Deneoux and Maghraoui point out, by leaving the prime minister and political parties the field of low politics, he could strengthen his position as supreme arbiter. By not getting involved in everyday politics, he could also focus on setting the general tone and philosophy of government policies and leaving to others the task of implementation. Most importantly, perhaps, he could focus his attention on issues of high politics such as security and foreign affairs, and decide on matters that demand a 'higher' authority.[134]

Not surprisingly, opposition *koutla* parties did not agree with these changes. They fell short of their expectations and were not elaborated with their input. Although it may have been clear that the King's prerogatives would not be reduced in any constitutional changes, still the issue of meaningful elections was insufficiently addressed as long as a third of the parliament was still indirectly elected. Although both the King and opposition parties were clearly seeking a compromise, this was not to be achieved at any price. Hence, the opposition called for a boycott of the 1992 constitutional referendum while the official participation rate of the referendum reached 97.2 per cent, with an approval rate of 99.97 per cent. Such a score again raised questions with regard to the King's seriousness.

From this perspective, by semantically replacing the idea of national consensus governments with that of alternance, the King, albeit timidly, went a step further towards the opposition in an attempt to seduce them into government. His 'offer' of an alternance government formulated in October 1993 was to rely on a strong showing of one of the opposition parties – Istiqlal or USFP – in the 1993 parliamentary election, in order to obtain a majority in parliament. In his words, 'We will nominate the Prime Minister who will present himself to you, honorable deputies, in order to solicit your confidence'.[135] Even if he was still free to appoint whoever he wanted, he affirmed that the 'logic' of the ballot box would be respected. Unfortunately for the first 'invitation' to form an alternance government, the *koutla* parties of USFP, Istiqlal and PPS did not win a majority: although these parties won 99 out of 222 seats that were filled by direct elections in June

1993 (45 per cent), it was the administration parties led by Constitutional Union that won an overwhelming majority of the remaining third of seats in the second round of indirect elections in September 1993 (76.6 per cent), reducing the *koutla*'s overall percentage of seats to 32 per cent.[136]

This discrepancy was seen as another indication of election rigging after the constitutional referendum. The official 99.97 per cent of yes votes, as well as the participation rate of 97.2 per cent of the Moroccan electorate in the referendum the year before, left a stained image on the Ministry of the Interior's electoral practices. Hence, the discrepancy was seen as another breach of trust between Hassan II and the opposition. As mentioned above, the electoral code had been subject to intense criticism by opposition parties the year before, as a third of deputies were elected indirectly by the local communes and chambers of commerce, and not by the people.

Under such circumstances, alternance was not possible both for 'arithmetical reasons' (Hassan II) and for reasons related to breach of trust (*koutla*). The *koutla* refused to enter the government and instead asked for a re-run of the indirect elections (and thereby official acknowledgement that they had been disadvantaged and there had been government interference), which, according to Hassan II, could not be granted as there was no constitutional basis for such a move. The crisis deepened in November 1993 as neither party seemed to be willing to compromise. The King still hoped to have *koutla* parties participate in the government, saying on 8 November 1993:

> Despite your electoral performance and even if the number of your deputies in parliament does not represent a majority, you deserve – quantitatively and qualitatively – to be invited in order to work next to Us.[137]

On the other hand, the two *koutla* parties, the Istiqlal and the USFP, insisted on the principle of democratic majorities, thereby questioning Article 24 and the King's right to appoint the prime minister regardless of electoral outcome. Interestingly, the King's own words of 8 October 1993, in which he affirmed that the prime minister had to win the trust of a majority in parliament, were used in their manoeuvring. It is significant to point out that, strengthened by what *koutla* parties perceived as a *de facto* electoral victory in direct elections, the USFP and Istiqlal gained more confidence and became more vocal as an opposition in parliament. As Waltz remarks, in 1994 the Istiqlal and the USFP introduced a bill in parliament that abrogated a royal *dahir* from 1935, which authorised the repression of public demonstration.[138] The tension was amplified when USFP leader Abderrahman Youssoufi went into self-imposed exile. Meantime, the King appointed the former Prime Minister Karim Lamrani to form his government.

Amid this political struggle, two contradicting understandings emerged. As El Mossadeq shows, a semantic battle over the meaning of *alternance* took place. On one hand, the King insisted on his constitutional right derived from Article 24 to appoint a prime minister and a government depending on the political circumstances, of which the elections were only one factor. This would be his imposed alternance, derived from his traditional role as arbiter, and opposition parties had to take it or leave it. On the other hand, early in the negotiations, the Istiqlal and the USFP insisted that the determining factor was free and fair elections, thereby reinforcing the idea of a contractual relationship through electoral alternance based on majorities to which Hassan II himself had made reference. The power of the *koutla* was derived from its common stance, but it was precisely on this contractual question that individual parties fell out.

Already in 1993, i.e. right at the beginning of the battle over the meaning of alternance, the PPS approved the idea of participation in a government regardless of whether or not a majority was achieved in parliament. This strengthened the role of the monarch, *not* elections, as that of arbiter.[139] When on 14 October 1994 the King further proposed to choose as prime minister the leader of a party of the 'former opposition' despite its electoral minority in parliament, the united front further weakened. Ali Yata, leader of the PPS, declared on 15 November 1994 that the King's speech was 'very important that we have welcomed very much'. In addition, it reflects 'the vision of His Majesty the King of the necessity of change and development'.[140] More clearly was the response of El Yazghi, designated leader of the USFP after Abderrahman Youssoufi's temporary departure: he embraced Hassan II's wish to consider 'the popular desire expressed during the [direct] June 1993 elections for change and renewal', and affirmed his wish to see a 'pact with His Majesty the King (protector of the constitution and guarantor of the stability and unity of the country)', in order to 'make the necessary step for the preparation of the democratic alternance'.[141] What became for *koutla* parties the most important factor was no longer the question of whether or not they would have a democratic majority and the re-run of the indirect elections, but rather the composition of the government. In particular, the main issue was whether or not Driss Basri would keep his 'super' Ministry of the Interior, Communication and Saharan Affairs, with many informal links to all higher echelons of the state. While the first attempt of 1993 failed on the question of electoral majority and premiership, it was on the question of governmental composition, *not* election rigging, that the second attempt of 1994 failed, as Driss Basri kept his post.

As a result, a *modus vivendi* needed to be found, and King Hassan's deteriorating health increased the stakes involved. Clearly, a successful alternance and a political consensus would guarantee a smooth transition of power to his son, Crown Prince Mohamed. The key was another constitutional reform under his supervision, which would allow significant face saving for *koutla* parties. In 1993, the electoral difficulty was the fact that one third of the parliament was elected indirectly, by trade unions, chambers of commerce and local communes. As conservative forces and administrative interference was higher here, the *koutla* suffered an electoral defeat that it blamed on election rigging. When Hassan II announced a constitutional revision in 1995, he suggested that a bicameral system would install a 299-member lower house of directly elected 'representatives' and a 270-seat upper house of indirectly elected 'councillors'. The formation of a new government could then occur after direct elections, where *koutla* parties had had a stronger showing. In turn, the more clearly pro-monarchical political forces could then be 'stored' in the upper house.

With this understanding but without any contractual relations between appointment of a government and prime minister on one hand, and elections and electoral results on the other, a consensus was found: for the first time since the 1962 constitution, the parties that now formed the *koutla* and that formed the nationalist movement before did not call for a boycott of the constitutional referendum, but instead supported it. This was despite the fact that, in reality, the upper house had exactly the same prerogatives as the lower house, and could block all pieces of legislation. Hence, the formerly one third of the parliament that was indirectly elected increased its power and was now on par with the remaining two thirds of directly elected deputies. In Deneoux and Maghraoui's words, the upper house could play the role of 'defender of the throne'.[142]

Consequently, the electoral process of 1997 reproduced similar results to the 1993 election. The *koutla* won 102 out of 299 seats in the lower house, whereas it remained in a marginal position in the upper house. However, as the lower House of Representatives was now directly elected, it seemed more important. In addition, it was a compromise with regard to *koutla*'s long-standing constitutional demand to have a directly elected parliament.[143] A consensus emerged among the political elite, which, along with El Yazghi of the USFP, could very well be described as a 'pact'. After the USFP became the strongest political party, with 52 seats out of 299 in the lower house, its leader Abderrahman Youssoufi returned from self-imposed exile in the south of France and was appointed prime minister on 4 February 1998. Even if *koutla* parties did not have a majority, the King called upon a loyal party, the MP, to support the *koutla* in exchange for ministerial positions. Hence, the alternance government was an extremely heterogeneous coalition of the USFP, Istiqlal, MP, PPS, Democratic and Socialist Party (PDS), with a large share of technocratic ministers especially in the 'key' areas of justice, interior, foreign affairs and religious affairs. Most importantly, the *koutla* accepted the formation of a government together with Driss Basri, the 'super' minister of the interior. Clearly, this was not the government that the *koutla* in 1993 claimed would be able to put Morocco on the path to substantive change: it was not accountable to the parliament, homogenous, nor a result of an electoral majority.[144] Its primary objective was still to pursue developmental policies but, ironically, this had been the same technocratic orientation of previous governments.

From this perspective, the alternance government, while creating significant hope and further political liberalisation towards the end of the 1990s, represented little but the ultimate success of what Tozy called 'defused' politics in the mid-1980s. Politics is not defined as a legitimate struggle for power. Questions of sovereignty or legitimacy are not raised in elections, nor in the appointment of government ministers. Instead, state–society relations are 'normalised', the absolute authority of the monarchy is accepted, and questions of accountability or disagreement over policies are no longer expressed. Compared with the period of the early 1960s, when questions of sovereignty and accountability were openly addressed in parliament, Morocco was left with an apolitical government and parliament *despite* the election of pluralist parties that, in rhetoric, allude to their own democratic credentials. For Maghraoui, this is a process of 'marginalisation of question of legitimacy or sovereignty and – in the Moroccan case especially – the concomitant political primacy given to economic issues'.[145] As rights-oriented questions were not taken up by Morocco's political institutions, it is not surprising that other non-governmental actors have increasingly challenged governmental political parties by initiating and fostering rights-oriented ideas and reform projects. Morocco's pluralist history as well as its increasing political and economic integration with Europe played an important role in non-governmental challenges to the state and political parties.

## 3.7 NGOs and the rise of new agendas

While religion became politicised by Islamic groups such as *Al 'Adl wal Ihssane* especially, more secular groups developed non-governmental organisations (NGOs) outside the immediate realm of politics. Prior to the establishment of these NGOs, newspaper projects such as *Lamalif* (1966–88) and *Kalima* (1983–87) had already been important tools for intellectuals and liberals, which challenged both party politics and state propaganda. Meantime, Morocco's socio-economic context of the late 1980s also emphasised private-sector initiatives in order to create more employment. Although Morocco never experienced a virtual guarantee of employment after university graduation as, for example, Egypt did in the 1970s, increasing un- and underemployment challenged the state's integrative role and its legitimacy based on Islam, nationalism and the King. New social and political means for the integration of an increasingly young and urban population needed to be found. The balance between on the one hand secular, modern associations and political currents, and traditional and Islamist currents on the other, became an important preoccupation for the state. Consequently, the late 1980s saw a reversal of the 1970s policy of supporting Islamist groups against secular, leftist groups. By the early 1990s, it seemed that secular association and 'civil society' were tolerated and increasingly supported in order to marginalise the threat of radical Islamism that the 1980s had brought.

There are three main areas in which secular, rights-oriented movements became increasingly active: minority rights, women's rights and human rights. Although associations in these areas existed from the early 1970s, their activism sharply increased by the end of the 1980s. It is worth mentioning that both human rights and women's rights had been embedded into party politics in the 1970s and 1980s, while from the late 1950s Amazigh rights had been listed as a concern by the leader of the MP party, Mahjoubi Aherdane. In all three instances, though, these rights remained marginalised. In the case of Amazigh rights, the MP almost from its inception was a vehicle for landowners, rural sheikhs and notables, who advanced their elite interests in the Ministry of the Interior. In the Istiqlal and USFP, human and women's rights were only promoted as long as they did not contradict overall party interests. Women's and human rights were never fully supported, and depended on the extent of the Istiqlal's and the USFP's cooperation with the monarchy.

For this reason, independence from both state and political parties became a major structural move by the end of the 1980s. In 1988, the OMDH was founded in response to the earlier AMDH's marginalisation and suppression. The AMDH's misfortunes were a result of party politics, i.e. its association with the radical wing of the USFP, which later formed the PADS.[146] A similar move occurred in women's rights organisations, the most important example being that of the Moroccan Association for Women's Rights (AMDF), which was originally the women's section of the communist PPS. In 1986, it became officially independent from the PPS, 'in order to develop its strategies independently from party strategies, in order to work more efficiently for its cause', according to one activist.[147] As with the OMDH, the question of independence from political parties became important. However, as with the OMDH, many high-ranking party members continued to be active in both these associations, which continued to cause conflicts between non-party members and party members – especially in the area of human rights. As Waltz remarked concerning the OMDH, its early independent activism in advancing human rights through petitions, and the state's early reaction of giving in to some of these demands such as the release of 35 prisoners from Kenitra Central Prison in 1989 – kept in prison after the infamous 1977 *Ilal Amam* trials – made rivalry with the USFP inevitable.

> During the USFP conference [in 1989] ... applause for OMDH observers recognized from the podium lasted some 10–12 minutes ... According to one participant, this was the moment of truth for Morocco's political parties: human rights were an issue around which Moroccans could be mobilized; by linking social and economic grievances to politics, the concept of human rights acquired enormous potential as a political weapon.[148]

This 'potential as a political weapon' did not remain unnoticed by the monarchy. As mentioned earlier, human rights became an important realm in which relaxed controls and political liberalisation could create a consensus that united the monarchy with political parties. The creation of the CCDH in May 1990 ensured integration of the political elite and its political concerns as it related to human rights in state-dominated institutions.

The articulation of women's rights in the early 1990s underwent a similar process, focusing on reforms of Morocco's conservative family code, the *moudawana*. Inspired by tribal and Islamic values that made much of the political-social fabric of the post-independence period, especially due to the rise of rural notables in political institutions,[149] this code required a father's or male next of kin's consent in a wide range of areas such as marriage, university enrolment or application for a passport. In addition, age restrictions on female marriage were lenient, polygamy was allowed, and inheritance laws were unequal in favour of males. Divorce was very difficult to obtain for women, while husbands could 'repudiate' their spouses by oral declaration. By 1993, the contradictions between such a male-dominated, *shari'a*-inspired family code, and lifestyles in urban areas and the rise of a class of professional women, resulted in first attempts at reformation by a women's rights movement.

In 1993, a campaign of collecting 1 million signatures to reform the *moudawana* led to a broad appeal for, and publicity of, women's rights activists' demands. In addition, they resulted in an increasing issue-based public discourse on rights. Spill-over effects, from women's rights to a broader discussion of human rights and vice versa, occurred. This was also due to the fact that many women's rights activists, such as the feminist writer Halima Zin Abidine, received death threats from radicalised Islamists. Religious charges of apostasy were frequent. As a result, human rights organisations such as the OMDH publicly defended the right of expression of these women's rights activists, against what one communiqué called 'intellectual terrorism' that *fatwas* pronouncing maledictions and sanctions represented.[150]

Similarly, Amazigh rights associations independent from Mahjoubi Aherdane's MP organised and challenged the state's official Arabic identity. In all of its constitutions prior to 2011, the Kingdom of Morocco affirms not only that it is a Muslim country, but also that its official language is Arabic and that it is part of the Great Arab Maghreb. Consequently, its Amazigh identity had been downplayed, Tamazight, its language, had not been taught in schools, and Tamazight has not been used in public activities. Arabisation of first and secondary school curricula since 1977 and partial Arabisation at universities amplified this tendency. This is despite the fact that between 40 and 50 per cent of Moroccans are Tamazight speakers,[151] a number that seems to be declining with the rural exodus from Tamazight-speaking rural areas and, concomitantly, rising urbanisation in mostly Arabic-speaking cities (semi-urban/provincial centres such as Khenifra, Midelt or Azrou excepted). The fact that the Arab nature of the state was emphasised was also a response to perceived divide-and-rule strategies by the French, who administratively separated Amazigh rural areas from Arab urban areas. The so-called Berber *dahir* of 1930 served as a rallying point for the nascent nationalist movement. Arabism, together with a return of the monarch's sovereign powers, gave the independence movement some cohesion, but it also alienated Amazigh tribes soon after independence was achieved.

The contradictions of this ideological emphasis on Arabism in a country with a substantial Tamazight-speaking population with its distinct culture very soon produced associations that aimed at defending the Amazigh character of Moroccan culture. Associations such as the Moroccan Association for Cultural Exchange (1967), the New Association for Culture and Popular Arts (1978), or the Université d'Eté d'Agadir (1979) avoided the use of 'Amazigh' as either word or language in their names, and Al Intiliqa Attaqafia (1978) even used Arabic. Political parties have not taken up minority rights issues or tried to create any minority rights associations. The MP served as a patron–client institution of ethnic Amazigh elites in relation to the monarchy. It is often referred to as a family that also relates to its chief Mahjoubi Aherdane's promotion of his own family members inside the party. What can be described as a process of gradual de-politicisation that took place within the political parties of the nationalist movement culminating in alternance was at the heart of the MP's political activity from its inception in 1959. This created from an earlier stage on independent Amazigh rights associations.[152]

In 1991, six Amazigh rights associations joined forces, and supported by human rights groups demanded a more explicit recognition of Amazigh language and culture. On 5 August 1991, Amazigh demands were for the first time explicitly formulated in the 'Charter of Agadir'. The charter denounced 'the systematic marginalisation of the Amazigh language and culture'. In addition, it declared its aim of promoting the recognition of Tamazight as an official language, and demanded the 'integration of the Amazigh language and cultures in various areas of cultural and educational ... programmes' and the 'right to have access to the mass media'.[153]

## Political reforms under Hassan II

As explained above, the political context of the early 1990s resulted in a state-led reform programme in the area of human rights. This became part and parcel of the project of alternance, as defending human rights does not directly question the monarch's political monopoly, but rather how its auxiliaries treat Moroccan citizens. Similarly, while questions of women's rights and minority rights had indirect repercussions on state authority, such as the principle of (male) primogeniture, patrimonialism, religion in politics, or the Arab (*shurfa*) descendants from the Prophet Mohamed, the promotion of these rights could also be used to illustrate Morocco's 'modern' image and laws that Hassan II increasingly emphasised. Hence, the 1990s saw a process in which 'neo-traditionalisation' was complemented by what Moroccans refer to as '*rationalisation*' – an emphasis on reform and modernity. This emphasis became an equally powerful means for the reproduction of authoritarianism, as it reinforced the role of the monarch as the personalised institution that grants rights, listens to the people's concerns, and reforms injustice beyond partisan politics. An important external dimension to this 'reform' has been noted by a Moroccan scholar in the following words.

> When our government officials travel abroad, and when they participate in international organisations, they do not like to be questioned about democratic deficits. As a result, they need to give democratic credentials, one of which is the existence, – or its appearance – of a dynamic civil society, independent from the authorities.[154]

While relaxed state controls evidenced by the authorisation of the OMDH in 1989 gave the appearance of this vibrant civil society, the state also responded to reform proposals initiated by these groups. This, too, provided for an important perception of political change through reform that the state increasingly embarked on. For example, the creation of the CCDH was to deal with human rights violations and reforms as understood by the state. Clearly, from the beginning the CCDH was limited by the nature of its decision making and the composition of its members, from state ministers to carefully selected technocratic, apolitical individuals. On its foundation on 8 May 1990, its mission was put by Hassan II in the following words:

> We have devoted this meeting … to the complementing of the rule of law, which will first and foremost put an end to the long palaver about human rights, so that we can settle this matter once and for all.[155]

Now a state structure was 'dealing' with the problem, and advised the King on the release of prisoners. The council collected data and wrote reports, organised conferences, and responded to national and international criticism, thereby helping improve how Morocco was perceived both domestically and internationally. More importantly, perhaps, the King created an institution other than the Ministry of the Interior that became the focal point of criticism. Hence, as with other institutions such as the Ministry of Human Rights, created in 1994, the council diverted attention away from the monarchy's and its interior ministry's responsibility for human rights abuses.

In the realm of women's rights, it was more difficult for the state to engage in similar activism. While the 1993 collection of 1 million signatures indicated strong support for a reform of Morocco's family code *moudawana*, the violent religious counter-attacks made the production of consensus a more difficult undertaking.[156] In addition, a reform of the family code may have had repercussions concerning the monarch's main sources of legitimacy: Islamic *shari'a* law is probably most explicit and most codified in the areas of divorce, tutorship, marriage and inheritance. Moreover, what is often perceived as declining public morality in Morocco, especially in towns, is intrinsically associated with decreasing family values, values that the family code prior to reform seemingly protected. More importantly, perhaps, is the monarchy's association with tribal values. This gave pre-eminence to the right of polygamy and other traditional practices that aim at preserving the status quo. A reform of the family code would have significant political, social and cultural repercussions.

While two women's rights association, the AMDF and the Feminine Action Union (UAF), became very vocal in their demands for changes to the family code, the state reacted cautiously while assuming its authority in this sensitive area. In 1994, the King invited selected personalities to discuss a legal reform, but excluded the main, publicly visible protagonists such as Latifa Jbabdi or Amina Lmrini. Instead, the state-controlled National Union of Moroccan Women (UNFM), created in 1969 and presided over by Princess Lalla Fatima Zohra, was the only association present. The actual reform, though, was to be discussed behind closed doors in a royal commission consisting of *'ulema*, representatives of the Ministry of Justice and the Ministry of Habous and Islamic Affairs.[157] In a publication of the newly created and state-controlled Council for the Integration of Women in Development, the King addresses women's rights activists:

> Certainly, there are obstacles that prevent Moroccan women from enjoying the full liberty to exercise their rights. When it comes to divorce and repudiation, Moroccan women are at the centre of concern, as the social security network is absent … If she does not enjoy the liberty of movement and the possibility of getting her passport without the permission of her husband … I consider this against the principles of our religion which is the basis of our constitution. Our constitution guarantees the liberty to move for all our citizens … In certain questions, such as polygamy, the Koran has posed certain conditions.[158]

Consequently, a 1995 reform of the *moudawana* concerned two aspects of the principle of male tutorship. Women needed the authorisation of their male tutor – father, husband or, in the case of a widow with no male parent, even the oldest son – to be involved in any aspects of public life. Starting with school and university enrolment, to signing a work contract, obtaining a passport, or marrying, women needed the authorisation of the designated tutor. The reform introduced two exceptions to this rule. While a male tutor was still necessary for many other areas (especially marriage), signing an employment contract and obtaining a passport were now exempted. As a first step towards the 'integration of women in development', later proposals picked up the question of legal empowerment through the dynamic created by the '*Plan d'Action pour l'Intégration de la Femme au Développement*' (1997–2000). This plan was sponsored by the World Bank and integrated more women's rights groups under the auspices of the Moroccan Ministry for Family and Social Affairs.

A similarly cautious state response concerned the question of minority rights. While the Amazigh rights association became more outspoken within the framework of political liberalisation introduced by Hassan II's policy of seeking a national consensus, it also experienced continuing and more controversial public repression. The most significant event after the Charter of Agadir (1991) was the 1 May 1994 arrest of seven members of the association *Tilleli* ('freedom' in Tamazight), in Goulmima in south-eastern Morocco. They displayed banners in Tamazight asking for the official recognition of the language.[159] While 17 days later four of them were released, the other three received prison sentences ranging from one to two years. They were convicted and found guilty of posing a 'threat to the sanctity of the state'.[160] After a widespread campaign launched by human rights activists, more than 400 lawyers volunteered on 29 June 1994 to defend these activists in an appeal. Four days later they were released, but, more importantly, King Hassan addressed some of their grievances. On 20 August 1994, he declared that Morocco's 'dialects' were 'one of the components of the authenticity of our history'. Concerning Arabic, he affirmed:

We have to hold to the language of the Koran but not at the expense of our authenticity and dialects especially since there is not one of us who cannot be sure that there is in his dynasty, blood, or body, a small or large amount of cells which came from an origin which speaks one of Morocco's dialects.[161]

Initial reforms included news bulletins that were now also broadcast in the three main dialects – reinforcing the idea of the absence of a unified 'language' Tamazight. Hassan II also issued a decree that authorised necessary changes in the national school curricula to teach the three different dialects at schools. By emphasising that dialects were a crucial component of Morocco's social fabric and history, he thereby responded to the prevalent ideological fear that the recognition of Morocco's linguistic divisions would lead to national divisions.

## Morocco's Islamists enter parliamentary politics

With alternance on the agenda, two new constitutions and referendums in 1992 and 1996, state-sponsored human rights activism, and the regime responding to women's and Amazigh rights demands with partial reform programmes, the Moroccan state of the 1990s resembled a construction site. As Leveau's well-noted essay 'Morocco at the Crossroads' argues, as the regime appeared to make important concessions to the former political opposition, a real opportunity appeared for a Spanish-style transition to democracy.[162] An important aspect of political liberalisation was the authorisation of Morocco's first Islamist party, the PJD, to participate in the 1997 elections. The modalities of this process represent a remarkable case study on how political forces work within a repressive regime and manage to carve out spheres of manoeuvre. In the last two years of Hassan II's rule, this led to a policy of appeasement between the state and more moderate Islamists, with the apparent aim of marginalising Yassine's more radical (and more popular) *Al 'Adl wal Ihssane* movement. Given Hassan II's often repeated denial that Islamists even existed in Morocco,[163] preferring to call them *integristes*, this accounted for a change in policy from exclusion to managed integration. It is worth pointing out that Yassine also benefited from this approach, as he was temporarily released from house arrest in 1995. He was put back under surveillance when, in his 15 December 1995 sermon, he alluded to the King's deteriorating health, stating that 'his adversary was punished by sickness'.[164]

In the early 1990s, the Islamist association *Al Islah wal Tajdid* applied for official recognition of its political party, *Hizb At Tajdid Al Watani*.[165] Even if this request was rejected by the Ministry of the Interior, it supported the different referendums that the King called for, starting with the 1989 referendum for an extension of parliamentary activity (and postponement of general elections), to the two constitutional reforms of 1992 and 1996. This attested not only to its pro-monarchical stance that the monarch could mobilise in order to divide Islamic opposition, but also to its ambition to become a political party that could enter Morocco's 'defused' political game.[166]

In 1996, Islah's leader Benkirane decided to open negotiations with the head of the defunct Democratic and Constitutional Popular Movement (MPDC), Abdelkrim Khattib. If the Ministry of the Interior did not allow the creation of an Islamist party, the alternative was to join an existing, weak party that lacked members. Khattib agreed under the condition that he remained officially the leader of the MPDC. The take-over took place on 2 June 1996 during an extraordinary congress of the MPDC, and it was preceded by a green light that Hassan II sent in an interview with a German national TV channel:

> These are Moroccans. As long as they are not involved in dividing Islam (*schisme*) or some other form of heresy, and as long as they follow the laws and the rules of the state, I will not intervene.[167]

The monarch's words were followed by deeds, and the MPDC was not outlawed. First, however, the Islamists inside the MPDC had to ensure that its cooperation with Abdelkrim Khattib would continue, as Khattib did not feel it appropriate for the party to field any candidates in the upcoming June 1997 municipal elections. As a splinter party from the mainstream MP, the MPDC had long boycotted elections and Khattib clearly wanted to determine the modalities of any policy changes. Interestingly, the Islah leadership around Abdallah Benkirane, Mohamed Yatim, Saadeddine El Othmani and the younger, more 'radical' Mustapha Ramid accepted the choice, and the decision was made to field independent candidates in the municipal elections. According to Benkirane, the strategic importance of continuing Islah's relations with Khattib was more significant than the tactical question of whether or not to participate in the municipal elections.[168] The real issue was the nationwide legislative elections of 14 November 1997, and here Khattib no longer objected to the party's participation, clearly as this may have meant an end to *Al Islah*'s union with the MPDC. In its first parliamentary election, the Islamists fielded candidates in only half of Morocco's constituencies, and they showed significant restraint in their usage of Islamic language, such as references to *shari'a*. Although the MPDC was accused by its competitors of using the mosque for political discourse, most observers contended that its campaign was remarkably well organised. Door-to-door campaigning was omnipresent; candidates who were selected had important local roots and were known for their high level of education. Most importantly, MPDC electoral activities were marked by an absence of what became Morocco's most important election and campaigning tool: the buying of votes. Although the MPDC, soon thereafter renamed the Justice and Development Party (PJD), only won a disappointing nine out of 325 seats, the political process that led to its participation was a clear success.

## 3.8 Succession and new leadership: the early years of Mohamed VI

A regular theme among Moroccans is that Mohamed VI's accession to the throne upon his father's death on 23 July 1999 accelerated political change and reform.

The 35-year-old man emphasised social welfare, and soon people started calling him King of the Poor. In addition, he apparently placed less emphasis on royal protocol such as the hand kiss. Together with his young age, all of this made him seem modern and a representative of a new generation. Further, when he dismissed Morocco's infamous Minister of the Interior Driss Basri in November 1999, he was viewed as a liberal, and when he called for a 'New Concept of Authority' on 12 October 1999 to change the nature of administration–citizen interaction, it appeared that he would steer Morocco away from authoritarianism to (more) democracy.

The release of Abdessalam Yassine from house arrest on 16 May 2000, as well as the return of Hassan II's most prominent opponent from forced exile in France, Abraham Serfaty, reinforced this appearance. Although Yassine immediately wrote an open letter to Mohamed VI, asking him not to repeat his father's wrongs and to return his father's wealth to Moroccans, his house arrest was not reimposed, even if his website remained banned.[169] Mohamed VI also encouraged women's rights activists when he addressed women's conditions on 20 August 1999. He questioned the rationale of keeping women as second-class citizens under the *moudawana* if Morocco wanted to achieve 'progress and prosperity'.[170] As the Moroccan government was involved in a series of women's rights reforms, the *Plan d'Action pour l'Intégration de la Femme au Développement*, this seemed to suggest that a new wave of liberalisation would also include a more substantial reform of Morocco's *moudawana*.

These events marked what the French journalist Jean-Pierre Tuquoi called the Spring of Rabat (*Printemps de Rabat*),[171] a generalised atmosphere of political opening and reform. The French journal *L'Express* had already run the headline *printemps marocain* on 17 June 1999, one month before Hassan's death, to describe this atmosphere. A new generation of newspapers, such as *Le Journal* and *Assahifa*, broadened the public space and critique. Given this context, it was not a large step to believe that Mohamed VI's accession to the throne might signify a devolution of power from the monarchy to elected government institutions. The governmental *Plan d'Action pour l'Intégration de la Femme au Développement* proved a very important symbol in this regard. After all, in 1999–2000 the government of alternance, even if it had only a fragile majority in parliament, seemed determined to change the *moudawana* as part of the *Plan d'Action*. New non-governmental leaders, both feminist and Islamist, organised two very well-attended public demonstrations in Casablanca and Rabat in March 2000. Latifa Jbabdi from the UAF, Rabia Naciri from Collectif 95 – Maghreb Egalité, and Amina Lmrini from AMDF faced the increasingly outspoken daughter of Abdessalam Yassine, Nadia Yassine from *Al 'Adl wal Ihssane*, who marched against the *Plan d'Action* side by side with the head of the PJD, Saadeddine El Othmani.

Given all this activity around the *moudawana* at the beginning of Mohamed VI's reign, there was a real chance that he would be outpaced by these actors and no longer in control of the domestic political scene. Consequently, in April 2000 the new King intervened, shelved the governmental plan, and created an inter-ministerial commission, which later became a royal commission. Given its potential for mobilisation of both modernists and Islamists alike, the reform process of the *moudawana* had to be controlled. More than three years later, in September 2003, a new, reformed *moudawana* was presented to the public and passed by the parliament, whose role was reduced to agreeing to the changes that had been negotiated behind closed doors. It appeared that, while the King might have agreed to reform in principle, this needed to come from his prerogatives as the Commander of the Faithful, at a time when he would have more institutional leverage and authority than in the first year of his reign.

The temporary withdrawal of the plan to reform the *moudawana*, and the creation of an unaccountable royal commission to deal with any changes, gave a first impression of the new King's vision for Morocco's political system: although substantial changes were underway that changed the content of politics, such as more autonomy and participation in new social and political actors, this was not to signify a rearrangement of powers or prerogatives. The King retained the key powers over the security forces. Trusted loyalists that he inherited from his father's era – General Benslimane and Laanigri amongst others – occupied the most sensitive posts in the regime's security network. The government was replicated in an informal 'shadow' cabinet, which held real powers thanks to its members' proximity to the King. A school friend of Mohamed VI, Fouad Ali El Himma, occupied the most sensitive position, the 'shadow' Ministry of the Interior. Hence, what Remy Leveau remarked with regard to Morocco under Hassan II remains valid after his death: the state's authority remained based on its ability to use coercion without significant constraint, which creates a sense of fear among opponents.

> To a large extent, Morocco's political life still rests upon domestic fear over the arbitrary use of power, a fear which is likely to disappear if its main vector – royal control over the interior portfolio – is put aside. The real effects of the Makhzen's arbitrary exploitation of power have greatly decreased in the past ten years but it has continued to be important to maintain the potential threat-perception that it represents in order to frighten off marginal elements that would like to sweep the system away.[172]

In addition to the monarch's continued control over the interior portfolio, a new rearrangement of the political field was marked by increasing his presence outside the, strictly speaking, state institutions: the increasing creation of para-governmental organisations. The creation of the CCDH in 1990 was one such para-governmental organisation par excellence. Already under Hassan II, these institutions were used as a way to bypass governmental institutions and to assert royal control in areas where the government seemed too bureaucratic – such as the League of Moroccan *'Ulema* (1960), the National Council of *'Ulema* (1980), the National Council of Youth and the Future (1994), and the Advisory Council for Social Dialogue (1994). Under Mohamed VI, the creation of the Hassan II Fund for Economic and Social Development (2001) reinvigorated this approach. The Hassan II Fund was charged with ensuring that revenues generated from Morocco's privatisation of 35 per cent of Maroc Telecom, and the licence for its second GSM line (1999) was used for specific, development-oriented purposes. This meant that state revenues were diverted from ministerial supervision and to royal supervision. Another major social fund was the Mohamed V Fund for Social Work (2001). Other ad hoc councils included the Instance for Truth and Arbitrage (1999), which was to determine indemnities for human rights violations committed under Hassan II's reign. Even in a key foreign policy issue, the Western Sahara dispute, such a council was reinvigorated in 2004: the Royal Advisory Council for Sahrawi Affairs (CORCAS). Together with the above-mentioned royal commission for the reform of the *moudawana*, and the integration of Amazigh militants such as Mohamed Chafik in the Royal Institute for Amazigh Culture (IRCAM) in 2002, the state initiated a process of integration of new actors of civil society in para-governmental organisations. Consequently, the state forged new partnerships with potential opponents.[173]

All of this illustrated that, under Mohamed VI, a process of accelerated readjustment was taking place. Human rights, social and economic rights of the poor, minority and women's rights have been made a priority and gained more visibility. Non-state actors have also been given more visibility as they have been increasingly integrated into the polity. The result, however, has been a strengthened presence of the monarchy in the political process. This weakened elected institutions of the state and political parties in the second half of the government of alternance (1998–2002) under Mohamed VI's reign. The country's strengthened civil society did not become a precursor for a pro-democracy movement and democratic transition, either, as some scholars suggested in the 1990s.[174] In addition to the continued monopolisation of coercion that Leveau remarked upon, major incentives were missing: after all, political integration also means access to patronage and social prestige, as well as working towards the realisation of some of these single-issue organisations' objectives. Consequently, the imprisonment of an increasing number of journalists and even a Facebook writer, hitting headlines worldwide, produced little domestic mobilisation in their favour. Lise Garon even speaks of a dangerous civil society–state alliance against civic liberties that the integration of new actors in Morocco's authoritarian regime produced.[175]

## 3.9 Democratisation

Despite the absence of meaningful political reforms that would change the balance of power since Mohamed VI's accession to the throne, the paradigm of democratisation continued to be used by Morocco's political elite. Even more, an important production of meaning accelerated around democratisation, in which the King and associated elites managed to dominate domestic discourse. In an interview with the French newspaper *Le Figaro* on 4 September 2001, Mohamed VI made reference to the democratic transition led by Spain's King Juan Carlos I after Francisco Franco's death in 1975. In the King's words:

People have not stopped ... comparing me with King Juan Carlos ... The Spanish monarchy has nothing in common with the Moroccan monarchy ... Moroccans want a strong, democratic, and executive monarchy.[176]

Although principles such as 'democratic' and 'executive' monarchies are difficult to reconcile, it is important to point out that Mohamed VI views executive monarchy as the popular, 'democratic' wish of Moroccans. For this reason, the regularity of elections and their fair and transparent process have been increasingly emphasised, at the expense of governmental accountability. After all, the government remained appointed by the King alone. This was clarified in his throne speech on 30 July 2002, two months before the September 2002 parliamentary elections:

> Of course, democratic competition is necessary. However, it stops where the superior interest of the nation commands it ... Hence, will politicians approach this electoral year with their dividing politicised logic, rendering election an end in itself? We assure you, no, as We are very concerned with the superior interests of the nation ... [Elections] will form a powerful support for the executive organs, and an efficient lever for integrated development ...[177]

Political parties and the monarchy agreed on a new semi-proportional electoral code prior to the September 2002 elections. Based on multi-candidacy proportional districts and the introduction of a 10 per cent women's list, the system ossified the already fragmented political forces presented in parliament. Up from 14 after the 1997 parliamentary election, 22 parties made it to the 2002 lower house, with the smallest party – the *Congrès Ittihati* – only receiving 0.3 per cent of votes and one seat. With 50 seats, the USFP only achieved a marginal victory over its main rival, the Istiqlal Party, which obtained 48 seats. While this was clearly disappointing for the USFP, the newcomer – the PJD – obtained 42 seats and therefore became overnight the third largest parliamentary group. This was despite the fact that it had only presented candidates in 56 of 92 constituencies. The Ministry of the Interior had apparently interfered and 'consulted' with the Islamists, thereby ensuring that they would not win an outright victory, which was still deemed politically unacceptable.[178]

Following the elections, King Mohamed surprised the political establishment when he appointed Driss Jettou as prime minister. He was an independent technocrat and former minister of the interior, and his appointment was the first major controversial move of King Mohamed. It revealed a number of major preoccupations of the monarch, and it underscored doubts about his commitment to democratic change. First, it was not the 'democratic' logic of majority that would legitimise the prime minister, but rather his performance as minister of the interior and his successful record as an entrepreneur. He had been a shoe manufacturer, member of the General Confederation of Moroccan Enterprises (CGEM), as well as the head of Morocco's most important public company, *Office Chérifien des Phosphates* (OCP). Second, by nominating an independent, technocratic prime minister, the King set an example for the future. He made it clear that he would not be bound by electoral results in his pursuit of the superior interests of *La Nation*. He thereby freed himself from expectations to the contrary, which could potentially result in democratic transition. Third, it illustrated the importance he gave to technocratic forms of governance to face Morocco's development challenges based on neo-liberal strategies. The appointment of a new generation of regional governors and *walis* in 2001, not consisting of traditional Ministry of the Interior personnel, followed the same logic. Jettou's prior appointment as minister of the interior was also a sign that the ministry, charged with all the ills of human rights abuses under Driss Basri and Hassan II, was relegated to second rank under Mohamed VI. After all, Jettou was not appointed from within the ministry's own ranks.

The appointment of Jettou divided the political scene into two camps. On one hand, the USFP criticised the appointment. In a statement it made it clear that 'nothing can justify the abrogation of the democratic logic', a position that became difficult to defend when it participated in the 2002–07 government.[179] On the other hand, the economic journal *La Vie Economique* ran the following headline taken from an opinion poll among Moroccan entrepreneurs: 'Following his nomination to the premiership, the business sector unanimously supports Jettou.'[180] His reputation as a good manager and technocrat gave so much confidence among businessmen that the Casablanca stock exchange witnessed a significant jump on the day of his appointment. Given this division, it is interesting to see the balance clearly shift in Jettou's favour when the Istiqlal, the PJD and the MP issued a joint statement in which they affirmed that the country needed a 'strong' and 'efficient' government that had both the trust of the King and the support of the Moroccan people.[181]

The critical role of elections and political party activism, i.e. ongoing 'democratisation' for the monarchy's legitimacy, has been further strengthened in public discourse since this controversial appointment. In 2007 the Moroccan government, sponsored by the United States Agency for International Development (USAID), engaged in a massive public relations campaign (Daba 2007), aimed at encouraging especially young voters to vote. This was partially a reaction to strong public criticism about intra-party practices, election rigging, vote buying and gerrymandering, at a time when voting age was decreased from 20 to 18 years. The monarch himself participated in this campaign, calling elections a practice of 'normalisation of democracy'. In his 2007 *discours du trône*, such support even transformed into open threats to those who criticised political parties and electoral processes:

> You will always find me, my dear and loyal people, at the frontline, at the head of those who are determined to thwart every discourse that aims at casting doubt on the importance of holding elections and on the utility itself of political parties. I will foil all those trendy practices that aim at posing a threat to their [the elections'] credibility. The political maturity that we have achieved requires from Us the duty to outlaw faulty, nihilist, and deceptive conceptions,

which attack the respect owed to the democratic verdict of the ballot boxes.[182]

Consequently, electoral politics have suffered from a fundamental dilemma: on one hand, opposition voices, especially those of the PJD, kept the governing elite consisting of co-opted political parties in line, and kept a check on corrupt practices, which were otherwise occasionally brought into the public realm. Yet, on the other hand, public, vocal opposition also tarnished the image that the King aimed to give elections and the King's reformist agenda, including important economic reforms. Concerning PJD opposition, a leading PJD politician and later government minister, Lahcen Daoudi, expressed this in the following words:

> The PJD was useful in the late 1990s and early 2000s for the image of Morocco as a democratic country. But please, we should not have too much power, as this would be bad for Morocco's image, for its corrupt political class, and especially for its international alliances.[183]

## Dealing with opposition

The stability of the system depends on all actors' acceptance of the rules of the game, yet there have been two main sources of constant criticism under Mohamed VI. The first source is Islamists; the second, liberal reformers who have used the country's liberalised media space to criticise the *status quo* and test the palace's 'red lines'. While both currents ostensibly share a commitment to principles of democracy and transparency and while both had been unhappy with the palace's domination of the state apparatus, their cultural visions are fundamentally opposed. Liberal reformers aim to establish a society based on the protection of liberal norms and values. Islamists, for their part, and often with a tinge of nationalism and anti-colonialism, view these liberal norms and values as a threat to authentic Moroccan values based on Islam, giving rise to sometimes intolerant views especially concerning homosexuality and moral conduct. In the words of PJD member of parliament Lahcen Daoudi, 'we did not kill millions of Jews, Tartars, or native Americans, and we don't need to take lessons from either Europe or the US about being intolerant … certainly the PJD will never allow homosexual marriages and we will counter the plans of these so-called liberals'.[184] Consequently, opposition to the government remains fundamentally fragmented. Interestingly, in its dealings with such political opposition, the second half of the 2000s saw the monarchy become more proactive and willing to interfere in order to diminish the importance of existing opposition, using the stick where the carrot had failed to produce results. This was possible due to its own relative strength and ability to take advantage of the divided opposition to fashion a preponderant amount of support from the civilian political establishment.

Recent years have witnessed increased restrictions on the freedom of press through the use of loyal judges and state-controlled courts where successful suits could be brought against individual journalists on accusations of defamation. One may observe that the banning of critical newspapers over the last decade always took place when individual publications faced a lack of support both in civil society and political parties. Both the francophone *Le Journal* and *Demain*, as well as the Arabophone *Assahifa* suffered from a widespread consensus in parliament and elsewhere (even in the journalists' own professional associations) that their activities were illegitimate, because their reports were primarily investigative rather than an analysis of official news. A high number of reports focused on the government's dysfunctionality, abuse of power and corruption, as well as human rights abuses. The monarchy, of course, could not be criticised, but these publications did seek to familiarise the public with topics like the palace's budget, which was definitely unacceptable to the authorities. The criticism most widely voiced was that these journalists lacked professional ethics, and consequently needed to be disciplined. One leading publicist, PPS politician and government minister in three governments (2002–07; 2007–11; 2011–16) Nabil Benabdallah, declared as early as 2002 that due to these newspapers' lack of 'ontology' he would 'fight each of these newspapers until they are all gone'.[185]

Dealing with the Islamist PJD has been more complex. Its criticism of the state has been more nuanced, and its activities in parliament have focused on criticising the coalition government as well as contradictions between Islamic principles and social practice, such as the selling of alcohol to Moroccan Muslims, especially in poor neighbourhoods. The PJD is careful to be anti-government, not anti-state. Even if this semantic division is not always clear in practice, the monarch symbolises the state while it is politicians who represent the government. It is also an opposition that can be quite functional, as long as it does not create short- and medium-term uncertainty that threatens other political goals and interests. After all, it puts pressure on the governmental coalition to work efficiently and to avoid infighting, in order to show unity in the face of a potent competitor for votes and political significance.

On the other hand, such competition is a potential menace for a traditional monarch, who represents a religio-political paradigm himself. Although Mohamed VI remains a traditional monarch, he is also perceived as a moderniser, as evidenced by the reform of the family code, his attendance at inter-religious services in the cathedral of Rabat in memory of the victims of 9/11, the integration of women *'ulema* in state-run mosques, the quota for women in parliament and on municipal councils, the public hearings of victims of torture organised by the Justice and Reconciliation Commission (IER), and the acknowledgement of Amazigh rights. In more contentious areas, he has also continued the path of his father Hassan II by expanding the tourism industry and being open to European lifestyles, including a 2010 rock concert by Elton John, and especially tolerating the widespread sale and consumption of alcohol in nightclubs.

While Morocco's Islamists inside the PJD do not seem to disagree with any of these projects *per se*, there is nevertheless substantial unease with the rapid pace of uneven and disruptive modernisation, which is felt particularly in the poorer neighbourhoods. Over the last couple of years, this unease has substantially grown, and while it is difficult to provide precise data for such concerns, the growing electoral success of the PJD, the attacks in Casablanca on 16 May 2003, as well as isolated yet persistent acts of Islamist-inspired violence in Marrakech, Casablanca and elsewhere, have all been important signs. Add to this the amount of unrest in towns such as Sefrou and Sidi Ifni in 2007–08, as well as the nationwide protests in 2011, and opposition expressed to the government and its policies has also been a challenge to the system, as it undermined the monarch's long-term vision for his kingdom.

Partially to counter the importance of the PJD, and partially to keep the political elite in political parties under control and to reinforce patron–client relations, Mohamed VI repeated his father's strategy of creating a political party in 2009: the Authenticity and Modernity Party (PAM), led by his childhood friend and closest royal councillor, Fouad El Himma.[186] While the popularity of the moderate Islamist party, the PJD, was hardly contained as evidenced by a remarkable increase in PJD parliamentarians from 46 to 107 members in the 2011–16 parliament, an important side effect of the PAM's creation was the containment of the Arab Spring, or rather the Moroccan movement it inspired, the 20 February Movement. This is because the PAM managed to represent a movement of 'gradual politicisation of civil society and entrepreneurs',[187] as witnessed by the incorporation in its leadership of key members of Morocco's leftist human rights organisations (such as Salah El Ouadi, Khadija Rouissi) and entrepreneurs who have sought, since the 1990s, a role in politics (Ali Belhaj, Abderrahim Lahjouji).

An important precursor of the PAM was Daba 2007, a large-scale public relations campaign that attempted to rally more popular support for electoral politics and, in particular, attempted to mobilise youth to join the elections as voters and candidates. As with the PAM in 2009–10, Daba 2007 organised public meetings and debates about people's concerns, all under slogans such as 'the politics of proximity' and 'the moralisation of public life' that appear close to civil society activists' concerns. As to the PAM and the Movement of All Democrats, the public meetings it organised in this spirit of 'the politics of proximity' appeared quite successful if judged by the exceptional turnout achieved.[188] Given the prestige of its leader, Fouad El Himma, the high-profile individuals who were invited to join, and the media coverage it thereby attained, this might hardly be surprising. Yet the effect was such that, when the to date only real pro-democracy movement appeared on Morocco's political centre stage from February to April 2011, Morocco's middle class and opinion makers, with their resources in universities, civil society, the media and the private sector, had already been absorbed into networks of patronage. This meant that the mass movement lacked leadership from well-known activists, and in turn allowed co-opted civil society actors to be involved in yet another of the King's projects to create a democratic façade of participation and integration in a new constitutional project that, as with the Movement of All Democrats and Daba 2007 before, was clouded in democratic rhetoric with little democratic content.

## *The rise of Islamist violence*

Amidst these political developments, international events after 11 September 2001 discredited Morocco's policy orientation, as well as its political elite. It made the electoral process appear increasingly meaningless as the country's elite became isolated from popular concerns. The 2002 voter turnout was at officially 52 per cent of registered voters, which decreased even further to officially 37 per cent in 2007. While the United States invaded Afghanistan and Iraq, Morocco kept its traditional position as a US ally, and co-opted parties did not pick up on the population's resentment. Although the US war efforts in Iraq and Afghanistan were not openly supported by Mohamed VI, US Secretaries Donald Rumsfeld, Condoleezza Rice and Colin Powell were all welcomed in the country, as was the 2003 US proposal for a US–Moroccan free trade agreement (FTA).

Meanwhile, authorisations to demonstrate on foreign policy issues were systematically refused, resulting in major clampdown campaigns against organisers who dared to protest without authorisation. The single exception was a massive April 2002 demonstration in Rabat prior to the US campaign against Iraq, which attracted about 1 million people against Israel's military incursions in the West Bank, notably in Jenin. Although no riots were reported, the widespread support for suicide bombers and Hamas activists displayed during the protest indicated the potential for radicalisation inside Morocco's Islamist milieu.

On 16 May 2003, 12 suicide bombers killed 45 people in Casablanca, including themselves, targeting a luxury hotel – a Spanish as well as Jewish cultural centre. Most suicide bombers came from one particular shanty town area in Casablanca called Sidi Moumen, which indicates that questions of wealth and the distribution thereof were one of the underlying reasons. In addition, while many commentators and Ministry of the Interior officials referred to a sophisticated network of Islamists who were involved, it is worth pointing out that no strategic or political locations such as touristic areas or governmental offices were targeted, but rather the closest site associated with conspicuous consumption, immorality and foreigners in Casablanca itself. Luxury hotels are often regarded as places of prostitution.

In addition to the disgruntled youth that lives in Morocco's shanty towns, important international connections existed to Afghanistan, Saudi Arabia and migrant communities living in Europe. Nebulous Al Qaeda networks led to the creation of Moroccan groups such as *Salafiyya Jihadiyya* and *Groupe Islamiste Combattants Marocains*, which were involved in the particularly lethal Madrid 2004 bombings. According to Spanish investigators, after the Madrid bombings, Moroccan authorities admitted that they had lost track of 400 of the 600 Moroccans who were trained in Afghan camps. In turn, Morocco's alliance with Saudi Arabia has also led to the increasing importance of Wahhabi clerics in Morocco, and brought these preachers' particular militancy that remained outside many official mosques.[189] What all of these actors seem to have in common is their fragmented nature, in which ad hoc political militancy leads to Islamist-inspired violence. The Spanish judge heading the Madrid investigation concluded in 2004 that 'the most serious problem that Europe has right now with this type of terrorism is in Morocco'.[190] Such concerns continued in the 2010s, when a remotely triggered bomb killed 17 people, mostly foreign nationals, at Marrakech's touristic Jemaa el-Fnaa square on 28 April 2011. The authorities blamed the attack on Al Qaeda-affiliated individuals. Since civil war broke out in Iraq and Syria, an estimated 2,000 Moroccan nationals are believed to have travelled to join ISIS (Islamic State in Iraq and Syria) and other Islamist militant groups.

The state's reaction after the Casablanca bombings was swift. Within a few days, an anti-terrorism bill was drafted by the government and passed in parliament, introducing a major legal loophole that persecutors could easily use: if charged with crimes related to terrorism, suspects could be kept in special detention for up to 12 days without seeing a lawyer. The original detention period had been fixed at 96 hours (four days), but it could be renewed twice with the approval of a judge. In addition, Mohamed VI heralded the end of an era of 'leniency' in a speech following these attacks,[191] linking political liberalisation with terrorist activities. There were even demands emanating from political parties and potentially suggested by the Ministry of the Interior that called for a ban on the PJD, as they were considered ideologically responsible. Up to 2,000 Islamists, 700 alone in the two months following 16 May 2003, were consequently arrested in a country-wide sweeping campaign.[192] Not surprisingly, confessions were extracted within the 12-day detention period. This was often the only evidence used to incriminate the accused.[193] Later testimonies in trials that confessions were extracted under torture were not investigated by judges. The judges' harsh sentences included four death penalties. In the aftermath of the 2011 Marrakech bombing, one individual was sentenced to death, and five others to prison terms ranging from ten years to life. In the meantime, the Moroccan parliament passed a law in 2014 criminalising Moroccan citizens for fighting in the ranks of ISIS and other groups in Iraq and Syria.

## *The politics of reform 1999–2011*

The events of 16 May 2003 gave more freedom of manoeuvre to Morocco's security forces. In addition to the anti-terrorism act, the Ministry of the Interior created a special task force called *Groupement Urbain de Securité* (GUS) in 2004. It was dismantled only two years later for its heavy-handed approach to suspects that led to a number of casualties and both international and domestic criticism. The 'end of the era of leniency', however, did not mean that the state's oppressive approach was not supplemented by incentives for Morocco's more secular elite to modernise the state and give more credibility to its elected institutions. Although the legislative function of the parliament remains fairly limited, partly due to lack of effective governmental accountability and public freedom, concerning its oversight function it has been given more leeway – significantly improving its image among stakeholders. Two unprecedented parliamentary inquiries into cases of top-level corruption in the public sector took place: in 2001–02, that of the *Crédit Immoblier et Hôtelier* (CIH) and in 2004 that of the *Caisse Nationale de Securité Sociale*

(CNSS). Both inquiries gave evidence of involvement of close protégés of the regime in the abuse of credit facilities and corruption, and their public reports named some of those involved. These reports also proposed a law that would make it punishable to refuse testimony to parliamentary fact-finding missions.[194] Both parliamentary missions strengthened the institution's credibility. One of Morocco's human rights associations, the OMDH, praised the fact-finding mission for its unprecedented work.[195] This was despite the fact that the subsequent public trial of the CIH's chief manager, Moulay Zine Zahidi, was regarded as a show trial as many of the King's advisers primarily responsible for 'ordering' credits remained untouched.[196]

Other major changes addressed Morocco's secular elite that remained out of the parliament – human rights, women's rights and Amazigh rights activists. Public policies aiming at appeasing human rights groups' criticism and integrating opposition into proto-governmental bodies had already taken place prior to Mohamed VI's accession to the throne. Still, the period of 2002–07 saw an accelerated series of policy reforms in all three areas in addition to a renewed focus on the poor in the form of human development.

Much attention focused on the reform of the family code, as well as on Morocco's introduction of a 10 per cent national list for female parliamentary candidates, later increased to 20 per cent.[197] After about three years of behind-the-scenes consultations in an ad hoc advisory council appointed by the King in 2000, substantial changes were introduced in September 2003. These changes included the abolition of the concept of tutorship in all respects, which meant that women could engage in administrative procedures, including marriage, without approval of their fathers, husbands or other male relatives. Effective since 2004, this has meant an end to Moroccan women's status as second-class citizens. Practically, this gave women the right to choose their own husbands, a decision formerly monopolised by the male head of the family. Other substantive changes to the family code included an end to the right of men to proclaim a divorce orally – repudiation – in favour of a decision proclaimed by a family court. This substantially decreased the threat of a unilateral divorce that women faced until then. In addition, the right to divorce is now equally given to both spouses – formerly women had little to no right to obtain a legal divorce without the consent of their spouses. Although polygamy remained allowed, it was made more difficult to obtain for it required the consent of the first spouse. On issues such as inheritance, however, no changes were introduced as here Islamic *shari'a* law seemed too specific and binding.

Whereas changes to the family code were introduced by a royal commission, subsequent to the government's proposed *Plan d'Action pour l'Intégration de la Femme au Développement*, it is important to point out that women's rights activists have been crucial in mobilising women, political parties and state functionaries behind this project. Although external support especially from the World Bank – which originally commissioned the plan – was central, it responded to activities in Morocco's increasingly vibrant non-governmental sector, which developed together with Morocco's political liberalisation of the 1990s. Despite increasing instrumentalisation of women's rights by linking it to economic development, King Mohamed VI also adopted the language of women's rights activists. His speech commemorating the introduction of the new family code echoes the religious arguments advanced by Moroccan women's rights activists. Polygamy is conditioned in the Koran by the duty of men to treat all wives equally, which, according to Muslim feminists, means in practice that polygamy is outlawed by Islam. Adopting this argument, the monarch advises in his own words to avoid polygamy if one fears being unjust. More than that, he renders polygamy quasi-illegal when he suggests that in reality no man can ever treat all his wives equally, despite one's apparent feelings.[198]

A similar dynamic can be detected in the state's response to increasing Amazigh militancy. The 2001 Kabilyan rebellion in neighbouring Algeria coincided with increasing calls inside Morocco for substantial reforms – especially as, six years after Hassan's announcement of teaching Tamazight in schools, no efforts had been undertaken. On the contrary, as the widely published 'Berber Manifesto', written by the Amazigh scholar Mohamed Chafik in March 2000, criticises, Hassan's promise 'did not have the smallest effect and, up till now, remains null and void'.[199] The manifesto further demands the introduction of compulsory teaching of Tamazight, the constitutional recognition of Tamazight as an official language, with its implications of Tamazight TV, official translators in hospitals and courts. The manifesto drew on support from heads of more than 200 Amazigh associations, some of whom, such as Rachid Raha from the Global Amazigh Committee (CMA), also evoked the idea of creating a political party. Given the potentially destabilising nature of Amazigh militancy, as the example of Kabilya made increasingly clear, and given some anti-state sentiments that were widespread in the northern Rif region in particular, the state had to ensure quickly that a cultural movement remained apolitical. In addition, by integrating Amazigh demands into a state-led policy of inclusion, the state could simultaneously re-establish a sense of national identity. Hence, on 23 July 2001, the second anniversary of his accession to the throne, the King announced the creation of IRCAM, which was to be the cultural basket of his New Concept of Authority introduced two years before. He explained that Moroccan identity was 'plural because it was built on diverse influences: Amazigh, Arab, Saharan, African and Andalusian'.[200] IRCAM had as its mission to promote Amazigh culture, and it spent most of its first five years of existence in standardising the three spoken dialects that are prevalent in Morocco into one written form of Tamazight. Meantime, Amazigh activists, especially through their use of the Internet, continue to challenge the lack of attention that Amazigh-speaking areas receive in terms of investment, schooling, literacy campaigns, and argue that Morocco remains as divided as before the creation of IRCAM. Clearly, though, through the appointment of Mohamed Chafik as the first head of IRCAM, the state succeeded in co-opting the moderate, less politicised part of the Amazigh rights movement into a proto-governmental institution. It is important to mention that Chafik used to be the director of the *Collège Royal* where Mohamed VI received part of his education.

De-emphasising Arabic also has been a way of decreasing the influence of Islamists in the aftermath of the 16 May attacks. Especially secular Amazigh have repeatedly pointed out that the state's prior focus on the Arabic language exposed it to Middle Eastern Islamist influence. This concern even triggered a response by Abdessalam Yassine in a book entitled *Dialogue with an Amazigh Friend*.[201]

By far the most important concession to modernists was the creation of the IER in 2004. Its creation was preceded by the appointment of Driss Benzekri to chair the CCDH. Benzekri not only was a former political prisoner (1974–91) and member of the *Ilal Amam* group, but also had been the head of a more radical human rights group, the Truth and Justice Forum (FVJ). Since 1999, the CCDH had been dealing with the question of indemnities to human rights victims, but it had been criticised, especially by the FVJ, for how it tried to determine indemnities and entitlements. Hence, by appointing the head of the FVJ as the president of the CCDH, a further attempt was made by the King at integrating critics into state-controlled structures. In turn, though, Driss Benzekri succeeded in his idea of creating the IER, which involved not only the determination of indemnities but more importantly public TV hearings of victims of human rights abuses prior to 1999, what is called in Moroccan parlance years of lead. Reconciliation did not mean to follow the South African example of confronting victims with perpetrators, and it did not include mentioning the names of the former torturers. As many of those were still in positions of power, this would have risked opening a Pandora's Box. After hundreds of hearings, indemnities were determined by a committee that also included the women's rights activist Latifa Jbabdi, and a final report written with recommendations of how to avoid human rights abuses. These recommendations included the separation of the three branches of government – hence constitutional reform.[202] Importantly, the IER limited its investigation and public hearings to victims under Hassan II's rule, giving the message that human rights abuses either no longer existed or were not important enough to be investigated. This had the effect of creating a powerful symbolic rupture between Hassan II's rule and that of Mohamed VI.

While all these policies addressed the concerns of Morocco's educated and secular elite as well as their representations in politics – political parties and rights-oriented movements – average Moroccans had little to gain from these changes. With support for radical Islamic solutions being relatively high, a more local, grassroots development plan was introduced. The plan meant to ensure popular support for the monarch as well as to prevent further terrorist activities. This link was made clear two years after the Casablanca bombings. On 18 May 2005, the King inaugurated the National Initiative for Human Development (INDH). He referred to it as his *projet de règne*, and to ensure both visibility and implementation, he has been busy inaugurating hundreds of associated projects. In 2007 alone, it received a budget of 3.3 billion dirhams (approximately €290 million), while in the same year some 7,000 projects were inaugurated.[203]

All of this represents a symbolic discontinuity that may be at the heart of what can be called the mask of Janus that has increasingly characterised changes under

Mohamed VI.[204] Compared with the first 30 years under Hassan II's rule, the period starting in 1992 has witnessed a surprising regularity of (direct) parliamentary elections in 1993, 1997, 2002, 2007 and 2011. This has been accompanied by increasing inclusion of former opposition figures, political prisoners and (moderate) Islamists. After the 2007 election, the monarchy showed its willingness to accept electoral outcomes: Mohamed VI appointed Abbes El Fassi as prime minister, the head of the Istiqlal Party. With 50 out of 325 seats it was the declared winner over both the USFP and PJD. Reforms in many non-political realms have also been prevalent. In education, Morocco instituted the now European standard of BA (Bac + 3) and MA (Bac + 5); in justice, Morocco is involved in increasing training for its judges to implement the new family code; in the economy, more and more branches are liberalised, and FTAs are signed with the EU, the United States, and other Middle Eastern states. The audiovisual media are slowly liberalising – new radio and TV channels obtained licences in 2007. In addition, development is no longer conceived as white elephant projects. Instead, the King's initiative focuses on 'human development', which emphasises the poor, the disabled, women and underdeveloped rural areas.

Yet, elections did not serve to select new governments, nor did they produce governmental accountability. Up until the critical reform of the constitution in 2011, the King alone had the constitutional right to select a prime minister and the government. Parliament has very few powers and patron–client relations make sure that even those powers are not used. The 2007 Prime Minister Abbes El Fassi, when asked about his government's programme, responded by saying that his programme was the King's parliament opening speech. Reforms in education have not tackled core problems such as linguistic divisions. While the audiovisual media sector experienced liberalisation, a council (the High Authority for Audiovisual Communication – HACA), appointed by and accountable to the King alone, oversees and sanctions its activities. Morocco's system of justice remains heavily corrupt and political interference is frequent, as all judges are appointed and promoted by the minister of justice, who is appointed by the King.[205] Poverty is at best stagnant and the urban poor and disgruntled youth continue to provide a receptive pool for radical Islamic ideas. Morocco's 2007 official voter turnout rate of 37 per cent was the lowest turnout in Moroccan history. While this may simply be evidence of increasing freedom and transparency, very high rates of spoilt ballots indicate a high level of frustration. These reached 32 per cent in Tangier and 30 per cent in Fes.[206] In addition, according to anecdotal evidence, many spoilt ballots were marked with insults. This clearly points towards soaring political disillusionment among average Moroccans.

In the aftermath of the 2007 parliamentary election, Morocco's political landscape continued to be marked by fragmented but mostly co-opted political parties and non-partisan pro-palace movements headed by close associates of the King. The most important was created right after the September 2007 elections by the King's school friend, Fouad El Himma. The second most powerful man in the country after the King himself had been the King's 'shadow' minister of the interior before he turned down his position and ran for election. After obtaining a seat, El Himma created the 'Movement of all Democrats', which weakened established political parties even further, and reinforced patron–client relations and royal control.

## 3.10 The Arab Spring and the 2011 constitutional reform

Under these circumstances, the protests that broke out in Morocco following the events in Egypt and Tunisia in January and February 2011 that culminated in a country-wide movement on 20 February 2011 (from which the subsequent protest organisers borrowed its name, the 20 February Movement) marked an unexpected turning point. They can only be understood as part of the enthusiasm that followed the fall of Zine Eddine Ben Ali and Hosni Mubarak in Tunisia and Egypt, respectively. Due to geographical and cultural proximity, and a shared history of French colonial rule, Moroccans were particularly affected by the fall of Ben Ali. The mass mobilisation inside Morocco illustrated that, in spite of appearances, the King's monopolisation of the reform process was not universally accepted. It also marked a fundamental break with the end of the 2000s. As illustrated above, in the period of 2006–10, there appeared very little room for further political reform, and the monarchy even started to control the political landscape by creating rival political parties and imposing limits on an increasingly liberal newspaper scene. Yet the content and scope of the protests in Morocco, as well as the responses from the state and its political elite, were strongly influenced by the modalities of reforms that took place under Mohamed VI in the first ten years of his reign.

First, Morocco can be considered one of the most politically liberal of all authoritarian systems in North Africa and the Middle East. The Moroccan monarchy did not react with even a fraction of the violence employed in other states in order to counter the 20 February Movement. Even the most violent crackdown, on 13 March 2011 in Casablanca, did not result in any deaths. Only one protester died from the actions of police in June 2011. This relative restraint reflected the reformist nature of the protests. While keywords such as *hogra* and 'rage' were used by the movement, it did not resonate among a larger Moroccan public as much as it did in neighbouring countries. Slogans such as *degage!*, as used in Tunisia, remained largely unthinkable. In turn, the relatively liberal reactions of the state, which included a new constitution and referendum on 1 July, did not galvanise the population as compared to other MENA countries, as evidenced by much lower turnout rates to calls for protests in September 2011. Effectively, in the summer of 2011 the state was able to avoid a confrontation, while Moroccans were swept with information about the misfortunes of their Libyan and Syrian neighbours, the uncertainty of Tunisian and Egyptian experiments, as well as the benefits of their new constitution.[207]

Second, throughout the 2000s the monarchy engaged in a series of political, economic and social reform projects that made the King arguably one of the most popular of all contemporary Arab rulers. An independent (and banned) survey of 2009 credited the King with an approval rate of more than 90 per cent.[208] While public support may partially have waned due to notorious high unemployment levels and poverty, the monarchy devised a political system in which elected politicians are increasingly charged with the day-to-day running of government, and therefore take the blame for any wrong-doing or failed policies. For example, unemployed graduates in Rabat routinely demonstrate in front of the elected parliament, not the palace, despite their being only 200 metres apart.

Third, partially reflecting his willingness to reform and a commitment to 'Moroccan-style' democracy, the monarchy could quickly adapt to the spirit of reform. On 9 March 2011, he announced the formation of a committee that would revise Morocco's constitution, and appointed trusted reformers and experts to draft Morocco's fifth constitution since it achieved independence in 1956. He thereby sent a message to the protesters that he understood, even championed their demands. He also illustrated his willingness to adapt to the new political reality that the Arab Spring had created. As the reformist weekly magazine *Tel Quel* succinctly headlined on 22 April, 'The Revolution is the King'. He also combined this pro-reform spirit with nationalist sentiments concerning Moroccan claims to the Western Sahara. After all, a new constitution was needed to ensure the partial decentralisation necessary for Morocco's autonomy plan in the Sahara. That he was not willing to hand over power to elected officials was also clear. It was not an elected assembly of politicians who were to draft the new constitution publicly, but rather an expert committee of royal appointees who would work behind closed doors. Clearly, they were accountable to the King alone.

## *One step forwards, two steps backwards*

Without any doubt, the constitution is the most liberal that Morocco has known since independence. It enshrines liberal principles, gives more independence to elected officials and the judiciary. It promotes gender equality and even creates an institution that is meant to oversee the actual implementation of gender equality. It also upgrades the importance of Tamazight to become Morocco's second 'official' language next to Arabic.

In terms of substance, however, the King's position as *Amir Al Mu'minin* remains intact. While Article 19 previously described his position as 'sacred', the new Article 46 makes his position 'inviolable' – a difference that constitutional lawyers may find difficult to ascertain. Consequently, his speeches remain, as in the past, not to be debated in public. In addition, he has to approve all legislation and governmental appointments, which gives him effective veto power. While he no longer chairs the Council of Government, which seems to imply more independence for the government, he still chairs a parallel organisation called the Council of Ministers. The most important concession, though, concerns the appointment of the prime minister. Article 47 stipulates that the King appoints as prime minister someone from the political party that has won the most seats in elections to Morocco's lower house, the house of representatives. While this does not necessarily mean that the individual who presides over the most powerful party shall be the prime minister, it is clear that this article inaugurates a new political and constitutional practice.

In terms of procedure, the organisation of a referendum on 1 July 2011, only two weeks after the presentation of the new constitution in mid-June, lacked the preparation that a credible and democratically legitimate constitutional referendum entails. Not only was a public debate avoided but the entire state apparatus was mobilised to ensure in two weeks a high approval rate. State TV disproportionately aired opinions in favour of the 'yes vote', and the King's personal televised support that included Koranic verses not only made public disagreement a crime according to the old (and new) constitution, but also a sacrilege. In addition, simple vote rigging, absence of 'no votes', lax identification and registration requirements, and the transport of voters in cars organised by local Ministry of the Interior officials, cast serious doubts on the fairness of the referendum. Not surprisingly, the approval rate of 98.5 per cent, and an official participation rate of 72 per cent, reminded observers of Hassanian practices during the 'years of lead'. Meantime, demonstrations of sometimes violent pro-monarchy loyalists and thugs further reminded 20 February activists of Egypt's infamous *baltagiyya*.[209]

Although mass mobilisation and repressive tactics continued, it seems that the monarchy scored important points in its dealing with the challenge of the Arab Spring. The monarch could compound his image as a reform-minded ruler, and political stability was reconfirmed before serious doubts could arise. The Arab Spring's revolutionary spirit was transformed into reform as understood and guided by the monarchical state. Not surprisingly, in 2011 Standard & Poor's credit outlook remained 'stable' and international support for its reforms and stability came from both the East, notably the Gulf Cooperation Council, and the West.

Still, the Arab Spring opened a Pandora's Box in Morocco. While protesters may be divided between Islamists, leftists, middle-class intellectuals, students, unemployed graduates and the country's poor, the question of the King's powers exited intellectual circles, academia and political party offices, and occupied the street. This was unprecedented. Consequently, as in other countries, the 'wall of fear' has been broken, and will inform street action, public discussions, newspaper editorials and electoral politics in coming years. This will include a critical questioning of the King's personality and role in political and economic marginalisation that many Moroccans experience. For example, in one of his songs, the Moroccan rapper Mouad Belghouat changed the country's slogan from 'God, Country, King' to 'God, Country, Freedom' (*Allah, Watan, Hurriyah*).[210] While Belghouat was arrested in September 2011 for having allegedly assaulted a regime loyalist, the public nature and distribution of such a song is a significant sign for changes that have occurred.

## *The PJD in government*

Although the monarchy may still feel powerful after this last constitutional coup, the nature of politics has fundamentally changed and has given rise to many more challenges. The first was the 25 November 2011 parliamentary elections, which saw the Arab Spring's third Islamist-dominated government take office (after the Muslim Brotherhood in Egypt and Ennahda in Tunisia). As in 2007, success and failure of the parliamentary election were linked to official voter turnout. The government registered fewer voters (down to 13.48 million from 15.46 million in 2007). Consequently, a similar number of actual voters (6.18 million as opposed to 5.72 million in 2007) yielded a higher registered voter turnout from 37 to 45 per cent. In contrast, turnout among the voting-age population only increased marginally from 27.83 to 28.65 per cent, indicating that disaffection and disenchantment with the electoral process remain equally problematic.[211]

Both the parliamentary election as well as the constitutional referendum may have been flawed for different reasons, yet the appointment of a PJD government following the 25 November 2011 elections means that the monarchy increased the stakes involved in electoral contest. After winning 107 seats in the now 395-member lower chamber, the King appointed Abdelilah Benkirane on 29 November, who established a heterogeneous coalition government with the Istiqlal Party, the MP and the PPS. As a sign of the slow dissolution of the 'ministries of sovereignty' (interior, defence, justice, foreign affairs, religious affairs), which were previously considered only for individuals close to the King without partisan affiliation, the new government included not only the PJD minister of justice, Mustapha Ramid, but also the PJD minister of foreign affairs, Saad Eddine El Othmani. The sensitive Ministry of the Interior went to Mohand Laenser of the MP. The Ministry of Education, traditionally an ideologically important ministry to Islamists, remained outside the reach of the PJD and was occupied by the Istiqlali Mohamed El Ouafa, before the King appointed the technocrat, Francophile and former minister of education Rachid Benmoukhtar in 2013. As the power of appointment continues to rest with the King, the prime minister needed to suggest three individuals for ministerial positions, of whom the King selected one. The new cabinet included only one woman (down from eight in the 2007–11 government); increased competition among politicians relegated women to secondary positions. This is quite ironic, as the new constitution promised to realise gender parity and to establish an authority that would oversee this principle (Article 19). It also shows the limited effect of the 2002-initiated female reserve list in parliament: while it doubled the number from 30 to 60 in 2011, the number of ministers went down dramatically.

In contrast to the Istiqlal Party, which has held governmental positions since Morocco gained independence, the PJD has evolved out of an opposition not just to the monarchy but, since 1998, to the preceding government coalitions that primarily included the USFP and the Istiqlal. As a consequence, the new government positioned itself in contrast to El Fassi's 2008 government, in which the Istiqlal's loyalty to the King was expressed by the prime minister's repeated assertion that the government's programme was that of the King. Clearly, tensions were looming. Yet, as with preceding governments, a royal cabinet with shadow ministers (and often more authority and power) continued to limit the government's

**TABLE 3.1** Voter turnout in elections to the lower house, 1977–2011

| Year | Official voter turnout (%) | Total vote | Registration | Voting-age population turnout (%) | Voting-age population | Population | Invalid votes (%) |
|---|---|---|---|---|---|---|---|
| 2011 | 45.40 | 6,117,847 | 13,475,435 | 28.65 | 21,356,831 | 31,968,361 | n/a |
| 2007 | 37.00 | 5,721,074 | 15,462,362 | 27.83 | 20,555,314 | 33,241,259 | 19 |
| 2002 | 51.61 | 7,165,206 | 13,884,467 | 39.98 | 17,923,815 | 30,645,305 | 17 |
| 1997 | 58.30 | 7,456,996 | 12,790,631 | 50.21 | 14,852,810 | 28,024,000 | 14 |
| 1993 | 62.75 | 7,153,211 | 11,398,987 | 51.77 | 13,816,570 | 26,069,000 | 13 |
| 1984 | 67.43 | 4,999,646 | 7,414,846 | 47.57 | 10,510,080 | 22,848,000 | 11 |
| 1977 | 82.36 | 5,369,431 | 6,519,301 | 73.12 | 7,343,600 | 18,359,000 | n/a |

Source: Institute for Democracy and Electoral Assistance, www.idea.int/vt/countryview.cfm?id=138

authority. A case in point is Minister of Foreign Affairs El Othmani, who has been flanked by the former minister, Taieb Fassi Fihri, and Youssef Amrani, a trusted royalist. Fassi Fihri occupies the position of royal adviser, and Amrani that of the delegate to the minister of foreign affairs. Whilst the constitution theoretically grants the government the authority to sign foreign treaties and nominate ambassadors, Mohamed VI nominated 28 new ambassadors on 6 December 2011 without anyone capable of opposing this gesture. Reflecting on this tension, El Othmani declared to the Moroccan press that the minister cannot be given instructions from the royal cabinet, yet in subsequent diplomatic manoeuvres, especially around the critical Western Sahara issue, El Othmani had been outpaced by the King and his advisers.[212] Another burning point was the question of Morocco's relations with Egypt given the ousting of the Muslim Brotherhood President Mohamed Morsi in July 2013, with whom the PJD shared substantial affinities based on moderate Islamism and democratic legitimacy. When the Istiqlal left the governmental coalition in 2013, El Othmani left his place to Salaheddine Mezouar in November, a former minister of economy and finance, and tensions surrounding this relationship subsided.

While such governmental transactions illustrate the limitations placed on governmental autonomy and the continuing authority of the monarch, a side effect of the constitutional change has been changes in the content of politics. Both the Istiqlal and the USFP have experienced leadership (and generational) changes in which more populist leaders, Hamid Chabat and Driss Lachguer, took over from the old guard and hierarchies – in the case of the Istiqlal Party especially the extended El Fassi family. The new Istiqlal leadership did not support the PJD finance minister's attempts to cut expenditure and address a budget that had been inflated in 2011 following the widespread protest movement as an attempt to appease labour demands and address basic economic grievances. As the minister of the economy, Nizar Baraka, was a member of the Istiqlal Party, the new leadership correctly believed that economic failure would weaken any further claims to governmental leadership in subsequent elections. Given that social protests continued to rock the entire country throughout 2012–13, the party's decision followed an electoral rationality. This illustrates that the party perceives, maybe for the first time, that its future no longer uniquely depends on its relation to the King.

## *Reinvigorating the politics of exclusion and inclusion*

Prior to the 2011 unrest across the Arab world, it was difficult to predict that the PJD would lead the Moroccan government, especially as the royal electoral alliance around the PAM was viewed as anti-Islamist. In addition, the monarch rejected any constitutional reform throughout the 2000s, in spite of the IER's recommendation to strengthen the rule of law and checks and balances. In fact, the 2000s were marked by a duality of reform and continuing authoritarianism leading to a complex situation in which a new type of conservatism – no changes to the way the monarch handles the transition – was built. Morocco's political construction site of the 1990s was complemented by a state-led discourse on reform in the 2000s that has co-opted and apparently seduced the country's political elite.

In 2011, the monarchy broke with its policy of rejecting a new constitution and excluding the PJD from governmental responsibility. Yet the process of inclusion and constitutional reform remained carefully controlled such that no legal or political challenge could arise to its own claims. Such control from above was complemented by a wide range of co-opted political actors who allowed the monarchy to handle the constitutional reform without public challenges. Patron–client relations extending to all branches of the Moroccan political system (tribes, mosques, universities, political parties, state-controlled press) were all mobilised to rescue the King from the potential threats that the Arab Spring represented. In the process, the monarchy managed to more fully include the PJD as a political newcomer in the system of alliances, which accepted its marginal role and did not attempt to engage in street politics in support of the 20 February Movement. This clearly was the condition on which it could expect to participate freely in elections and obtain limited governmental responsibility. The monarchy thereby illustrated its capacity to integrate newcomers flexibly, and to reverse its policies of exclusion: after all, the royal move of creating the PAM in 2009 was aimed at excluding the PJD from electoral victory and governmental authority.

It remains questionable that the political elite, driven by patron–client relations, manages to introduce any substantial change to the status quo. Morocco remains a complex system of alliances, and so far the political elite seems far more threatened by potentially radicalised youth groups and Islamists rather than by the monarchical state. In addition, it is doubtful that political parties are able to rally popular support on a platform of constitutional change that reduces the power to the King. In the media, the King is portrayed as the active leader, the representative of a young, non-corrupt generation, which contrasts with old, inactive political party leaders who only talk. As a result, voter turnout studies have illustrated that low participation rates are not so much a reflection of popular discontent with the country's primary leader, but rather with its political parties and *elected* institutions.[213]

Since the mid-1980s, the rise of radical Islamism and its socio-economic basis have been a threat to Morocco's urban socio-economic elite – best illustrated by the 2003 Casablanca and the 2011 Marrakech bombings. This has provided both the monarchy and its elite with a powerful incentive to mend fences and to form a strategic alliance in exchange for power sharing and political liberalisation. Reforms in the areas analysed in this chapter supported political liberalisation: they underscored the ideologies of the secular, modernist faction, whilst offering the conservative, Islamist factions of Morocco's elite an avenue for political participation and power sharing. Since the Arab Spring gave rise to regional instability, the interest in the status quo among a fairly broad spectrum of the political and economic elite and population has arguably increased, especially as the constitutional reform appeared as a political success for the monarch. Not only ensuring that no challenge to his claim to power can emanate from any changes, the monarch has thereby appropriated a major reform project, and converted a challenge into a success story of regime adaptation. Conservative rule in Morocco, based on the inclusion of different segments of the country's elite in exchange for their acceptance of the political status quo based on the sacredness of the monarchy, has thereby been reproduced.

## 3.11 Summary

This chapter illustrated how the Moroccan political system developed in response to a series of domestic challenges. The key has been to find a balance between including some of the political protagonists of these challenges and punishing selected individuals if they were too much of a threat to the status quo. The most significant political period in which this was tried and tested was from 1972 to 1977, as the two preceding coup attempts illustrated the fragility inherent in the monarchy's isolation. Fuelled by diplomatic success in Western Sahara, and especially the Green March, vague nationalist feelings provided the King with a much needed political resource. The 1980s saw a prolonged political crisis, which was partly due to economic restructuring and a profound financial crisis. However, instead of isolating itself from the political field by having recourse to authoritarian measures alone, the monarchy aimed at including the political elite in a long period of negotiations. The 1990–91 Gulf crisis, strengthened Islamist movements, as well as civil war in neighbouring Algeria after 1992, led to a renewal of the politics of inclusion, which culminated in the historical government of alternance (1998–2002).

After 2002, the politics of inclusion seemed to have reached its limits until the Arab Spring dramatically changed the equation. Throughout the 2000s, the King refused to address the fundamental question of constitutional changes despite continuing emphasis on political reforms. Similarly, whilst the Islamist PJD was increasingly tolerated, in 2007 the monarchical establishment decided to counter it with the creation of its own party, the PAM. Both areas of establishing limits on political changes were compounded by increasing the pressure on the autonomous press, which was disappearing by the end of the 2000s.

Recent reforms, including constitutional reform and the appointment of the PJD government in 2011, have only perpetuated the lack of meaningful political participation and supported authoritarianism. Ironically, reforms have multiplied the resources available to Morocco's monarchical institution to control the political sphere, creating the image of the Janus yet also an impasse. While it is difficult to see any meaning in many young Moroccans' active support for terrorist activities inside Morocco and abroad, such support may respond precisely to this impasse, i.e. a lack of any political alternatives among the large number of linguistically, economically and socially excluded Moroccans.

On the other hand, there is little doubt that Moroccan politicians are increasingly facing electoral competition in which they will have to address the large number of excluded voters. If the recent potentially populist transformations inside the two leading parties, the Istiqlal and the USFP, lead to an increasing mobilisation of voters, this may ultimately increase their democratic legitimacy and claims to leadership. Clearly, with the 2008 creation of the pro-monarchy PAM, the monarchy under Mohamed VI has already prepared to compound its religious and traditional legitimacy with electoral and procedural legitimacy. Given its successful dealing with the PJD in government over recent years, as well as the constitutional challenge in 2011, the monarchy appears to be much more in control than ever before. Yet, there continue to be cracks in the control that the monarch is able to exercise. His reformist image is by no means undisputed inside and outside Morocco, and the monarchy has as often responded to criticism and challenges to its image with brute force and legal manipulation,[214] as it has with reform and legal change.

## Notes

1. J. Waterbury, *The Commander of the Faithful. The Moroccan Political Elite – A Study in Segmented Politics*, London: Weidenfeld and Nicolson, 1970.
2. M. Tozy, 'Représentation/Intercession. Les Enjeux de Pouvoir dans les "champs politiques désamorcés" au Maroc' in *Annuaire de l'Afrique du Nord*, Vol. 28, CNRS, 1989.
3. L. Anderson, 'Dynasts and Nationalists: Why Monarchies Survive' in J. Kostiner (ed.) *Middle East Monarchies. The Challenge of Modernity*, Boulder, CO: Lynne Rienner, 2000.
4. A. Gaudio, *Allal El Fassi ou L'Histoire de l'Istiqlal*, Paris: Alain Moreau, 1972, p. 116.
5. Ibid.
6. Ibid.
7. R. Leveau, 'Islam et contrôle politique au Maroc' in E. Gellner and J.-C. Vatin, *Islam et Politique au Maghreb*, Paris: CNRS, 1981, p. 273.
8. Cited in ibid., p. 273, original emphasis.
9. Ibid., pp. 275–276.
10. Hassan II, translated in I.W. Zartman, *Man, State and Society in the Contemporary Maghreb*, London and New York: Praeger Publishers, 1973, p. 119.

11  Hassan II, *The Challenge: The Memoirs of King Hassan II of Morocco*, London: Macmillan, 1978, pp. 67–68, cited in L. Storm, *Democratisation in Morocco. The Political Elite and Struggles for Power in the Post-Independence State*, Abingdon, Oxon. and New York: Routledge, 2007, p. 18.
12  Cited in M. Bennouna, *Heros sans Gloire. Echec d'une Révolution*, Paris: Tarik Editions, 2002, p. 57.
13  Ibid.
14  The Moroccan constitution provided for an electoral system in which only about half the parliamentarians were directly elected. The other half were indirectly elected through electoral colleges. These consisted of local assemblies, chambers of commerce, trade unions and other bodies. This division is at the origin of its contemporary bicameral parliamentary system.
15  M. Bouaziz, *Aux Origins de la Koutla Démocratique*, Casablanca: Editions de la Faculté des Lettres Aïn-Chock, 1997, p. 143.
16  Hassan II, translated in Zartman, op. cit., p. 122.
17  Bouaziz, op. cit., p. 144.
18  Ibid.
19  Ibid.
20  Commenting on this, Claisse writes that 'this concept has nothing to do with either the Islamic tradition or Western constitutional law. It stems rather from European monarchical theories of the eighteenth century, which saw the king as an incarnation of the whole nation'. A. Claisse, 'Makhzen Traditions and Administrative Channels' in I.W. Zartman, *The Political Economy of Morocco*, New York: Praeger, 1987, p. 39.
21  I.W. Zartman, 'King Hassan's New Morocco' in I.W. Zartman, *The Political Economy of Morocco*, New York: Praeger, 1987, pp. 1–33.
22  M. Raiss, *De Skhirat à Tazmamart. Retour du Bout de l'Enfer*, Casablanca: Afrique Orient, 2002, p. 48. This alleged reason for the mission made perfect sense at the time. Morocco witnessed urban warfare against the symbols of power. For a portrait of one of its main protagonists, Fqih Basri, see B. Belouchi, *Portraits d'Hommes Politiques du Maroc*, Casablanca: Afrique-Orient, 2002, pp. 133–137. See also Bennouna, op. cit.
23  Raiss, op. cit., p. 48.
24  Officially, it was suicide, which he committed inside the palace.
25  Interview with the director of LMDH Diouri, quoted in Mohammed Karem, 'La notion des droits de l'Homme au Maghreb. Essai sur une nouvelle culture politique', Thèse de Doctorat, Université de Droits, d'Economie et de Science Politique d'Aix-Marseille, 1991, pp. 153–154.
26  The 'option révolutionnaire' was Mehdi Ben Barka's key text that he presented in June 1962 to the UNFP congress. Influenced by the failure to achieve effective power sharing with the monarchy in the 1956–62 period, Mehdi Ben Barka was also influenced by pan-Arab revolutionary movements in the Arab East. He was also supported by other communist-inspired regimes and movements. On Bouabid's changing strategy, see R. Gallison, 'Illusion révolutionnaire et contre-révolution monarchique' in Bennouna, op. cit., p. 10.
27  Bennouna, op. cit., p. 200.
28  Zartman, 1987, op. cit., p. 7.
29  Ibid., p. 8.
30  Hassan II, *La Mémoire d'un Roi. Entretiens avec Eric Laurent*, Paris: Librairie Plon, 1993, p. 175.
31  Claisse, op. cit., p. 49.
32  Dahir 1-72-258 du 19 août 1972 relatifs à la suppression du Ministère de la Défense nationale et des fonctions de Major général et de Major général Adjoint, cited in Association des Familles des Victimes des Evenements de Skhirat, *Le Massacre de Skhirat 10 juillet 1971 'crime contre l'humanité'*, Rabat: Editions A.F.V.E.S, 2002, p. 232.
33  Cited in Gaudio, op. cit., p. 277.

34 See M. Rousset, 'Changements institutionnels et équilibre des forces politiques au Maroc: un essai d'interprétation' in J. Leca, *Développement Politique au Maghreb*, Paris: Centre National de la Recherche Scientifique, 1979, pp. 189–213.
35 Ibid., pp. 193–195.
36 Ibid., p. 194.
37 J. Damis, 'The Impact of the Western Sahara Dispute on Moroccan Foreign and Domestic Policy' in I.W. Zartman, *The Political Economy of Morocco*, New York: Praeger, 1987, p. 204.
38 Rousset, op. cit., p. 198.
39 J.N. Sater, 'The Dynamics of State and Civil Society in Morocco' in *The Journal of North African Studies*, Vol. 7, No. 3, Autumn 2002, pp. 101–118.
40 Tozy, op. cit.
41 J.C. Santucci, 'Les élections législatives marocaines de juin 1977' in J. Leca, op. cit., p. 231.
42 Ibid., p. 228.
43 Rousset, op. cit., pp. 204–205.
44 Ibid., p. 210.
45 Storm, op. cit., chapter 3.
46 Cited in Rousset, op. cit., p. 207.
47 See M. El Mansour, 'Salafis and Modernists in the Moroccan Nationalist Movement' in J. Ruedy (ed.) *Islamism and Secularism in North Africa*, London: Macmillan, 1996, pp. 53–72.
48 J.C. Santucci, *Les Partis Politiques Marocains a l'Epreuve du Pouvoir*, Publications de la Revue Marocaine d'Administration Locale et de Développement, No. 24, 2001, p. 13.
49 Ibid.
50 M. Tozy, 'Monopolisation de la production symbolique et hiérarchisation du camp politico-religieux au Maroc' in *Annuaire de l'Afrique du Nord, 1979*, Paris: CNRS, 1981, pp. 219–234, cited in Santucci, 2001, op. cit., p. 13.
51 E. Hermassi, *Leadership and National Development in North Africa*, Berkeley, CA and London: University of California Press, 1972, p. 143.
52 See A. Hammoudi, *Master and Disciple. The Cultural Foundations of Moroccan Authoritarianism*, London and Chicago, IL: The University of Chicago Press, 1997, chapter 2.
53 M. Tozy, 'Champ et contre champ politico-religieux au Maroc', unpublished PhD thesis, Université de Droit, d'Economie et des Sciences d'Aix-Marseille, 1984.
54 Ibid., p. 41.
55 See H. Munson, Jr., *Religion and Power in Morocco*, New Haven, CT and London: Yale University Press, 1993, p. 9.
56 *Maroc Soir*, 7 January 1982, cited in M. Tozy, *Monarchie et Islam Politique au Maroc*. 2ème édition, Paris: Presses de la Fondation Nationale des Sciences Politiques, 1999a, p. 82.
57 D. Hart, 'Moroccan Dynastic *Shurfa*'-hood in Two Historical Contexts: Idrisid Cult and 'Alawid Power' in *The Journal of North African Studies*, Vol. 6, No. 2, Summer 2001, p. 91.
58 Tozy, 1984, op. cit., p. 45.
59 Ibid., 35; see also J.N. Sater, *Civil Society and Political Change in Morocco*, Abingdon and New York: Routledge, 2007, chapter 3.
60 M. Tozy, 'Islam and the State' in I.W. Zartman and W.M. Habeeb (eds) *Polity and Society in Contemporary North Africa*, Boulder, CO: Westview Press, 1993, p. 103.
61 Tozy, 1984, op. cit., p. 44.
62 See Waterbury, op. cit., chapters 3 and 7.
63 Hassan II, cited in Waterbury, ibid., p. 146.
64 Abdelaziz Bennani, Abdellah Eloualladi, Jammal Eddine Naji and Said Essoulami, *Liberté de la Presse et de l'Information au Maroc*, Rabat: OMDH, 1995, p. 6. This modification came only a few months after the director of the newspaper *Attahrir* was arrested.

65  Ibid.
66  Ibid. See also Sater, 2007, op. cit., pp. 46–47. These modifications were introduced after the attempted *coup d'état* of 16 August 1972, and some weeks after the arrest of a number of UNFP figures who wanted to found the USFP.
67  Hassan II, quoted in Waterbury, op. cit., p. 150.
68  Claisse, op. cit., p. 39.
69  Ibid., pp. 39–40.
70  See M.E. Combs-Schilling, 'Performing Monarchy, Staging Nation' in R. Bourqia and S. Gilson Miller (eds) *In the Shadow of the Sultan. Culture, Power, and Politics in Morocco*, Cambridge, MA: Harvard University Press, 1999, pp. 176–214.
71  Claisse, op. cit., p. 44.
72  Cited in E. Ahmad and S. Schaar, 'Human Rights in Morocco and Tunisia: A Critique of State Department Findings' in *MERIP Report*, No. 67, 1978, p. 16.
73  Ibid.
74  Cited in Claisse, op. cit., p. 45.
75  M.J. Willis, 'Political Parties in the Maghrib: The Illusion of Significance?' in *The Journal of North African Studies*, Vol. 7, No. 2, Summer 2002, p. 6.
76  Karem, op. cit., pp. 162–163.
77  J.-F. Clement and J. Paul, 'Trade Unions and Moroccan Politics' in *MERIP Reports*, No. 127, October 1984, p. 24; P. Vermeren, *Histoire du Maroc depuis l'Independance*, Paris: La Decouverte, 2002a, p. 87.
78  Tozy, 1989, op. cit., p. 165.
79  Quoted in B. Korany, 'Monarchical Islam with a Democratic Veneer: Morocco' in B. Korany, R. Brynen and P. Noble (eds) *Political Liberalization and Democratization in the Arab World: Vol. 2*, Boulder, CO: Lynne Rienner, 1998, p. 157.
80  Vermeren, op. cit., p. 85.
81  A. Laroui, *Idéologie Arabe Contemporaine*, Paris: La Decouverte, 1983.
82  Z. Daoud, *Les Années Lamalif*, Casablanca: Tarik Editions, 2007, p. 127.
83  See Korany, op. cit., p. 163.
84  See El Mansour, op. cit., pp. 53–72.
85  Cited in Tozy, 1999a, op. cit., p. 27.
86  See Combs-Schilling, op. cit.
87  See Tozy, 1999a, op. cit., pp. 40–49.
88  Ibid., pp. 129–167.
89  Anthony Giddens would even postulate the question of uncertainty as the 'core' aspect of modernity itself. See Tozy, 1999a, op. cit., pp. 170–174. I would add to this that uncertainty is heightened in countries experiencing late development, as new forms of 'solidarity' do not yet replace older ones. The most significant indicator seems to be the large informal sector that employed around 39 per cent of the urban population in 2000. See R.M. Alami, 'Le Secteur Informel au Maroc: 1954–2004', www.rdh50.ma/fr/pdf/contributions/GT3-7.pdf (accessed 15 April 2008), p. 435.
90  It may be pointed out that Morocco's main Islamist leader, Abdessalam Yassine, emphasises this idea in his book *Islamiser La Modernité*, n.p., Al Ofok, 1998.
91  Tozy, 1999a, op. cit., p. 172.
92  J.P. Entelis, 'Political Islam in the Maghreb: The Non-violent Dimension' in J.P. Entelis (ed.) *Islam, Democracy and the State in North Africa*, Bloomington and Indianapolis: Indiana University Press, 1997, pp. 43–74.
93  M.J. Deeb, 'Islam and the State in Algeria and Morocco: A Dialectical Model' in J. Ruedy (ed.), op. cit., p. 279.
94  T. Chadi and A. Amar, 'La chabiba Islamiya. Nid de terroristes?' in *Le Journal Hebdomadaire*, 1–7 March 2008, p. 26.
95  Ibid.
96  Entelis, op. cit., p. 53.
97  Ibid.

98 Mohamed Yatim, quoted in M. Tozy, 'Reformes politiques et transition démocratique' in *Monde Arabe Maghreb-Machrek*, No. 164, April–June 1999b, pp. 79–80.
99 Entelis, op. cit., p. 53.
100 A. Amar, T. Chadi and F. Tounassi, 'Complot Islamiste?' in *Le Journal Hebdomadaire*, 23–20 February 2008, pp. 22–25.
101 A. Lamchichi, *Islam et Contestation au Maghreb*, cited in Korany, op. cit., p. 180.
102 Tozy, 1999a, op. cit., p. 193.
103 See Yassine, op. cit., chapter 1.
104 www.yassine.net
105 E.E. Shahin, 'Secularism and Nationalism: The Political Discourse of Abd al-Salam Yassin' in J. Ruedy (ed.), op. cit., pp. 170–176.
106 Tozy, 1999a, op. cit., pp. 194–195; Shahin, op. cit., p. 169.
107 P. Vermeren, *Ecole, élite et pouvoir au Maroc et en Tunisie au XXe siècle*, Rabat: Alizés, 2002b, p. 433.
108 Tozy, 1999a, op. cit., p. 108.
109 Ibid., p. 107.
110 Vermeren, 2002b, op. cit., p. 428.
111 Ibid., p. 435.
112 Ibid., p. 447.
113 The French cultural mission attempted to break up this system as fewer Moroccan students from modest backgrounds made it to French elite universities, the *Ecoles d'Ingénieurs*. France started to finance preparatory classes in normal high schools. In 1999 these numbered 70 in nine Moroccan high schools around the country. Ibid., p. 464.
114 Ibid., p. 467.
115 Haute Commissariat du Plan, 'Horloge de la population: Historique de la Population du Maroc par Milieu de Résidence de 1960 à 2004 au Milieu de l'Année', www.hcp.ma/frmInd.aspx?id=0404000000&vara=10 (accessed 1 August 2008).
116 D. Bensaid, 'L'Etudiant et l'Institution' in R. Bourqia, M. El Harras and D. Bensaid (eds) *Jeunesse Estudiantine Marocaine*, Series Essais et Etudes No. 14, Rabat: Faculté des Lettres et des Sciences Humaines, Université Mohamed V, 1995, p. 13.
117 M. Bennani-Chraibi, *Soumis et Rebelles. Les Jeunes au Maroc*, Casablanca: Le Fennec, 1995, p. 15.
118 Bensaid, op. cit., p. 25.
119 Cited in Bennani-Chraibi, op. cit., p. 138.
120 J.P. Entelis, op. cit., p. 51.
121 Bennani-Chraibi, op. cit., p. 145.
122 J.-F. Bayart, *L'Etat en Afrique. La Politique du Ventre*, Paris: Fayard, 1989, cited in Bennani-Chraibi, op. cit., p. 159; Entelis, op. cit., p. 51.
123 Dale F. Eickelman, 'Re-imagining Religion and Politics: Moroccan Elections in the 1990s' in John Ruedy (ed.), op. cit., p. 254.
124 Y.H. Zoubir, 'Reactions in the Maghreb to the Gulf Crisis and War' in *Arab Studies Quarterly*, Vol. 15, No. 1, Winter 1993, p. 92.
125 G. Perrault, *Notre Ami Le Roi*, Paris: Gallimard, 1990.
126 Human Rights Advisory Council, *10 Years in the Service of Human Rights. The Royal High Instructions, Legislative and Statutory Texts, Advisory Opinions*, Rabat: Royaume du Maroc, 2001, p. 15.
127 Ibid.
128 Ahmed Marzouki, *Tazmamart, Cellule 10*, Paris: Paris-Méditerranée and Tarik, 2000.
129 D. Basri (ed.), *Le Maroc et Les Droits de l'Homme: Position, Réalisations et Perspectives*, Paris: L'Harmattan, 1994.
130 Eickelman, op. cit., p. 264.
131 Ibid., p. 256.
132 Cited in A. Saaf, *La Transition au Maroc. L'Invitation*, Casablanca: Eddif Editions, 2001, p. 27.

133 R. El Moussadeq, *Les Labyrinthes de l'Alternance. Rupture ou Continuité?* Casablanca: Souchepress, 1998, p. 23.
134 G. Deneoux and A. Maghraoui, 'King Hassan's Strategy of Political Dualism' in *Middle East Policy*, Vol. 5, No. 4, January 1998, p. 108.
135 Hassan II, discourse du 8 octobre 1993, cited in Saaf, op. cit., p. 31.
136 G. Joffé, 'Elections and Reform in Morocco' in Richard Gillespie (ed.) *Mediterranean Politics*, Vol. I, London: Pinter Publishers, 1994, p. 216.
137 Hassan II, cited in El Moussadeq, op. cit., 1998, p. 51.
138 S.E. Waltz, 'Interpreting Political Reform in Morocco' in R. Bourqia and S. Gilson Miller, op. cit., p. 298.
139 Ali Yata affirmed in October 1993 that 'the logic of numbers that is the automatic right to form a government would lead to an explosive situation. This logic needs to be avoided as the Koutla, even if it does not have an arithmetic majority, disposes of an unquestionable popular majority'. Cited in El Moussadeq, op. cit., pp. 84–85.
140 Ali Yata, cited in El Moussadeq, op. cit., p. 87.
141 El Yazgi, cited in ibid., p. 68.
142 Deneoux and Maghraoui, op. cit., p. 114.
143 El Moussadeq, op. cit., p. 110.
144 In an open letter to the King, on 5 November 1993, these characteristics were enumerated. Cited in El Moussadeq, op. cit., p. 106.
145 A. Maghraoui, 'Depoliticization in Morocco' in *Journal of Democracy*, Vol. 13, No. 4, October 2002, p. 24.
146 S.E. Waltz, *Human Rights and Reform. Changing the Face of North African Politics*, London and Berkeley, CA: University of California Press, 1995, p. 145.
147 Cited in Sater, 2007, op. cit., p. 57.
148 Waltz, 1995, op. cit., p. 148.
149 See M.M. Charrad, *States and Women's Rights: The Making of Postcolonial Tunisia, Algeria, and Morocco*, Berkeley, CA: University of California Press, 2001, chapter 7.
150 OMDH, 'Déclaration au sujet de la revendication de modification des dispositions du code de statut personnel', 23 June 1992, cited in S. Hegasy, *Staat, Öffentlichkeit und Zivilgesellschaft*, Hamburg: Deutsches Orient Institut, 1997, p. 191.
151 To my knowledge, no Moroccan census has ever asked questions concerning usage of any of the three Amazigh dialects. The well-known British anthropologist David M. Hart estimates the Tamazight-speaking population to be around 40–45 per cent. See D.M. Hart, 'Scratch a Moroccan, find a Berber' in D.M. Hart, *Tribe and Society in Rural Morocco*, London: Frank Cass Publishers, 2000, p. 23.
152 Sater, 2007, op. cit., p. 61.
153 B. Maddy-Weitzman, 'Contested Identities: Berbers, "Berberism" and the State in North Africa' in *The Journal of North African Studies*, Vol. 6, No. 3, Autumn 2000, p. 31.
154 Cited in G. Deneoux and L. Gateaux, 'L'Essor des Associations au Maroc. A la recherche de la citoyenneté?' in *Monde Arabe Maghreb-Machrek*, No. 150, October–December 1995, p. 31.
155 Royal speech delivered on 8 May 1990, printed in Kingdom of Morocco, Human Rights Advisory Council, *10 Years in the Service of Human Rights. The Royal High Instructions, Legislative and Statutory Texts, Advisory Opinions*, Rabat: Imprimerie El Maarif Al Jadida, 2000, p. 14.
156 For a review of the discussion, see M. al-Ahnaf, 'Maroc. Le Code du Statut Personnel' in *Monde Arabe Maghreb-Machrek*, No. 145, July–September 1994, pp. 3–26.
157 Hegasy, op. cit., pp. 191–192.
158 King Hassan, in Cellule Intégration de la Femme au Developpement, *La Femme Marocaine*, Rabat: n.p., 1992, p. 36, cited in Hegasy, op. cit., p. 268.
159 Apparently, they shouted slogans against the teaching of Hebrew at Moroccan universities when that of Tamazight was banned. *Courier International*, No. 550, 17–22 May 2001.

160 US State Department, 'Morocco Human Rights Practices for the Year 1994', February 1994.
161 Quoted in Maddy-Weitzman, op. cit., p. 32.
162 R. Leveau, 'Morocco at the Crossroads' in *Mediterranean Politics*, Vol. 2, No. 2, Autumn 1997, pp. 95–113.
163 See Hassan II, *La Memoire d'un Roi. Entretiens avec Eric Laurent*, Paris: Librairie Plon, 1993, p. 242.
164 M. Tozy, 'L'islamisme à l'épreuve du politique' in *Confluences Méditerranée*, No. 31, Autumn 1999c, p. 105.
165 Ibid., pp. 95–96.
166 Ibid., pp. 97–98.
167 Ibid., pp. 98.
168 M.J. Willis, 'Between Alternance and the Makhzen: *Al Tawhid wa Al Islah*'s Entry into Moroccan Politics' in *The Journal of North African Studies*, Vol. 4, No. 3, Autumn 1999, p. 50.
169 www.aljamaa.org (accessed 10 June 2008); another of Yassine's websites is www.yassine.net.
170 Royal speeches can be consulted online at www.maroc.ma.
171 Jean-Pierre Tuquoi, *Le Dernier Roi. Crépuscule d'une Dynastie*, Paris: Editions Grasset & Fasquelle, 2001, pp. 167–190.
172 Leveau, 1997, op. cit., p. 111.
173 See Sater, 2007, op. cit., pp. 122–158.
174 See A.R. Norton (ed.), *Civil Society in the Middle East*. Vol. I, Leiden: E.J. Brill, 1995.
175 L. Garon, *Dangerous Alliances: Civil Society, the Media and Democratic Transition in North Africa*, London and New York: Zed Books, 2003.
176 www.maroc.ma
177 www.maroc.ma
178 See M.J. Willis, 'Morocco's Islamists and the Legislative Elections of 2002: The Strange Case of the Party that Did Not Want to Win' in *Mediterranean Politics*, Vol. 9, No. 1, 2004.
179 *Libération*, 11 October 2002.
180 *La Vie Economique*, 11 October 2002.
181 *L'Opinion*, 10 October 2002.
182 King Mohamed VI, 30 July 2007.
183 Interview with the author, Rabat, 14 September 2010.
184 Lahcen Daoudi, PJD, deputy secretary-general, interview with the author, Rabat, 14 September 2010.
185 Interview with the author, Rabat, 22 May 2002.
186 James N. Sater, 'New Wine in Old Bottles: Political Parties Under Mohammed VI' in Bruce Maddy-Weitzman and Danny Zisenwine (eds) *Contemporary Morocco: State, Politics, and Society Under Mohammed VI*, Abingdon: Routledge, 2012, pp. 9–23; James N. Sater, 'Patronage and Democratic Citizenship in Morocco' in Nils Butenschon and Roel Meijer (eds) *Citizenship in the Middle East:: History Theory and Practice*, Leiden: Brill, forthcoming.
187 Ferdinand Eibl, 'The Party of Authenticity and Modernity (PAM). Trajectory of a Political *Deus Ex Machina*' in *The Journal of North African Studies*, Vol. 17, No. 1, 2012, p. 52.
188 Ibid,, pp. 48–49.
189 J.P. Entelis, 'Democratic Desires and the Authoritarian Temptation in the Central Maghreb' in Y.H. Zoubir and H. Amirah-Fernandez, *North Africa. Politics, Region, and the Limits of Transformation*, Abingdon and New York: Routledge, 2008, pp. 20–21.
190 Ibid., p. 21.
191 See his speech delivered on 29 May 2003, www.maroc.ma (accessed 10 April 2008).
192 '52 in Court Over Suicide Bombings', *The Guardian*, 22 July 2003, www.guardian.co.uk/world/2003/jul/22/alqaida.terrorism (accessed 10 April 2008).

193 See Amnesty International, 'Torture in the "Anti-terrorism" Campaign – the Case of Témara Detention Centre', www.amnesty.org/en/library/asset/MDE29/004/2004/en/dom-MDE290042004en.pdf (accessed 8 April 2008).
194 G.P. Deneoux and H.R. Desfosses, 'Rethinking the Moroccan Parliament: The Kingdom's Legislative Development Imperative' in *The Journal of North African Studies*, Vol. 12, No. 1, March 2007, pp. 94–96.
195 OMDH, 'Communique au Sujet de la Commission d'Enquete sur le CIH', Rabat, 27 January 2001, www.omdh.org/newomdh/def.asp?codelangue=23&info=784 (accessed 8 April 2008). See also A. Benchemsi, 'CIH: jusqu'où ira le scandale?' in *Jeune Afrique*, 13 February 2001, www.jeuneafrique.com/jeune_afrique/article_jeune_afrique.asp?art_cle=LIN13023cihjueladna0 (accessed 12 June 2008).
196 Transparency Maroc, 'Royal Power and Judicial Independence in Morocco' in Transparency International, *Global Corruption Report 2007 Part Two – Country Reports on Judicial Corruption*, www.transparency.org/content/download/18702/255302 (accessed 12 June 2008).
197 B. Maddy-Weitzman, 'Women, Islam, and the Moroccan State: The Struggle over the Personal Status Law' in *Middle East Journal*, Vol. 59, No. 3, Summer 2005; J.N. Sater, 'Changing Politics from Below? Women Parliamentarians in Morocco' in *Journal of Democratization*, Vol. 14, No. 4, August 2007.
198 Mohamed VI, *Discours de Sa Majesté le Roi Mohammed VI que Dieu l'Assiste à l'Occasion de l'Ouverture de la Deuxième Année Legislative de la VIIe Legislature*, Rabat, 1 October 2003, p. 5.
199 M. Chafik, 'Le Manifeste Berbere', unpublished manifesto, 2000, p. 13.
200 Cited in *l'Economiste*, 1 August 2001.
201 Cited in www.aljamaa.net/fr/Cheminement4.asp (accessed 2 April 2008).
202 Royaume du Maroc, Instance Equité et Réconciliation, 'Synthèse du rapport final', www.ier.ma/article.php3?id_article=1496 (accessed 5 April 2008).
203 *Le Journal Hebdomadaire*, 17–23 May 2008, p. 6.
204 I borrow this expression from Michael Willis and George Joffé who discussed this idea at a conference on 'Reforms in the Arab World' on 2–3 May 2008 at St Antony's College, Oxford.
205 See James N. Sater, 'Reforming the Rule of Law in Morocco: Multiple Meanings and Problematic Realities' in *Mediterranean Politics*, Vol. 13, No. 2, July 2009, pp. 181–193. According to an undisclosed survey conducted by Al Akhawayn University in Ifrane in 2007, 50 per cent of Moroccans do not trust the courts. According to an IFES survey, 25 per cent of Moroccans believe that bribery is common among judges. See I. Shalhoub, *Comparative Report on the State of the Judiciary in Egypt, Jordan, Lebanon and Morocco*, Washington, DC: IFES, May 2007, p. 5, www.eldis.org/assets/Docs/33831.html (accessed 5 April 2008).
206 www.elections.gov.ma (accessed 10 November 2007).
207 'Morocco's "Arab" Spring' in *Middle East Institute*, Viewpoint Series, Revolutions and Political Transformations in the Middle East, October, www.mei.edu/LinkClick.aspx?fileticket=QnpP0vmNOX8%3d&tabid=541.
208 TelQuel 2009, 'Le Peuble juge son Roi' in *Le Monde*, 3 August 2009.
209 Paul Silverstein, 'Weighing Morocco's New Constitution' in *Middle East Report*, Vol. 260, 5 July 2011, www.merip.org/mero/mero070511.
210 monde-arabe.arte.tv/en/#/video_3269_mouad-belghouat-alias-haqed-the-fanatical-one
211 Institute for Democracy and Electoral Assistance (IDEA), 'Voter Turnout Data for Morocco', www.idea.int/vt/countryview.cfm?id=138.
212 Thierry Desrues and Irene Fernández Molina, 'L'expérience gouvernementale du Parti de la Justice et du Développement: les islamistes au pouvoir?' in *Année du Maghreb*, Vol. IX, 2013, pp. 345–365, anneemaghreb.revues.org/1954.
213 See J.N. Sater, 'Elections and Authoritarian Rule in Morocco' in *Middle East Journal*, Vol. 63, No. 3, Summer 2009, pp. 381–400.

214 I make reference to the monarchy's successful attempt to discredit Eric Laurent and Catherine Graciet. In a classic set-up that involved the French police, both journalists found themselves accused of extortion after having been offered €3 million to prevent a publication about the personal life of King Mohamed VI. Eric Laurent et Le Roi du Maroc, 'C'est une tentation, pas un chantage' in *Le Monde*, 30 August 2015.

# 4

# THE CHALLENGE OF ECONOMIC DEVELOPMENT

Morocco is prosperous in natural resources. Fishing resources off its 1,835 km coastline (excluding Western Sahara) are particularly rich; phosphate resources have made it the world's largest exporter of this mineral; and fertile agricultural soil north of the Atlas Mountain range was once believed to turn Morocco into the granary of Africa.

Morocco also enjoys favourable climatic conditions and geographical proximity to Europe, from which it is separated by only 13 km of water. Compared to many of its neighbours, it has good infrastructure – both in terms of communication and transport and in financial services – as well as a sizeable proportion of the urban workforce that can be considered educated. Yet, with a per capita income of about US$3,030 in 2013 (gross national income, Atlas Method), compared to a MENA average of $8,596,[1] rampant illiteracy and high unemployment rates, Morocco scores particularly poorly not only in the production of wealth but also in human development (ranking 129 out of 187 in 2014).[2] As a governmental report on the occasion of Morocco's 50th anniversary of independence euphemistically puts it, in 'the key issue as to whether or not, over these 50 years, it might have been possible to do things better: [the] answer would most likely be a straightforward "yes"'.[3] While it is too simplistic to assert a direct relationship between poverty and religious extremism or, after the Arab Spring, support for democratic regime change, both lines of analysis have driven Moroccan decision makers: the state significantly emphasised the question of poverty after the Casablanca attacks of 16 May 2003. Two poverty maps were produced by the government in 2004 and 2005, identifying the most vulnerable regions and neighbourhoods, and the National Initiative for Human Development (INDH) specifically targets education, health care and basic infrastructure as a way to increase the standard of living among Morocco's poor. In turn, public-sector as well as industry minimum wages received a 15 per cent raise in 2011, partially in response to strong trade union activism during the nationwide protests, partially to weaken social support for more radical changes.[4]

This chapter aims to illustrate the challenge of economic development and how Morocco has approached the question since independence. Although Morocco's population growth of 3 per cent annually until the late 1980s was reduced to about 1 per cent in 2014, reaching 34 million, with an average of 1.7 per cent between 1990 and 2003,[5] the World Bank estimates that Morocco needs to have a minimum annual average growth rate of 5 per cent to prevent current levels of poverty and unemployment from deteriorating. Given its population growth and rural exodus, and especially the unequal distribution of wealth, poverty alleviation and real improvements on the labour market may only be achieved with growth rates of 7 to 8 per cent.[6] Already in the 1960s, a World Bank report eloquently remarked with reference to population growth that 'Morocco will continuously … need to run faster in order to stand still'.[7]

French colonialism has left the Moroccan economy internally divided and externally linked to France and Europe. At the time of independence, its relatively modern urban and rural economic structures were so linked with the French metropolis that the future of both economic model and economic relations with France was of primary nationalist concern. Although Morocco officially gained independence, its bureaucracy, agriculture, education system, public and private enterprise continued to be dominated by the French and their relations to French firms and administrations. On the other hand, most of Morocco's agricultural sector and countryside remained traditional, untouched by colonisation and modern means of farming. More than 70 per cent of Morocco's 10 million inhabitants at independence lived in rural areas, most in deplorable economic conditions.

As a result, Moroccan politicians and public debate were primarily concerned with two sets of questions: first, what type of agricultural reform should the country undergo, should Morocco adopt import substitution industrialisation (ISI), inspired by socialist reformers, and what type of indigenisation policy should the country adopt? Second, what should be the role of private-sector and market economics, and should the country continue its policy of export-oriented agrarian growth – agrarian capitalism – that the French had introduced? Ultimately, what path to economic, social and educational development should the country adopt? Given its social fabric and the traditional claims to power by the King, policies tended to favour slow change and preservation of the status quo over more radical changes, thereby compounding some fundamental economic disequilibria. Especially as population growth continued to cut out a significant share of economic growth, attempts at creating balanced agricultural and non-agricultural growth and development have remained a precarious political undertaking.

## 4.1 Agriculture: from tentative reform to *laissez-faire* and perpetual crisis

The problem that Morocco's agricultural sector has faced since independence can be put into some simple aggregate figures. In 1956, more than 70 per cent of

Moroccans were rural inhabitants, who contributed to only 40 per cent of gross domestic product (GDP). On average, the added value produced by Morocco's farming sector was four and a half times less than that of the manufacturing sector.[8] By 1983, 57.3 per cent of Moroccans were rural inhabitants, and they contributed to only 11 per cent of GDP.[9] This amounts to rural impoverishment: a decline in rural per capita income from about $400 to about $200, in a period in which overall GDP per capita grew from $690 to about $1,000.[10]

The meaning of these figures is amplified if patterns of land ownership and means of production are considered. At independence, of the 14 million acres (5.7 million hectares) of agricultural land north of the Atlas Mountains, 11 million were owned by 1 million families, accounting for an inhabitant per acre ratio of about 1/1. This is subsistence farming, in which farmers directly live off the yields of their labour, with no mechanical tools or property enabling them to accrue any surplus for trading. Side by side in the modern sector, only 7,000 families, three quarters of which were European, to whom a significant part was distributed in the process of French colonial conquest, owned the remaining 4 million acres (1.6 million hectares). Of these 4 million acres about 250,000 acres (100,000 hectares) were irrigated by dam projects that the French initiated.[11]

Excluding colonial land, an examination of Moroccan private ownership (*melk*) at independence gives an even starker picture. About 5–10 per cent of all private Moroccan landlords owned about 60 per cent of all *melk*; 50–55 per cent owned less than 40 per cent; and 40 per cent owned nothing or less than an acre. Most of the Moroccan-owned land was laboured by share-croppers and share-tenants, resulting in quasi-feudal relations.[12]

> The large landowners – an estimated 7,500 holding four million acres including pastures – often bore opprobrium along with their riches under the name of the 'feudals' and, although the term is strictly inaccurate, in many respects their relations with their one fifth contract workers are medieval. Although the group is not homogeneous, it does include many whom nationalists consider collaborators with the Protectorate, among them numerous *shiukh* (local administrators) who had enriched themselves more rapaciously than the *colons* at the expense of their citizens.[13]

This not only created a major socio-economic divide between rural and urban areas, but also created profound divisions among Moroccan farmers: a large, landless or land-poor majority was subject to weather conditions for their economic well-being. In turn, a small, modern, Europeanised sector owned all irrigated land and a disproportional share of all agricultural land, able to use mechanised labour, accrue surplus and serve as a foundation in export-led growth strategies.

The question then became what to do to alleviate the plight of Morocco's traditional farming sector, boost productivity and increase revenues. The Moroccan left advocated land reform as in neighbouring Algeria: Moroccanisation of European-held farmland and a redistribution of all land over a certain limit, possibly nationalisation and collective farming. The socialist politician, Minister of Labour and Prime Minister (1958–60) Abdallah Ibrahim, in a speech delivered in the summer of 1961 in the Gharb region, referred to privately owned land in the hands of large landowners as 'adjacent land that really belongs to you, the [landless] peasants'. He spoke to the Union Syndicale des Agriculteurs, which represented poor and/or traditional farmers. The union advocated land reforms and resisted further privatisation – *melkisation* – of state or tribally owned property that would have advantaged larger holdings or absentee *melk* landlords.[14] While these ideas were popular among the Moroccan left, Morocco's bourgeoisie and nationalist movement far from shared these ideas. After all, some of them were large landowners themselves, such as the Istiqlal's agriculture minister, Omar Abdeljalil, in the first post-independence government.[15]

The first attempt at modernisation under the title Operation Plough (1957–60) illustrated all the political obstacles that technocratic improvements and change, however well intended, would bring. The plan was simple: introducing mechanisation and fertilisation in areas where small-plot farmers could be brought together in collectives. It only touched 5 per cent of all agricultural land, though, and even here it was resisted by medium-sized farmers and increasingly powerful large landowners who feared that the state would take away their land. On one occasion, King Mohamed V attempted to reassure them by driving a tractor along the dividing line of two plots, giving symbolic legitimacy to private property.[16] In its first year, the yield in those areas that participated (400,000 acres; 160,000 hectares) dramatically increased, the surplus ranging from 30 to 50 per cent. Consequently, in its second year, overambitious state administrators forced more farmers to participate in the plan, when 750,000 acres (300,000 hectares) of land was under Operation Plough. However, as the bad year of 1958 resulted in less than expected crop yields in comparison with areas that did not participate in the campaign, local farmers refused to participate in the third and fourth years of the campaign – suspicious of modern equipment and state interference by mostly urban, young and educated state administrators. Hence, in 1959 and 1960, the programme fell to 490,000 and 433,000 acres (200,000 hectares and 175,000 hectares), respectively.[17] In subsequent years the plan was shelved. Through the political ascendency of landowners, especially through the Ministry of the Interior and the MP, other ambitious plans of redistribution of land along more egalitarian lines were shelved as well, such as the first 1960–64 five-year plan.[18]

Real change took place elsewhere: first, the slow but steady redistribution of colonial land benefited large landowners, which only amplified the unequal distribution of land. Second, Hassan II gave increasing importance to irrigated land through his high-profile agricultural dam project, the *politique des barrages*. Both developments increased the farming sector's division into a small surplus-generating and value-adding agricultural sector possessing large plots next to a large, poor and dependent traditional and impoverished sector.

In 1963, the Moroccan state expropriated 250,000 hectares out of about 1 million hectares of French-held land. Although it was expected that this land would be redistributed to poor peasants, the state leased most of the land to large landowners or it remained under some form of state management. The consequence of this was a wave of sales of the remaining foreign-held profitable farmland that had been privately acquired by foreigners in the colonial period, which was accelerated when Hassan announced that 728,000 hectares of foreign-held land would be expropriated: 400,000 hectares changed hands to larger landowners before the state could lay claim to it. In one fertile region, the Gharb, about 10 per cent of buyers bought plots of more than 100 hectares, accounting for some 60 per cent of all land that was sold.[19] A decree of September 1963 that aimed at limiting these land transactions between foreigners and Moroccans was only selectively applied to smaller farmers and not to the larger, powerful rural elite that became so politically important in Hassan II's state-building efforts. The result was that almost half of the 1 million hectares of land controlled by foreigners went into private, wealthy Moroccan hands without state regulations being able to affect these – leading to a further concentration of land among the few.[20]

Modernisation of Morocco's agriculture through irrigation without land reform was advocated not only by large landowners, but also by the World Bank. A 1966 report recommended the increase of the amount of cash crops over both food crops and industrialisation projects, in order to create much-needed foreign currency earnings. As a result of this rationality and the economic interests of large landowners, between 1968 and 1972, 85 per cent of agricultural investments went into irrigated zones, and 50 per cent of all public expenditure in agriculture went into the country's dam projects. Five dams were constructed in the same period, increasing the amount of irrigated land to 177,000 hectares.[21] The aim was to create 1 million hectares of irrigated land by the year 2000 by building 20 dams nationwide – an aim effectively achieved. The side effect of this was the concentration of more land in the hands of even fewer owners. The stipulations of the dam modernisation project required farmers to acquire modern techniques and cash crops, as the overall aim was to transform traditional farmland into modern, surplus-producing export-oriented agrarian capitalism. Hence, small farmers were expropriated if their land was under the threshold of 5 hectares, and their land redistributed to modern farmers if they failed to live up to this commitment. In one case, the state expropriated 97 per cent of collectively owned land where each farmer held less than 5 hectares, to the benefit of large landowners. These included not only young and modern rural entrepreneurs, but also old rural notables.[22] In addition, the state's *laissez-faire* policy of not assisting small farmers to adapt led to pressure on small farmers to sell their land to larger farmers. Clearly, loans, subsidies and other resources were only available to organised, modern landowners with knowledge of, and access to, administrative channels. The increasing concentration of land was added to by land speculation. Larger farmers bought as much land as possible from smaller farmers as soon as plans for a new irrigation dam became known to them. As Douad reports, this is how in the Souss region 40 per cent of the land was bought by three people before the Massa dam was constructed.[23] This agricultural policy became even more profitable for large landowners due to generous tax allowances. The traditional *tertib* tax was abolished as part of the policy, and agricultural activities were increasingly under-taxed. In the late 1970s, agriculture provided the Moroccan state with about one tenth of the income it provided immediately after independence. On the contrary, capital investments were channelled into irrigation plans, and starting in 1984, and renewed in 2000, a comprehensive tax exemption regime was established that included all agricultural activities.[24]

Importantly, neither the increasing concentration of land, nor the state's massive agricultural investments through dams and irrigation networks and tax cuts, had the effect of increasing Morocco's overall agricultural productivity, nor of decreasing its dependency on imports for cereals and other primary commodities. From 1960 to 1971, agricultural output as a percentage of overall GDP dropped by about 30 per cent, from 28.8 per cent to 19.9 per cent. In the same period, the rural population only decreased from 70.7 per cent to 65 per cent, illustrating relative per capita economic decline. In 2000, agriculture accounted for 13.5 per cent of GDP, while the rural population was at 47 per cent.[25]

This trend has been sharpened by the irrigation projects that supported export-oriented growth, especially in citrus fruits, to the disadvantage of domestically consumed cereal that forms part of Moroccans' basic diet. The per capita production of cereal was at 300 kg in 1960, only to fall to 150 kg in 1981. Similarly, the agricultural balance of trade was positive until 1973, but became increasingly negative to reach a deficit of 2 billion Moroccan dirhams (MAD) by 1982.[26] In 1998–2000, Morocco imported 54.1 per cent of the overall cereal consumed.[27]

Consequently, what has been termed Morocco's perpetual agricultural crisis has been largely man-made. While declining precipitation and restricted access to European markets have contributed to declining agricultural growth, these are not the main reasons. Morocco continued French colonial policy of emphasising export-oriented agricultural growth especially in citrus fruit and tomatoes. By 1981, Morocco became the third largest exporter of oranges, accounting for some 13 per cent of the world supply.[28] Predictably, though, the accession of Portugal and Spain to the European Economic Community (EEC) in 1986 reduced the number of oranges and tomatoes that Morocco was able to export to its main market. Already in 1984 oranges were down to 541,000 tons from 772,000 tons in 1981, whereas tomatoes were down to 69,000 tons in 1984 from 253,000 tons in 1980.[29]

Efficient cereal production through modernisation in the traditional sector, however, has been neglected, despite the fact that it provided income for 90 per cent of farmers on around 70 per cent of all cultivated land.[30] In fact, despite Morocco's food needs in these staples, domestic market prices have been kept artificially low, decreasing incentives for higher production. This policy deviated resources to the more lucrative export business or the fruit sector, where price controls do not exist. As Swearingen points out, in order to keep the price of wheat in urban areas artificially low, the traditional sector is being discriminated against, whereas policies through inexpensive water supply, subsidies and tax cuts, loans and fertilisers have benefited the modern sector with its large landowners. This further undermined investments and modernisation in Morocco's traditional agricultural sector, leading to chronically low cereal productivity. This low productivity constantly stagnated at less than 50 per cent of the world average. This was about 9.0 quintals per hectare between 1979 and 2002,[31] compared with a world average of about 19 quintals per hectare in the early 1980s.[32] When Morocco achieved a record output of 19.3 quintals in 2013, this compared with a world average of 38.5.[33] Fluctuations are mainly due to rainfall, as cereal production predominates in the traditional farming sector.

Due to population growth, the hard currency bill that Morocco increasingly paid has become a major source of financial constraint. Not only did Morocco increase its agricultural imports of mostly cereal, vegetable oil and sugar, from MAD 241 million in 1960, MAD 3.1 billion in 1980, to MAD 11 billion in 2002,[34] but governmental subsidies of these imports through the *Caisse de Compensation* increased the government's budget and significantly contributed to the country's debt crisis of the early 1980s. With world food prices soaring in the late 2000s, the government again attempted to increase mechanisation in the traditional sector and to distribute seeds more efficiently. In 2014, the number of tractors rose to 7 per 1,000 hectares from 5 per 1,000 hectares in 2005, compared to a world average of 20.[35] Yet due to irrigation and pricing inefficiencies, such programmes fail to address the core problem.

Consequently, increasing exports to the EU since the 1980s, such as the 216,000 tons of tomatoes or 580,000 tons of oranges in 2006,[36] while having a positive impact on GDP growth, may have only a very small impact on employment due to the prevalence of capital-intensive production processes in the modern sector. In addition, while it generates substantial revenues, these are not distributed evenly across the agricultural sector. Hence, Morocco's modernisation and reform in the countryside failed to address the most important economic questions of an agricultural economy based on subsistence-level farming, and instead led to economic deprivation and rural exodus. While legal migration to France, the Netherlands, Belgium, Italy and Germany was a partial solution up until the mid-1980s, most Moroccans started to fill the increasing number of shanty towns in urban centres, especially around Casablanca. As it became increasingly difficult to control these urban areas, as urban riots in Casablanca, Fes, Tangier and Al Hoceima testified in the 1980s, these urban dwellers' needs to sustain low prices in staples were prioritised over the introduction of a pricing mechanism that would allow for Morocco's poor, mostly cereal-producing traditional sector to invest and modernise with the assistance of the state. Hence, a vicious cycle was put in place in which the countryside continued to be impoverished, only to produce new migrants to the cities. In turn, these volatile migrants ensured that the cereal price mechanism remained as it was, forestalling any more substantive reforms that, ultimately, might put an end to rural exodus. Meantime, Morocco's wealthy farmers' interests, including those of the royal family, became intrinsically linked with the interests of the state to prefer short-term solutions to more substantive reforms. The political empowerment of these rural notables due to their intermediate role between the state and the peasantry on one hand, and as a counterbalance to the urban nationalists and more liberal segments of the elite on the other hand, has so far perpetuated Morocco's agricultural crisis.

## 4.2 From import substitution to debt crisis and structural adjustment

As in agriculture, Morocco's industrial and bureaucratic modernisation plans led to a significant polarisation between its traditional bourgeoisie and newcomers to the cities from the countryside. The main reason for this is that the independent but contested state, dominated by the political elite *makhzen*, needed an important ally to consolidate its weak social basis. As a result, as much as its agricultural policy was a consequence to assure rural notables' support, its ostensibly liberal approach to economic development was also meant to serve the interests of Morocco's rising, urban, commercial bourgeoisie. The side effect of this was to separate the conservative, bourgeois elements of the independence movement from the socialist elements – a tactic that led to the Istiqlal Party's split in 1959.

The first five-year plan (1960–65), in which ISI along with agrarian reform and redistribution were key elements to achieve 'economic independence', was quickly shelved after only six months, when King Mohamed V and Crown Prince Hassan ended the short-lived socialist Ibrahim government in May 1960. Instead, the three-year plan of 1964 no longer included industrialisation or economic independence as a priority, and adopted agricultural modernisation (i.e. irrigation) as the country's economic priority.[37] In 1967, Finance Minister Mamoun Tahiri, at a World Bank conference, declared that 'Morocco chose the liberal path to development and it will serve as an example for the entire African continent'.[38] Due to the absence of an indigenous industrial bourgeoisie – the manufacturing sector, first of all, was controlled by the French and, second, accounted for not more than 16 per cent of GDP[39] – the role of the Moroccan state was nevertheless reinforced despite its liberal overtone, and the following two decades saw Morocco sliding into ISI strategies. This meant that Moroccan 'liberalism' did not lead to the creation of a strong, independent private sector, nor did it limit the state's central role in economic activities. The state created new public institutions, such as the National Economic Development Bank (1959), which made available cheap credit, leading to a significant amount of state patronage. While favourable investment codes, tax benefits, and protectionist tariffs, implemented between 1958 and 1960, helped create small-scale industries such as in textiles and leather, they generally did not result in any large-scale investment necessary for heavy industries. Private funds needed for these more extensive industries were not yet available. Hence, the state directly took over, as in the case of the oil refinery SAMIR or the car assembly plant SOMACA.[40] As in neighbouring Algeria, the state occupied centre stage and a 'social pact' between the country's traditional urban bourgeoisie and the state developed. As the Moroccan economist Driss Ben Ali describes,

Institutional measures were taken to encourage these families to enrich themselves and to accumulate wealth (tariff protections contingent on local industries, subsidies and fiscal incentives, creation of state institutions that support industrialisation and that would provide cheap credits …). On the other hand, the state would become an immense market for their products. Effectively, the inflation of operational expenses, the renewing of equipment, the creation of middle class consumerism with significant spending power based on state salaries, all of this would turn the state into an immense market.[41]

The same author concludes that the relations established between the urban bourgeoisie and the state were entirely based on profits: the state allowed the bourgeoisie to occupy a privileged position among those providers of services and equipment for both the administration and public companies.[42] The country's budget deficit of about 10 per cent of GDP in 1961, peaking in 1977 at 16 per cent, therefore followed the political rationality of serving the interests of an increasingly state-dependent bourgeoisie. This dependency was not only indirect – the state as the main market – but increasingly direct: in 1971, the budget ratio of investment vs. salaries was already at 1/2.5, a trend that deteriorated to 1/3.8 by 2000.[43] The state has become not only the country's biggest investor and market, but also the main employer with the notable exception of agriculture.

Much to nationalists' disappointment, though, up to the early 1970s, economic independence from the French was not achieved, nor was it a stated objective. Still, the traditional, older, merchant-based Fassi class became increasingly involved in business after more and more French left and sold their businesses at low prices. Like many agricultural properties that were sold to well-established families such as the Kabbaj, Nejjai, Gueddari and Bekkai families, fortunes were quickly made by those with some liquid assets.[44] Overall, however, the economy continued to be dominated by foreigners. The best example was the French Banque de Paris et des Pays Bas, which controlled more than 50 companies through the kingdom's largest holding company, ONA. Up until the early 1970s, sectors that were under the control of ONA included tourism, mining, transport, sales agencies, as well as construction. A survey of a sample of 160 private industrial enterprises conducted in 1970 discovered that only 13 per cent of directors were Moroccan. Not limited to the private sector, 1,500 of 6,000 top public posts were held by foreigners. From higher education to medical care and engineering, foreigners remained the leading force. Given the overall lucrative potential of Moroccanisation for the Moroccan bourgeoisie, the early 1970s saw a resurgence of nationalist sentiments around this issue, and after the coup attempts of 1971 and 1972, the monarchy reacted. Unlike in rural areas, however, the urban population that stood to benefit had become more mobile and diversified. It comprised not only the older elite but also a new class of shopkeepers, restaurant and hotel owners from the southern Souss area. In addition, the state took a more active part by buying a good number of the 1,500 companies (out of the originally 4,000 companies identified) listed in the Moroccanisation act. The state-owned bank Société Nationale d'Investissement bought companies such as Lesieur (vegetable oil), Brasseries du Maroc (soft drinks and beer), Lafarge Maroc (cement), Forges Canaud, and sold shares to broader groups – not only to the established class. As a result, not only was the Casablanca stock exchange reinvigorated in the mid-1970s, but the benefits of Moroccanisation were less monopolised by the established elite. By the end of the 1970s, the Moroccan bourgeoisie included many Soussi families. This was best evidenced by increasing intermarriages between Soussis and Fassis – in Morocco marriages traditionally follow business logic.[45]

Other than Moroccanisation, more sources that could be redistributed resulted from the rise in phosphate prices and generous lending policies that followed the flooding of international financial markets with petro-dollars during the post-1973 price hike in crude oil. The price of Morocco's main export commodity, phosphate, tripled from 1973 to 1974, from around $14 to $42, only to reach $68 in 1975 – a 500 per cent increase in three years. As the third largest producer and the world's largest exporter of phosphate through the state-owned OCP, the monarchy expected to gain significantly from this unexpected windfall, and it engaged in an ill-fated public spending boom. It increased salaries of public-sector employees and subsidies on essential food items. Between 1974 and 1976, government expenditure doubled and public investment increased by 340 per cent between 1974 and 1978. Partly a result of Moroccanisation but certainly encouraged by phosphate revenues, 250 public companies were created in the same period. Consequently, the ratio of government expenditure to GDP increased from 20 per cent to 40 per cent from 1973 to 1977.[46] As Rhazaoui points out, most new investments went into ISI, such as oil refineries, sugar, fertiliser, pulp and paper, which are capital intensive. This had the consequence of important growth in the construction sector, but it did not yield any short- or medium-term increases in output levels that would offset the economic costs of these investments, such as in exports.[47] Similarly, a massive recruitment in the public sector – while increasing the burden on the Moroccan economy – did not increase output levels either. Over a 20-year period from 1960 to about 1980, the public sector increased in size from 50,000 employees to 500,000.[48]

Despite this period of economic expansion, the benefits were very unevenly distributed. As already noted above, due to the focus on large-scale import substitution projects, the main beneficiary was the construction sector and the new middle classes associated with this boom. In turn, the expansion had little effect on low-income groups in both urban and rural areas, and therefore did not create any of the demand necessary for successful import substitution. Unemployment and underemployment rates reached critical levels of about 29 per cent by the late 1970s. Although poverty estimates vary as much as unemployment figures, a World Bank report put the poverty figure as high as 45 per cent of the total population. This included all those who lived under the poverty threshold of $238 per capita per annum in 1983. Unequal access to post-independence expansion of services meant that adult literacy only reached an estimated 35 per cent in 1982 (see Table 4.1). In the late 1970s, primary education was only available to 29 per cent of children in rural areas. This is without counting drop-out rates that, together with low-quality teaching, have since perpetuated Morocco's exceptionally low literacy rates compared to other middle-income countries such as Algeria or Tunisia.[49] As recently as 2005, a World Bank report mentioned that only 25 per cent of those who finished primary school could be considered literate and numerate.[50] Similarly, even if Morocco's infant mortality rate dropped from 149 per thousand births in the early 1962s to 47.9 per thousand births in 2004, it remains exceptionally high in rural areas (see Table 4.2).

What can still be termed Morocco's 'bonanza' compared to the period that followed came to a sudden end in 1976, when the international price for phosphates reached the same level as in 1973. The government's spending plans failed to adjust accordingly – despite first austerity measures in 1978.[51] Consequently, borrowing from abroad became the major, if unsustainable, source of financing the growing gap between revenue and expenditure. Private credits were supplemented by official balance of payment and project assistance such as the first financial protocol obtained from the EEC in 1976. Regardless, compounded by the growing cost of the war in Western Sahara – estimated at US$1 billion per year in the 1980s[52] – as well as several poor agricultural seasons, especially in 1981 and 1982, foreign debt rose from US$2.3 billion in 1976 to US$7.9 billion in 1979, reaching US$11.8 billion in 1983. In 1983, this represented 300 per cent of Morocco's export earnings and 84 per cent of GDP.[53] In March 1983, Morocco's foreign exchange earnings were almost exhausted: the country was near bankruptcy; it could no longer service its debt, nor pay for critical imports. Morocco joined the list of the 15 most indebted countries worldwide.

Subsequent rescheduling of debts, increasing IMF and World Bank involvement in, and control of, Morocco's Structural Adjustment Programme (SAP) led to a changing social pact. Even if the pact's consequences were not as ideologically important as in neighbouring countries, such as Algeria and Tunisia, where

**TABLE 4.1** Illiteracy rates by gender and region (adults and children over ten years old), 1960–2004 (%)

|      | Urban | Rural | Male | Female | Total |
| --- | --- | --- | --- | --- | --- |
| 1960 | n/a | n/a | n/a | n/a | 87 |
| 1971 | n/a | n/a | n/a | n/a | 75 |
| 1982 | 44 | 82 | 51 | 78 | 65 |
| 1994 | 37 | 75 | 41 | 67 | 55 |
| 2004 | 29.4 | 60.5 | 30.8 | 54.7 | 43 |

Source: Secrétaire d'Etat Chargé de l'Alphabétisation et de l'Education non Formelle, *Recensement Général de la Population et de l'Habitat* (Rabat, 1982, 1994, 2004); www.alpha.gov.ma; Institut Universitaire de la Recherche Scientifique, *Rapport du Social 2000, Bulletin Economique et Social* (Rabat: Okad, 2000), p. 94; Lahcen Madi, 'L'alphabétisation et l'éducation des adultes', www.rdh50.ma/fr/pdf/contributions/GT4-9.pdf, p. 311

**TABLE 4.2** Infant mortality rate, 1962–2004 (per thousand births)

|      | Rural | Urban | Total |
|------|-------|-------|-------|
| 1962 | 170   | 100   | 149   |
| 1970 | n/a   | n/a   | 119   |
| 1990 | n/a   | n/a   | 69    |
| 2004 | 56.7  | 38.6  | 47.9  |

Source: Royaume du Maroc, '50 ans de développement humain & perspectives 2025, Chapitre I: Evolution du potentiel humain, population, mutations sociales et dynamique culturelle', p. 6; UNICEF, 'At a Glance: Morocco', www.unicef.org/infobycountry/morocco_statistics.html#47; UNDP, *2007–8 Human Development Report Morocco*, hdrstats.undp.org/countries/data_sheets/cty_ds_MAR.html

development and social progress were more central for the single party state and its ruling elite's legitimacy, it still led to serious riots (1981 and 1984) and a legitimacy crisis. Amongst others, this was evidenced in both the Istiqlal's and the USFP's absence from government following the 1984 election, after the initial honeymoon period following the Green March. Direct state involvement in the economy remarkably diminished since structural adjustment and the post-1988 policy of privatisation, but this change was quite in keeping with the monarchy's expressed liberal ideology based on free enterprise. As Joffé points out, together with allegedly democratic political structures, this has always been part of the rhetoric associated with 'Hassanian democracy'.[54] It is worth pointing out, though, that, in contrast to its neighbours in the Maghreb and the Mashreq, Morocco's implicit social contract in which the regime provided for its citizens economically in return for their loyalty was less populist and has been biased towards the wealthy and urban areas,[55] as seen from the country's poor social indicators. Clearly, it was from the more wealthy, urban strata that the monarch had traditionally encountered most resistance – before the new period of urban riots and the rise of political Islam. Still, the period of privatisation and restructuring post-1983, while it changed the economic nature of the social contract, was not inherently incompatible with continuing state protection that the wealthy strata enjoyed.

After signing the first stand-by agreement with the IMF in 1983, which granted Morocco US$200 million of Special Drawing Rights, the World Bank provided Morocco with US$600 million in structural adjustment assistance. Consequently, the creation of public jobs was limited to 10,000 per year post-1983, compared to 40,000 to 50,000 per year prior to the IMF intervention. In higher education, recruitment was limited and criteria for state grants were tightened. From 1982 to 1985, the price of sugar increased by 30 per cent, cooking oil by 52 per cent, and wheat by 87 per cent. Starting from 1983, the prices for electricity, water and public transport were revised, and the beginning of a privatisation campaign threatened to increase the already very high unemployment rate – estimated at 24 per cent in 1983.[56]

## 4.3 Economic changes and the development of a new ruling pact

Despite these SAP measures, GDP did not experience a significant decline all through the second half of the 1980s. A period of good agricultural years after 1980–81 droughts provided for both GDP growth and increasing employment rates. Growth in agriculture was on average 8 per cent per year until the early 1990s, when a period of sustained drought hit the economy. This paradox of overall declining state investment accompanied by increasing employment until the early 1990s illustrates one continuing feature of the Moroccan economy: for the basic questions of poverty and employment, it continues to be dependent on its agricultural sector and more specifically on rainfall due to the importance of the non-irrigated sector for both employment and wealth creation of poorer strata. The vexed question, however, has become that of growing unemployment among its university graduates, which touched the new middle classes due to the limitations placed on public-sector expansion. This has been despite the fact that government data on unemployment and poverty indicate falling rates (in 2007, Morocco had an official unemployment rate of 10 per cent, compared to more than 20 per cent in 1983). As a result of all this, the previous 'ruling pact' between state and society underwent some critical changes.

First, the 1980s saw the rise of a new, better-educated, younger and more technocratic elite due to the monarchy's increasing reliance on international institutions such as the IMF and World Bank to reschedule its debt. As the 1981 and 1984 riots illustrated, its former reliance on rural notables to uphold social order as well as appeasing the wealthy urban sector was leading to an impasse. The political rise of this new technocratic elite was best evidenced by the sudden ascendance of a political party of technocrats, the Constitutional Union (UC) in the 1984 parliamentary election. As overall debt increased to an alarming US$14.6 billion in 1986 – despite IMF intervention – Morocco had to convince the external financial community that overall policies were in line with the new Washington Consensus. These new technocrats implemented IMF recommendations such as a devaluation of the dirham, more balanced budgets, and privatisation after 1988. After trade liberalisation and joining the General Agreement on Tariffs and Trade (GATT), the elite in the inner circle of Minister of Privatisation Moulay Zine Zahid convinced the monarchy to become a founding member of the World Trade Organization (WTO), not coincidentally founded in Marrakech in 1994.[57]

Second, the reduction of the size of the state was felt differently across income strata. It did not directly lead to the sudden creation of a new pool of urban poor. Mostly due to agricultural growth in the 1980s, actual poverty declined from 21 per cent in 1984 to 13 per cent in 1991 (see Table 4.3). In addition, although the government cut subsidies, reduced investments, as well as salaries in the public sector all along the 1980s, it often reversed decisions once it was challenged by organised protests or riots. These were frequent: all through the 1980s and early 1990s, parliamentary opposition criticised the budgets as anti-social. Prisons, full with political prisoners who were jailed following the 1984 riots, were constant venues of hunger strikes. In turn, international human rights organisations and the European Parliament in 1992 criticised the state's human rights abuses and its harsh treatment of protests. In 1989 labour unrest, such as the four-day seizure by 400 miners of the Jerada coalfields, was followed by strikes in flour milling and petroleum refining industries. Bank employees went on a strike in support of higher wages the same year, a demand that the state responded to by increasing the wages of the higher civil servants in an apparent attempt to co-opt its ringleaders.[58]

The state's slow retreat from the economy affected most strongly a new, educated generation of what can be grouped together as the lower middle class. It had been this class that had experienced rapid social mobility in the 1970s, and it now expected upward social mobility for its offspring. The new, better-educated generation, however, found itself locked out of the public sector. Instead, permanent underemployment, temporary jobs and dependency on the informal sector became widespread. The annual public-sector intake no longer went above a couple of thousand. In turn, the nascent, often unregulated private sector was not yet ready to create meaningful graduate employment. The best indicator of this has been the rise of the phenomenon of graduate unemployment since the late 1980s, including those with doctoral degrees. This increased from 6.5 per cent in 1984 to 26.2 per cent in 1995. Unemployment among high school graduates doubled from 14.6 per cent in 1984 to 31.2 per cent in 1993. Concomitantly, unemployment became increasingly urban: 90 per cent of the unemployed were urban in 1993, whereas urban unemployment accounted for about 50 per cent ten years before – the ratio of urban vs. rural only changed from about 45/55 to 50/50 in the same period.[59] A qualitative dimension was the 1992 foundation of the Unemployed Graduates' Association, which has been remarkably active and selectively repressed up to this date.

Third, it is important to point out one constant: Morocco remains an agricultural economy, and most of the country's GDP growth is dependent on rainfall and other climatic conditions. Figure 4.1 illustrates how agricultural growth is the main stimulator for overall GDP growth, and the fact that the numerical index of poverty increased all through the 1990s can be mainly attributed to the particularly bad climatic conditions that Morocco experienced at that time (one drought every two years). While the SAP had an impact on public-sector spending in Morocco's

**TABLE 4.3** Population living in poverty (%)

| 1984 | 1991 | 2000 | 2005 |
|------|------|------|------|
| 21   | 13   | 19   | 14 (19★) |

Note: ★ Denotes a 2004 World Bank estimate, whereas all other estimates were released by the Moroccan government.
Source: J. Harrigan and H. El Said, *Royaume du Maroc: 50 ans de développement humain & perspectives 2025* (Rabat: Royaume du Maroc, 2007), p. 24. Updated data put a 2007 World Bank estimate at 8.9 per cent, but it is not included in this table as it appears as an outlier. See data.worldbank.org/country/morocco

urban, formal sector, the rural poor have been hardly affected by economic reform or cuts in social expenditure – given the already very low provisions of any type of social services in rural areas. Morocco's expenditure on health services remained stable at around 1 per cent of GDP, as did the country's expenditure on education, which decreased only slightly from about 6.2 per cent to about 5.3 per cent of GDP between 1982 and 1991.[60] As a result, it has not been the absolute number of poor or other poverty indices that are a challenge to the regime, but the existence of strata in *urban* areas that are affected by governmental policies. In 1993, rural exodus reached a critical level when, for the first time, more than 50 per cent of the country was classified as urban, reaching 60 per cent in the 2000s and 65 per cent in the 2010s. For this reason, the government has increasingly focused on limiting rural exodus and the spread of shanty towns or *bidonvilles*, especially from the more unruly north of Morocco. This is also why Morocco has at times been hesitant to effectively fight illegal emigration and drug trafficking to Europe, especially from its northern shores, given its positive effect on migratory pressures to its own cities.

The main benefit of a stable macro-economic environment and low inflation was to attract one major source of revenue back into Morocco: remittances. Morocco long neglected its migrant communities abroad (which numbered some 2.5 million in the 2000s), and has only recently tried to redress the balance with the creation of an elected migrant council – partly due to the increasing economic importance of these remittances. Already in 1991, migrant remittances accounted for 11 per cent of private consumption and 7.5 per cent of GDP. World Bank estimates of the time suggest that, if it were not for these remittances, 180,000 or 5 per cent of the estimated poor in 1991 would be added to the total number of poor.[61] Ever since, remittances have become more important for both GDP and, especially, the balance of payments. A chronic trade deficit in agriculture, raw materials, manufactured goods and capital goods has only been offset by these remittances and by tourism, the country's main service industry. These have

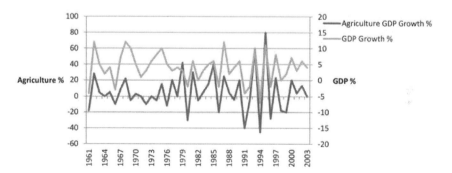

**FIGURE 4.1** GDP growth and agricultural growth, 1961–2003
Source: Adapted from Kingdom of Morocco, *50 ans de développement humain & perspectives 2025* (Rabat: Royaume du Maroc, 2007), p. 18

substantially contributed to hard currency income and secured balanced economic accounts until 2007. As Table 4.4 indicates, with the rising cost of imports especially in food stuff, the balance of payments reached a deficit MAD 80 billion in 2012, bringing the state's debt burden near breaking point.

Finally, the SAP had as one of its main consequences not only initially more balanced accounts and an end to state expansion, but also the start of a privatisation campaign. The goal has been to give Moroccan entrepreneurs more responsibility for the creation of wealth and employment and – in line with the rise of a new technocratic elite – a more important role in the decision-making process. This became crucial in the second phase of the SAP which started in 1996 with the signing of Morocco's association agreement with the EU. One of the main commitments of the EU has been to sponsor a '*mise à niveau*' programme as part of the Barcelona Process to ensure that Morocco's private sector is fit for increasing foreign competition. This commitment was achieved in exchange for Morocco's commitment to liberalise its trade relations with the EU until 2012, and to dismantle its tariffs on EU imports in areas until then protected, such as in manufacturing.

## *Privatisation*

While privatisation offered the monarchical state another source of patronage for a new generation of Morocco's political and economic elite, leading to increased if different state control over the private sector, in its legitimatisation process it generated a different view of private responsibilities and the state's ultimate political disengagement from economic activities. Both contradictory trends can be detected in the privatisation process, which started in April 1988 when the King publicly announced that legislation for a wave of privatisation was under way, expressing his wish to see all public companies privatised – the 'commanding heights of the economy' such as the phosphate industry, rail networks, air transport, as well as utilities and telecoms excepted.[62] While the SAP rationale for privatisation was to offer for sale companies that were not run efficiently and therefore posed a burden to the state budget, the Moroccan state – in its 1989 law on privatisation – listed companies that had been quite profitable and well run. As Joffé remarks, of the 75 companies (excluding hotels from the original list of 112) slated for privatisation, only 13 were loss making in 1988. In addition, of the remaining 61 that reported profits (one did not report results), 34 reported rates of return below 10 per cent, while 17 had rates of return between 10 and 15 per cent. Another 17 companies had rates of return exceeding 15 per cent.[63] Although the telecom sector was initially excluded, in 1999 the government negotiated a contract to sell its second GSM licence to a consortium led by Spanish Telefónica and the Banque Marocaine du Commerce Exterieur (BMCE), owned by one of Morocco's financial giants from the traditional Fassi merchant class, the Benjelloun family. The success in obtaining $1.1 billion for the GSM licence, as well as the surge in international interest in the telecom sector based on the anticipation of very high rates of return,

**TABLE 4.4** Remittances and balance of payments, 2003–14 (in million MAD)

| | 2003 | 2004 | 2005 | 2006 | 2007 | 2008 | 2009 | 2010 | 2011 | 2012 | 2013 | 2014 |
|---|---|---|---|---|---|---|---|---|---|---|---|---|
| Remittances | 34,581 | 37,422 | 40,737 | 47,833 | 55,000 | 53,072 | 50,210 | 54,387 | 58,385 | 58,751 | 57,867 | 59,946 |
| Balance of trade | -52,182 | -70,024 | -85,114 | -98,574 | -135,770 | -170,302 | -150,961 | -148,380 | -182,775 | -202,064 | -198,333 | -186,105 |
| Tourists receipts | 30,881 | 34,793 | 40,967 | 52,485 | 58,673 | 55,550 | 52,833 | 56,421 | 58,904 | 57,835 | 57,614 | 59,308 |
| FDI/capital receipts | 23,256 | 9,484 | 26,707 | 26,070 | 37,959 | 27,963 | 25,249 | 35,068 | 26,060 | 32,091 | 39,076 | 36,460 |
| Balance of payments | 15,732 | 16,790 | 9,431 | 12,423 | -411 | -35,936 | -39,873 | -34,321 | -64,602 | -80,647 | -69,182 | -52,336 |

Source: Office des Changes, *Balance des Paiements* (various years), in particular *Balance des Paiements 2011*, pp. 137–144, *Tableau de bord annuel 2003 à 2014*, www.oc.gov.ma

made the Moroccan state change its former attitude towards the partial privatisation of the state monopoly Maroc Telecom (Itissalat Al Maghreb – IAM). In 2001 it sold 35 per cent of its share to the French company Vivendi Universal for approximately US$3 billion (MAD 25 billion).

Both mega-deals illustrate that privatisation has first of all had the impact of filling the state's coffers to bridge financial gaps that have been accumulated elsewhere. The creation of the royal-controlled Mohamed VI Fund for Solidarity in 1999 (not part of the government's regular budget) or Hassan II Fund in 2001, funded by the privatisation campaign, has expanded direct monarchical patronage into the social services. Privatisation also had the effect of multiplying state patronage over the bourgeoisie and the nascent private sector, due to a lack of transparency and independent oversight. Rumours and speculation about closed deals and preferential treatment have caused Morocco's corruption index established by Transparency International to drop from 4.1 to 3.2 (out of 10) between 1999 and 2004, behind Egypt and Saudi Arabia, and on par with Algeria. As indicated in Table 4.5 Morocco's position in the corruption index has remained at the bottom part of the international ranking throughout the last 15 years.[64] This indicates that privatisation became another formidable resource for patronage, consolidating the technocratic elements of the class that was created by Moroccanisation, all of this legitimised in a discourse marked by liberal concepts based on efficiency.

Most importantly, perhaps, the royal family's own majority share in the most important *private* holding, the ONA, since the early 1980s has made King Hassan II and, since his death, King Mohamed VI the most important businessman in the country. Not surprisingly, deregulation in areas such as the retail market (Marjane, Acima) or banking (Attarijawafa) has greatly increased the monarchy's own economic interests in the private sector. This regularly creates conflicts of interest – from state subsidies on products in which ONA companies trade (Lesieur, vegetable oil; Centrale Laitière, dairy products), to deregulation of insurance or banking services, such as the lucrative remittances service.[65] Recent transactions, including

**TABLE 4.5** Morocco's position in the corruption index, 2000–14

| Year | Index | Global ranking |
| --- | --- | --- |
| 2000 | 4.7/10 | 37 |
| 2002 | 3.7/10 | 52 |
| 2004 | 3.2/10 | 77 |
| 2006 | 3.2/10 | 79 |
| 2008 | 3.5/10 | 80 |
| 2010 | 3.4/10 | 85 |
| 2012 | 37/100 | 88 |
| 2014 | 39/100 | 80 |

Source: Transparency International, www.transparency.org, various years

the fusion of the ONA with another royal holding, Société Nationale d'Investissement (SNI), and its withdrawal from the Casablanca stock exchange, have raised questions about transparency in this monarchical commercial entity. Together with the sale of less profitable food sectors and investment in more profitable telecoms – reversing the ONA's initial inability to match the investment offers for Maroc Telecom and Meditel made by the French Vivendi Universal and the Spanish Telefónica groups in the late 1990s[66] – such moves may have aimed at rendering the King's economic investments not just more profitable, but also less visible. With the King's personal revenues skyrocketing, with an estimated wealth of US$2.5 billion making him the world's eighth richest monarch,[67] the visibility of his economic interests in everyday household items such as milk and oil started to make him subject to criticism. During the 20 February demonstrations, calls for the dismissal of Mounir Majidi, the King's personal secretary in charge of his business interests, as well as calls for an end of the ONA, were frequently heard.

## *The rise of Morocco's entrepreneurial class*

As has been shown in the previous section, privatisation offered a resource for royal patronage as well as a possibility for increased royal involvement in the private sector. At the same time, though, privatisation was clouded in a language that gave entrepreneurs and the private sector a more important role in the running of the economy: throughout the 1990s, it became clear that the state was no longer able to provide jobs for the country's graduates, nor quality education, which became increasingly privatised. Neither was the state the only provider of key services – such as telecommunications – and many other public services (waste collection, public transport) also saw the involvement of private, sometimes foreign companies. All of this was publicly endorsed by King Hassan II when he launched the privatisation campaign in 1988: 'The goal pursued through the coming operations is to give *these men their chances, to open the door of responsibilities, chances and risks.*'[68] The public discourse that accompanied the privatisation campaign resulted in a new set of legitimacy that Bras summarised as 'Nation, State, and Enterprise'.[69] Declining public investments, declining protectionism from foreign competition, resulted in what Deneoux and Maghraoui describe as a 'progressive reevaluation of certain dogma, such as the belief that government is responsible for maintaining minimum standards of living or that it has a duty to protect national industries against foreign competition'. Instead:

> New concepts such as 'individual initiative,' 'economic efficiency,' 'competitiveness' 'austerity' and 'productivity' entered the arena of public debate. The country slowly began to question its earlier belief in 'dirigisme' and 'Etat providence'.[70]

The other side of the coin was that the state was also increasingly questioned, especially the political interference of the state in economic matters. As a result, a dynamic was created in which an increasingly vocal entrepreneurial class rejected political interference, claimed its autonomy, and demanded in turn political participation. If it was to be responsible for the creation of the nation's wealth, then it needed to be consulted, subject to transparent rules and the rule of law, and ultimately participate in the decision-making process.

With the exception of significant numbers of urban riots, there are few political-economic events that are as crucial as the anti-corruption campaign of 1995–96, which led to the rise of the entrepreneurial federation CGEM. When a political malaise hit the country due to the King's failed attempts to create alternance, a confidential World Bank report on corruption and tax evasion was leaked to the French press. According to the most famous phrase used in one of these 1995 World Bank reports, Morocco was approaching an 'economic heart attack' if it did not change direction.[71] These reports illustrated that the private interests that were generated during the privatisation campaign remained unregulated and that this had disastrous consequences for the economy. During the 1995 opening session of parliament, the King announced: 'I read these reports and find painful their eloquence and numbers. The comparisons that are made prevent every person with a bit of conscience from falling asleep.'[72] Six weeks later, *Le Monde* published a report by the Paris-based Observatoire Géopolitique des Drogues, in which it accused the palace of complacency with Morocco's drug lords and of unwillingness to prevent the export of hashish. Morocco had become the world's leading exporter of cannabis. King Hassan was furious about accusations of being surrounded by drug lords and thugs, and *Le Monde* issues were seized in the country.[73]

The ensuing anti-corruption campaign dubbed the 'sanitation campaign' was different in nature from previous attempts at fighting corruption and contraband. Starting in December 1995 after the constitution of an inter-ministerial commission (Ministries of Justice, Commerce and the Interior), headed by the all-powerful Minister of the Interior Driss Basri, thousands of companies were inspected, high-profile trials condemned apparently protected businessmen to high fines and imprisonment. As Deneoux remarks, '[n]ever before had the regime engaged in such a highly publicised effort to "moralise" public life. For the first time ... the government's actions seemed to reflect its rhetoric, at least for a while'.[74] The result was that the prevalent failure to respect non-enforced legal stipulations created a mass panic in the private sector. After all, failure to abide by tax laws had been endemic given the absence of effective, public and accountable institutions. Everybody could be charged, the system of justice could be used to pursue private entrepreneurs who had ostensibly abused the rules of the game as defined by the regime. Consequently, public opinion understood that the state attempted to impose its rules as a reminder that the economic class had to obey the political imperatives of the regime.[75]

The sanitation campaign backfired. In a televised debate on 12 February 1996, the president of the employers' federation, Abderrahman Lahjouji, opposed the head of the anti-corruption campaign, Driss Basri, telling him that the campaign and the jailing of entrepreneurs did harm to the economy.[76] This was unprecedented, as was the fact that Casablanca's port activity almost came to a halt as nobody dared to pick up merchandise that may have violated some of Morocco's customs laws. The campaign had to stop, the regime could not be accused of damaging the economy, and some guarantees had to be found to prevent the over-zealous, political use of courts against entrepreneurs. On 2 March 1996 King Hassan attempted to find a compromise by insisting that the campaign served a good purpose, and that it would continue without any excess and within the rule of law.[77] Integration and acceptance of the entrepreneurs' importance for Morocco's economic future became more explicit when Hassan II met with a delegation of the CGEM, and declared that 'today we receive you to make you part of our care and expectations. We are part of the same team and our common objective is to face the social and economic challenge to regain Morocco's dignity'.[78] An agreement between the two conflicting parties was quickly found, and the position and importance of the entrepreneurial class acknowledged. The campaign ended as quickly as it had begun: businessmen who had been jailed were released, and the regime promised more independence of the courts and a revision of the judges' training programme (thereby acknowledging the lack of judicial independence). In turn, the CGEM was given the responsibility to help fight corruption, first by awareness campaigns among its members, and second by supervising the import-export sector.

It must be pointed out that this was not simply an incident of co-optation that targeted Morocco's entrepreneurial class. The CGEM's president, Lahjouji, became a very important symbol of challenge to the regime and the nascent independent Moroccan press celebrated his stubbornness and courage. His successor, Hassan Chami (2000–06), also led a more independent direction vis-à-vis the regime. In the summer of 2005, Chami severely criticised the lack of transparency and good governance in an interview with the Moroccan newspaper *La Verité*. Pro-monarchy currents quickly criticised him as too openly political,[79] and after the monarchy seemed to orchestrate an internal division of the CGEM in autumn 2005,[80] a fight for control over the CGEM resulted in the 'election' of Moulay Hafid Elalami in June 2006. He was the only candidate, a former director of the ONA and a reputed royalist. Since his election, he has led the CGEM on a course of non-interference in political matters. This earned him a place not only on *Forbes'* list as Africa's 40th wealthiest individual in 2014, but also in the Ministry of Trade in the 2011–16 government.

Taken together, the last two decades saw a significant mutation of the former ruling pact. The landed elite and its organisation, the MP, have lost in importance, partially because a rural exodus has made this group less politically significant. In turn, a younger technocratic entrepreneurial class has become more present, while a significant proportion of the ascending middle class has seen its social mobility significantly reduced with the limitations placed on the state's expansion. The dual challenge therefore has been how to continue a reform-minded agenda that serves the interests of the economic elite to modernise and expand, while at the same time containing urban underemployment that in the form of radical Islamism regularly challenges the omnipresent symbols of modernity and wealth. To achieve this, King Mohamed VI accelerated Hassan's free trade policy, culminating in Tanger-Med, a giant port facility that includes customs free zones. At the same time, though, he gave more symbolic value to poverty eradication, traditional caring for the poor, and small-scale income-generating activities. While Morocco resembles an economic construction site, the monarchical state's economic position has been reinforced while the monarchy's emphasis on mutual responsibility and participation has made it less predisposed to accusations of mismanagement and failure.

## 4.4 The INDH, free trade and the future of Morocco's economic reform agenda

As has been shown in the previous sections, structural adjustment policies, privatisation and deregulation have not had the effect of reducing the state's central position vis-à-vis the country's economic elite. This has been partly because the monarchy itself exercises private economic power over Morocco's bourgeoisie. This was the case even if the private sector does not seem directly dependent on the state. Royal patronage extends into the country's most important economic institutions; it is being reproduced in privatisation campaigns as well as in power struggles within the CGEM.

For this reason, the economic class has often embraced the political leadership's decisions without much criticism, accepting arguments about free trade that led in 2004 to a comprehensive FTA with the United States. This came after the monarch's previous commitment to open up trade with the EU by 2012. It can also be argued that the uncertainties and risks of a global economy and its institutions – markets, trade regimes and financial regulators – in which the Moroccan economy has become increasingly integrated, emphasise the state's managerial qualities and de-emphasise ideological conflicts along with questions of internal distribution. Even if the country witnessed rumblings within the entrepreneurial class as illustrated above, its ultimate integration in the decision-making process quickly defused any tensions and created an overall consensual approach between capital and state, which extended to relations between capital and labour.[81]

On the other hand, the country's overall socio-economic record remains utterly poor, and occasional 'success stories' in the banking sector, aeronautics and even in tourism remain deceptive. As major rioting in provincial towns such as Sefrou (October 2007) and Sidi Ifni (June 2008), as well as the socio-economic demands of the Tangier protesters and the violence among Al Hoceima protesters (February 2011), illustrate, Morocco's largely agricultural economy that employs almost half of all labour remains unaffected by increasing economic prosperity among Casablanca's elite. The price of basic foodstuff – bread, wheat, sugar and vegetable oil – as well as the availability of affordable housing in the cities has a direct impact on the economic welfare of a vast majority of Moroccans. In comparison, increasing exports of tomatoes, oranges, or joint ventures between Spanish and Moroccan enterprises in food processing or fishing – the latter involving high-ranking members of Morocco's army – only have a marginal impact on employment and wealth distribution. The modern sector remains more capital intensive in which a few employment possibilities are high in added value. Salaries that reach European levels diminish any 'trickle-down' effect. Tourism and Morocco's increasing geographical attractiveness for wealthy Europeans, especially in the towns of Marrakech and Essaouira, may benefit a small proportion of Moroccans. However, what has been felt more are strong inflationary pressures on the housing market. The booming real estate market may only give testimony to a parallel economy: construction, especially in the north, launders money obtained through the illicit drug trade as the country remains one of the world's largest exporters of cannabis. Hence, despite entrepreneurial dynamism witnessed in Casablanca's financial sector as well as in its 2001 inaugurated *technopark*, Morocco's human development ranking has consistently been the fifth worst in the Arab world – in 2014 only Yemen (154), Mauritania (161), Sudan (166) and Djibouti (170) fared worse.

Addressing the reality of such a divided economy, the King launched a major social programme called the National Initiative for Human Development (INDH) on 18 May 2005. Making reference to religious extremism, he explained that it has been *la misère sociale* that renders itself to such unethical and unacceptable political exploitations. While the political overtone was clear, two years almost to the day after the Casablanca attacks of 16 May 2003, the King's focus on human development also meant to respond to World Bank and United Nations Development Programme (UNDP) criticism of overall disappointing performance and divisions, referred to in Moroccan parlance as *Le Maroc à deux vitesses*. Hence his explicit statement that 'in the long term, My ambition … is to raise the index of human development in our dear fatherland'.[82] The initiative was applauded by all actors of society with great enthusiasm. Morocco's 'King of the Poor' was now focused on the 'human' and no longer exclusively on infrastructure development projects that may mean more to the country's elite than to its average population, such as motorways. Development itself was redefined to include the human, and no longer exclusively focused on economic growth. Targeting specifically 250 urban shanty towns and ancient town centres, *medinas*, as well as 360 of the poorest rural communities, it meant both to decrease rural exodus to overcrowded cities whilst increasing the standard of living there too.

The three more specific objectives were: first to 'eradicate the social deficit' through health and education projects, the provision of electricity and water, and the creation of cultural, sportive and religious infrastructures especially for the younger generation; second to 'promote stable income generating activities' whilst finding a 'creative' solution for the informal sector; and third to 'assist vulnerable persons' to enable them to preserve their dignity and to avoid them sliding into crime and social isolation associated with '*précarité*'.[83] A project-based, hands-on approach was to show immediate results, and national attention was virtually guaranteed by involving the King himself in many inaugurations that occurred in subsequent years. The INDH is what the King called a '*chantier de règne*' – an ongoing process that would define his reign and which required constant, not periodic, mobilisation and attention.

To this end, 1,104 projects were identified for the remainder of 2005 and MAD 250 million (€20 million) was allocated in the same year. For the period 2006–10, MAD 10 billion (€900 million) was earmarked.[84] Under the supervision of the Ministry of the Interior and local governors – the core of royal administrative control – local committees were established to select projects for financing, monitoring and evaluation.[85] Clearly, priority was placed on efficient control and quick execution. After all, the bias in favour of the Ministry of the Interior in contrast to local elected representatives reflects the ministry's superior resources and organisation, and is not simply political. Still, one of the INDH's possibly unintended consequences was that the Ministry of Social Affairs and the Ministry of the Economy were stripped of their core responsibility. Also, as it was to be financed solely from existing governmental resources, it diverted resources from other ministries. The King explicitly stated that no new taxes would be created, 'either for the citizen or for companies', thereby responding to fears that Morocco's wealthy strata may finance the initiative. Overall, the King emphasised that this project-based approach was not to depart from overall economic directions based on macro-economic stability, growth and trade liberalisation. In his words:

> even if economic growth is not sufficient in itself and even if its dividends are distributed unequally among the population and across the regions, ... this does not mean that the social inclusion aimed for can be achieved in a simplistic way, i.e. as a burden that is placed on growth. After all, it is growth that is both condition and the engine with which to achieve the desired social inclusion.[86]

Critical evaluations of the INDH by journalists quickly emphasised that the quantity of grassroots projects was given pre-eminence over quality. Projects that were underway in the Ministry of Planning, Health and Education were suddenly under the authority of the Ministry of the Interior. The state-controlled media focused on royal activities, which seemed to indicate that it was now the King who was initiating all that is social in the country. While it served to enhance the visibility of the state's social projects, it did not mobilise new resources nor was it accompanied by an evaluation of overall development plans and strategies. In order to fend off such criticism, a scientific evaluation committee was appointed and headed by an engineer and former minister of education, Rachid Benmoukhtar. Over the last ten years, only one public evaluation has been released by this committee in which the lack of progress in any of the goals of the INDH was confirmed. While the political means employed in the INDH were assessed as overwhelming, on the financial side the report observes more soberly that the MAD 14.6 billion project over 2005–10 represented a redistribution of a mere 0.4 per cent of Morocco's annual gross national product (GNP).[87]

While it is indicative of the sensitivity surrounding the King's project that the report was released in 2013, i.e. eight years after the launch of the project and three years after the period that it meant to cover (2005–10), it is also indicative that the observatory's first non-released study undertaken and presented to the King was one of different social strata perceptions of the INDH.[88] This reinforces the idea that a primary concern of the campaign headed by the King is that of public appearance. An internal audit was drafted by the Inspection Générale des Finances and Inspection Générale de l'Administration Territoriale, attached to the Ministry of Finance and Ministry of the Interior, respectively. It identified a lack of transparency and participation and proper planning at the local level, which had the effect of favouring ready-made infrastructure projects often without the personnel to run them.[89] Although it has been made available to the public, the report's content has received hardly any media attention in spite of the high-profile nature of the project. Meantime, Morocco's human development index has not moved, which in the summer of 2008 earned the UNDP criticism from Morocco's High Planning Commission (HCP)[90] and by the kingdom's official newspaper *Le Matin du Sahara et du Maghreb* for the way in which it is calculated. Not recognising recent improvements that 'all impartial observers recognise', *Le Matin* concludes that 'the way the human development index is calculated is completely wrong and absurd'.[91]

The INDH attempts to eradicate poverty and increase human development, defined as enhancement of people's choices. It does so, however, without re-evaluation of overall development strategies, and by making it clear that a redistribution of wealth through taxation is not an option, nor a questioning of Morocco's commitment to free trade. Free trade itself, often referred to with the euphemism 'opening' – *l'ouverture* – (which also has positive political connotations), has indeed become a core commitment. It is through free trade that Morocco hoped to boost sales in Europe and in the United States as it hoped to become more competitive by allowing foreign access to its own market.

Clearly, Morocco faces a trade dilemma, which is reflected in its internal production processes and capacity. The EU is Morocco's principal export market and provider of goods ranging from tissues, chemicals and consumer goods to machinery, oil and gas products, and wheat. In 2001, Morocco received 56 per cent of its imports from member states of the EU while its exports to the EU amounted to 73 per cent of its overall exports. With 33.7 per cent of Moroccan exports, and 25 per cent of its imports in 2001, France has traditionally been its main trading partner, even if in 2013 it had to cede its place to Spain.[92] The large majority of its exports to the EU are textiles and knitwear. Small electronic items (transistors), canned fish, shellfish, phosphates, citrus fruit and tomatoes form other important exported items. In most of these areas, especially textiles, knitwear, citrus fruit and tomatoes, Morocco is subject to EU quotas that have become more restrictive since the early 1980s with the accession of Portugal, Spain and Greece to the EU. With EU restrictions, industrialisation in adjacent areas such as food processing plants did not occur at a large scale and, consequently, food processing industries primarily serve the domestic market. For small consumer and industrial goods, Morocco enjoyed until the late 1990s unreciprocated free access to the EU market, but, as it did not have a comparative advantage in these areas, its export performance was modest. Consequently, with quotas restricting the exports in which it had a comparative advantage, Morocco has had a chronic trade deficit primarily with the EU, but also with its other trading partners such as the United States, Saudi Arabia, Iraq and Russia.

Boosting sales abroad has therefore become a priority and it became clear that an export strategy based on the results of the privatisation process needed to be developed. Meantime, as a part of the Euro-Mediterranean Partnership Initiative (also called the Barcelona Process) that the EU initiated in 1995, the EU proposed a new generation of Association Agreement to replace the 1976 Cooperation Agreement that had been the framework for Morocco's commercial exchanges and quotas with the EU, including financial assistance. Part of the EU's ambitious project was to create a Mediterranean FTA by 2010, and in its Association Agreement it proposed bilateral agreements in exchange for more substantial financial assistance programmes. These programmes were called MEDA, an acronym from the French *mésures d'ajustements*. They specifically targeted the private sector – as protectionist customs duties were gradually dismantled, Moroccan industries needed to become more competitive to face increasing foreign competition.

Morocco was gambling high, and King Hassan's personal belief in anchoring Morocco's economic and political future with that of Europe – going as far as applying for EU membership in 1987 – may have been the ultimate reason for accepting what may seem utterly unfair: an unreciprocated dismantling of customs duties and opening up its market to EU firms that have a competitive advantage, while accepting continuous EU protectionist measures in those areas where Morocco had a comparative advantage – textiles, food processing and agriculture.

The immediate effect was a reduction of state income through tariff reduction. In 2002, Morocco received about 17 per cent of its state revenue from customs accounting for 1.9 per cent of GDP.[93] Starting on 1 March 2004, tariffs on locally produced goods were lifted at a rate of 10 per cent until their complete dismantlement on 1 March 2012, while tariffs on capital goods, raw materials, spare parts and non-locally produced goods were completely lifted by 1 March 2003. In 2002, the loss in state revenues was estimated at €225 million, which exceeded by far the €142 million commitment for the same year under MEDA. Estimates put the loss for each subsequent annual 10 per cent tariff reduction at €50 million,[94] putting a hypothetical, cumulative loss of state revenue between 2002 and 2012 at €5 billion – i.e. more than five times the value of the entire 2006–10 INDH programme.

Two sets of questions about these measures' effects became the most prominent: first, how would firms producing for the local market adapt to new competition should international competitors decide to reduce their prices and sell more of their products on the Moroccan market? Would there be significant job losses or other adaptations such as an increase in informal employment to reduce costs and to face competition? Alternatively, would the EU's *mise à niveau* programme and Morocco's new entrepreneurial class increase its productivity, protect its own market share, and possibly be able to improve its export performance itself?

Second, how would the Moroccan state achieve a balanced budget if a major source of revenue was no longer available? Would it tap into domestic sources by taxing the economy, thereby potentially undermining its competitiveness? Would it reduce expenditure by cutting jobs or slashing social programmes? Would it sell more state-owned companies and use the revenue to buy some time? Or would it revert to borrowing and thereby delay the decision of how to adjust in the expectation that by the time a decision was necessary the Moroccan economy might have grown and increased the Moroccan state's revenue base, as happened in member states of the EU?

To give a tentative answer to the first set of questions, one may examine trade statistics between Morocco and the EU from the early 2000s up to today. Between 2001 and 2014, Morocco's trade deficit with the EU witnessed a five-fold increase from €1,228 million to €6,897 million. EU exports to Morocco more than doubled from €7,562 million to €17,787 million, compared to a low increase of Moroccan exports to the EU from €6,334 million to €10,890 million. A more focused analysis of Spanish–Moroccan trade further reveals that, while Morocco's export-import ratio with Spain was quite balanced with a cover rate of 0.94 in 2005, this rate deteriorated quite dramatically to 0.58 in 2012, before becoming slightly more balanced in 2014 (see Table 4.6). This indicates that Morocco's export capability has not been significantly strengthened through the EU's *mise à niveau* programme. Meantime, Morocco has signed FTAs with Turkey (2003), the United States (2004), and Jordan, Tunisia, Egypt (Agadir Agreement in 2004), again in the hopes of seeing its export performance increase. Although the costs of these agreements have been significantly less than the Association Agreement with the EU, and the potential benefit of attracting foreign investors to serve these markets a lot higher, subsequent trade with these countries has again increased Morocco's trade deficit. With Turkey, imports more than tripled from MAD 2,009 million to MAD 6,933 million, whereas exports increased less spectacularly from MAD 469.2 to 1,102.3 in the period from 2003 to 2007, adding to Morocco's trade deficit. The same picture can be drawn from Morocco's trade with Agadir partners: combined imports increased from MAD 1,873 million to MAD 4,514.9 million, whereas Morocco's exports only increased from MAD 797 million to MAD 1273.5 million, its main export items being paper and fish products. Similarly, in its trade relations with the United States, the United States could increase its exports from MAD 6,501.4 to MAD 15,740 million between 2004 and 2007, whereas Moroccan exports to the United States even declined from MAD 3,418.7 million to MAD 2,837.5 million, of which a good third were phosphates and despite an increased world market price for phosphates.[95] Meantime, some success has been reported from Morocco's telecoms giant IAM and its state-owned airline Royal Air Maroc (RAM), which have expanded activities on the African continent. Both IAM and RAM became majority shareholders of Mauritel (Mauritania, 2001), Onatel (Burkina Faso, 2006), Gabon Telecoms (2007) and Air Senegal (2000).

**TABLE 4.6** Moroccan trade with Europe, France, Spain, 2001–14 (in million €)

| | 2001 | 2002 | 2003 | 2004 | 2005 | 2006 | 2007 | 2008 | 2009 | 2010 | 2011 | 2012 | 2013 | 2014* |
|---|---|---|---|---|---|---|---|---|---|---|---|---|---|---|
| Exports to EU | 6,334 | 6,403 | 6,347 | 6,558 | 9,061 | 7,167 | 8,024 | 8,311 | 6,510 | 7,693 | 8,769 | 9,201 | 9,918 | 10,890 |
| Imports from EU | 7,562 | 7,782 | 8,141 | 8,876 | 11,770 | 10,401 | 12,274 | 14,332 | 11,924 | 13,599 | 15,168 | 16,633 | 16,804 | 17,787 |
| Trade balance | -1,228 | -1,379 | -1,794 | -2,318 | -2,709 | -3,234 | -4,250 | -6,021 | -5,414 | -5,906 | -6,399 | -7,432 | -6,886 | -6,897 |
| Cover rate | 0.83 | 0.82 | 0.77 | 0.73 | 0.76 | 0.68 | 0.65 | 0.57 | 0.54 | 0.56 | 0.57 | 0.55 | 0.59 | 0.61 |
| Exports to France | 2,543 | 2,505 | 2,450 | 2,409 | 4,691 | 2,383 | 2,460 | 2,506 | 2,142 | 2,410 | 2,683 | 2,865 | 2,882 | 3,193 |
| Imports from France | 2,821 | 2,720 | 2,807 | 2,876 | 5,570 | 3,189 | 3,503 | 4,224 | 3,455 | 4,110 | 4,436 | 4,074 | 3,884 | 4,249 |
| Trade balance | -278 | -215 | -357 | -467 | -879 | -806 | -1,043 | -1,718 | -1,313 | -1,700 | -1,753 | -1,209 | -1,002 | -1,056 |
| Cover rate | 0.90 | 0.92 | 0.87 | 0.83 | 0.84 | 0.74 | 0.70 | 0.59 | 0.61 | 0.58 | 0.60 | 0.70 | 0.74 | 0.75 |
| Exports to Spain | 1,187 | 1,338 | 1,550 | 1,822 | 2,052 | 2,388 | 2,920 | 2,765 | 2,340 | 2,682 | 3,078 | 3,060 | 3,437 | 4,018 |
| Imports from Spain | 1,468 | 1,639 | 1,796 | 2,115 | 2,175 | 2,529 | 2,979 | 3,568 | 3,007 | 3,416 | 4,110 | 5,260 | 5,489 | 5,800 |
| Trade balance | -281 | -301 | -246 | -293 | -123 | -141 | -59 | -803 | -667 | -734 | -1,032 | -2,200 | -2,052 | -1,782 |
| Cover rate | 0.80 | 0.81 | 0.86 | 0.86 | 0.94 | 0.94 | 0.98 | 0.77 | 0.77 | 0.78 | 0.74 | 0.58 | 0.62 | 0.69 |

Source: Office des Changes, *Balance Commerciale*, 2001–2007, www.oc.gov.ma European Commission, *eurostat*, ec.europa.eu

Note: * Trade recorded by Office des Changes concerns the 25 EU member states, trade recorded since 2009 concerns 28 EU member states, and source is eurostat. The Moroccan Office des Changes ceased to publish a breakdown of its trade with the EU.

Although it is difficult to assess the implications for job losses in Morocco's economy from these trade statistics, it is clear that the pressure on domestic market shares in the industrial sector has increased with the rising trade deficit. Even if official Moroccan statistics give evidence of declining unemployment rates, from about 13.6 per cent in 2000 to 9.1 per cent in 2010, these figures need to be taken with a pinch of salt and may be indicative of the rise of the low-paying, unstable informal sector. A conservative estimate by the Moroccan statistical body Direction de la Statistique put the percentage of the informal urban economy at 39 per cent in 2000,[96] while a 2004 World Bank report indicates that 'poverty and presumably inequality, and urban unemployment have continued to climb. The increase is disproportionately among the young and educated which register unemployment rates of 32 per cent and 27 per cent respectively'.[97] The most alarming figure about the informal sector was recently calculated by the Moroccan economist Lahcen Achy. Using statistics from the HCP, he calculates that 79 per cent of all jobs created between 2004 and 2008 had neither a written contract nor any kind of verbal agreement, compared to a mere 10 per cent that were written and open ended.[98] Morocco has been able to obtain capital only through an unexpected rise in migrant remittances and tourism that fuelled the largely informal construction sector.

It is therefore not surprising that Morocco's formal manufacturing sector made major adjustments when in December 2003 the CGEM managed to introduce a new labour code that reduced the rights of those workers who remain employed in the private formal economy. It restricted the right to strike and increased employment flexibility by suppressing long-term contract status after 12 months of continuous work, thereby extending temporary job status for a period of up to 24 months. Likewise, the probation period for new workers has been extended, no provisions were included for pegging wages to price increases, and finally employers were given the right to reduce the annual working period to 75 days without financial compensation.[99] As to safety standards, tragic accidents regularly make headlines throughout the country.[100]

While export-led growth is still far from being realised, the state resorted to a combination of new debts, continuing privatisation, release of public-sector workers, and broadening of tax base to finance the budgetary gap that tariff reductions have brought. The state sold another 16 per cent of IAM to Vivendi Universal in January 2005 for MAD 12.4 billion (€1 billion).[101] With external debts becoming internationally problematic, internal debts became a new resource for the Moroccan government. Internal debts reached 62 per cent of GDP in 2005, but recognition of this problem led to its reduction to 58 and 55 per cent in 2006 and 2007, respectively, partly thanks to the IAM deal.[102] Still, in 2007 servicing interior debts absorbed MAD 59 billion of the government's budget, in contrast to 44.4 billion in 2006, more than twice as much as the budget reserved for investments, which was at MAD 26 billion in 2007.[103] In addition to windfall revenues such as the rise of the international price for phosphates since 2007, up to $250 per ton from previously $40, and an $800 million cheque from Morocco's Arab Gulf allies, a more durable yet risky source has been internal taxation.[104] While tax revenues increased by 3 per cent of GDP in 2007 compared to the previous year,[105] the erratic, unpredictable way of collecting them may set Morocco back even further in the international struggle to attract foreign direct investments (FDI). As the Moroccan economist Larbi Jaidi criticises: 'One year, they milk the banking sector, another year insurances, and then it's the turn of another sector. Fiscal revenues are regarded a source that is collected whenever the needs of the moment demand it. This is absurd.'[106]

Reducing the government's share in GDP and budget expenditure proved more difficult, as entrenched interests made lay-offs difficult to realise. Towards the end of the 2000s, the solution was an ironic 'win-win' situation with entrenched, well-organised interests: financial incentives of 20 months' salary were given to public-sector employees who asked for an early retirement. In 2005, 39,000 state employees were thereby released from state service into early retirement, against an initial cost of MAD 11 billion, i.e. an average per employee of about MAD 300,000 ($40,000). To be released, an employee had to get approval from his or her superior, and show that his or her departure would not harm the running of the sector in which he or she worked, typically education or health care. Although the result has been a noticeable decline in basic state services, especially at the higher echelons of the administration, the government reduced its recurrent salary bill to MAD 59 billion in 2006, down from MAD 64 billion.[107]

While all of these measures may have helped Morocco partly to cover the decline in revenues that its FTA with the EU brought about, the rise in oil and gas prices throughout the 2000s as well as the unprecedented price hike in basic staples since 2006 due to the world food crisis brought these efforts to a standstill. As the government subsidises basic food items such as wheat and sugar, in addition to gas and oil products, the overall bill of the *Caisse de Compensation* increased dramatically from MAD 4 billion to MAD 40 billion between 2006 and 2008.[108] Given the volatile political situation and riots among the urban poor compounded by the Arab Spring, recent attempts at cutting down these subsidies were quickly withdrawn.

When Morocco signed an Association Agreement with the EU in 1996, it may have expected that in the long run the EU would alter its Common Agricultural Policy (CAP), considering its significant burden on EU taxpayers as well as EU expansion. A second consideration was to increase Morocco's relations with the EU at all costs, given the importance of Morocco's migrant community in the EU, the state's hope to involve the EU further in its development policies, and its overall ambition to attract FDI and European tourists to Morocco. The latter gained momentum when Morocco signed an open sky agreement with the EU, which liberalised its air transport. All in all, this could be exchanged for diplomatic support concerning its number-one foreign policy priority, recognition of its claims over the Western Sahara.

While the CAP has not yet been significantly reformed, and relaxed import quotas would mainly serve the interests of Morocco's modern agricultural sector, paradoxically continued EU protectionism served Morocco's largest export industry – textiles – temporarily very well. When the multi-fibre agreement came to an end on 1 January 2005, all WTO members including China were to be granted free access to each other's textile markets. The EU invoked the Textile Specific Safeguard Clause with which it limited Chinese imports according to specific quotas until 2008. Although this gave Morocco more time to adjust, the country's vulnerability in a global market that is increasingly dominated by low-cost Chinese manufacturers became all too evident in 2009 when Moroccan exports to the EU dropped by almost €2 billion from 2008 to 2009. This indicates that, throughout the 2000s, Morocco's own success in attracting foreign investors outside portfolio investments remained limited.[109] Both in terms of tax regimes and cost of labour, as well as in terms of rule of law and administrative transparency, international surveys regularly point to severe limitations.[110] Although Morocco's aim has been to capitalise on its geographical proximity to Europe, the cost of transportation and the timeline associated with its cumbersome maritime transportation system have so far not been to its advantage.

The development of the northern modern Tanger-Med deep-water port facility, the biggest on the African continent, together with the privatisation of its main cargo fleet COMANAV, was intended to remedy this problem. Not only did the Moroccan state invest heavily in this facility together with rail tracks and a high-speed train project connecting Casablanca to Tangier, but it also provided a free trade zone to simplify import/export free of customs, passed a regulation guaranteeing no corporate tax for five years and a reduced rate of 8.2 per cent for the subsequent 20 years in the zone, inspired by the Mexican *maquiladora* and other free zones across the world. The state even provided Renault with land, free of charge, to start its largest North African assembly plant at Meloussa. The French car manufacturer started producing about 100,000 vehicles per year until 2013, with an expansion underway to produce 300,000 vehicles, of which 90 per cent was to be exported to Morocco's many free trade partners. In 2014, Renault employed some 5,000 workers. The Tangier Free Zones claimed to employ 50,000 Moroccans in the various activities associated with the new economic hub. The same year, the Tanger-Med Port Authority reported total container trade of 3 million twenty-foot equivalent (ETU), compared to 4.6 million ETU in Algeciras across the Straits of Gibraltar. While the new terminal Tanger-Med II will increase the capacity to 5 million ETU, such capacity will need to rely more heavily on Morocco's export capacity, if its economic growth in logistics is not to depend on world trade and increasing competition from other ports in the Mediterranean.

In spite of such important and visible activities that meant to boost Morocco's economy, the balance of payment and trade statistics indicate that deficits have expanded. In addition to domestic debts, the Moroccan finance minister has continuously sought credit from abroad, recently also introducing Islamic banking to attract new funds. In a recent credit note, Bloomberg reports that Standard & Poor's still considers Moroccan bonds investment grade, yet at BBB– they remain on the fringe of junk status.[111] It seems that, for the time being, the economic balance of the country rests on the uncertainty of workers' remittances, which, due to the ageing, integrating and maturing Moroccan communities in Europe, may fail to keep up their commitment to support Morocco's fragile public accounts.

## 4.5 Summary

Beyond doubt, Morocco has been undergoing significant economic reforms to face the main challenges since the early 1980s: finding employment and revenues for its young and increasingly educated population. The legacy of its timid steps towards ISI, Moroccanisation and especially agricultural dam projects are still felt in all areas of economic activity: a well-developed rural and urban elite lives side by side with a large majority of an economically excluded and deprived population that feeds the large informal sector. Three specific problems, however, can be identified that seem to hamper more substantial economic reform.

First, all economic reform plans need to take into account that Morocco has a substantial agricultural population and a very important agricultural economy. Both in terms of employment and in terms of GDP growth, which have knock-on effects in other aspects of the economy, state expenditure, subsidies, etc., agricultural output is crucial. As the world was experiencing an economic recession in 2008, Morocco reported record growth rates of 6.2 per cent due to good climatic conditions. In agriculture, Morocco's dam project has not only had negative repercussions on water levels in non-irrigated areas, which have led to dried-out lakes since the early 1980s and a decline in its forestry, but it has also diverted resources away from economic activities on which a majority of Morocco's population depend for revenue and consumption: the production of staples. Modernisation of Morocco's traditional, non-export-oriented farming sector will require large-scale investment in, and education of, Morocco's poor and traditional peasants, as well as a meaningful reorganisation of property rights and land use. Although education and infrastructure such as roads may increase in the short-term rural exodus of a more mobile and educated population, it may also create incentives for Morocco's peasants to stay and to increase productivity, thereby meeting domestic demand and acting as consumers of domestically produced goods.

Second, educational reforms need to focus on finding remedies to the country's linguistic divisions and the low quality of mass education. From training to ministerial management, Morocco's education sector is poorly funded and equipped, and state employees have few incentives for improving educational programmes and teaching styles. Emphasis is placed on memorisation of a large quantity of information that is only useful for exams, without the development of critical thinking skills typical of more advanced education systems. The result is what Moroccans recognise as a large quantity of semi-skilled, polyglot-illiterate and semi-educated high school and university graduates. While it is impossible to extrapolate directly from trade statistics the reasons for Morocco's poor international competitiveness, education certainly is a core problem. Whatever dynamic the country's foreign-trained, young and well-educated elite in the formal sector illustrates, the reality of a large quantity of semi-educated workers and employees who work without any legal securities or formal contracts produces at best mediocre results across all economic sectors. Crucially, as Achy remarks, the large majority of informal economic activities puts additional pressure on formal labour and undercuts its competitiveness in the local market.[112] As to international capital investments, it appears clear that the high entrance costs due to large-scale royal economic interests remain an additional obstacle. In the absence of such large-scale investments that could take advantage of infrastructure and Morocco's geopolitical stable environment, Tanger-Med risks running below full capacity, thereby decreasing cost efficiency and losing out to Spain's Algeciras container port.

Third, all plans and reforms create two types of extreme response in Morocco's public arena: complete support or complete criticism, with the two camps being divided into pro-monarchical, often state-dependent elites and a small number of independent thinkers and, especially, journalists. This means that there is no critical evaluation among the decision makers themselves in which they may respond to criticism and critically reflect on their policies. When two large-scale development projects were launched in 2005, the *Plan d'Emergence* (industrialisation) and the *Plan Maroc Vert* (agricultural modernisation), the details were not made public. What restrictively circulated was a small number of PowerPoint presentations, which, not surprisingly, did not encourage a credible domestic discussion in either parliament or among stakeholders.[113] As illustrated above, even the high-profile INDH has failed to initiate a general discussion about what development should achieve in Morocco: on one hand, a co-opted published opinion follows the royal plan, while on the other independent journalists reject it as a public relations exercise by a monarchy in despair. Meantime, the monarchy's strong hold over economic policy, including export-oriented growth strategies and new large-scale infrastructure projects such as Tanger-Med and the high-speed train connecting Tangier with Casablanca, has led to an uncritical understanding that this should and must be the only viable option for Morocco, creating a Moroccan-style *pensée unique*. This may be fatal, as, in the process of Morocco's increasing integration in the world economy through trade, its complex economic structure remains misrepresented, its problems understated, and the outcomes skewed to serve the interests of the few.

## Notes

1 World Bank data, data.worldbank.org/indicator/NY.GNP.PCAP.CD/countries/MA-XQ-ZQ?display=graph.
2 United Nations Development Programme, *Human Development Report 2014*, p. 18, hdr.undp.org/sites/default/files/hdr14-summary-en.pdf.
3 Cited in Iván Martín, 'Morocco Wakes Up to Human Development' in *Mediterranean Politics*, Vol. 11, No. 3, November 2007, p. 437.
4 Matt Buehler, 'Labour Demands, Regime Concessions: Moroccan Unions and the Arab Uprising' in *British Journal of Middle Eastern Studies*, 2014, DOI: 10.1080/13530194.2015.973189.
5 The World Bank, *World Development Indicators*, Washington, DC: International Bank for Reconstruction and Development, 2005, p. 49; data.worldbank.org/country/morocco.

6 Cited in J. Harrigan and H. El Said, 'Economic Reform, Social Welfare, Civil Society and Islamists in Morocco', iicas.ucsd.edu/research/projects/dwds/papers/El-Said_Social%20Capital%20in%20Morocco.pdf, p. 18.
7 Cited in G. Sabagh, 'The Challenge of Population Growth in Morocco' in *Middle East Report*, March–April 1993, p. 30.
8 I.W. Zartman, 'Farming and Land Ownership in Morocco' in *Land Economics*, Vol. 39, No. 2, May 1963, p. 187.
9 www.hcp.ma/frmInd.aspx?id=0404000000&vara=10; Will D. Swearingen, 'Morocco's Agricultural Crisis' in I.W. Zartman, *The Political Economy of Morocco*, New York: Praeger, 1987, p. 162.
10 Kingdom of Morocco, *50 Ans de Développement Humain & Perspectives 2025*, Rabat: Royaume du Maroc, 2007, p. 19.
11 Zartman, 1963, op. cit., pp. 188–189.
12 Ibid., pp. 192–193.
13 Ibid., p. 198.
14 Ibid., p. 195.
15 C.R. Pennel, *Morocco Since 1830. A History*, London: Hurst and Company, 2000, p. 306.
16 Zartman, 1963, op. cit., p. 195.
17 Ibid., p. 189.
18 Z. Daouad, 'Agrarian Capitalism and the Moroccan Crisis' in *MERIP Reports*, September 1981, p. 29.
19 Ibid., p. 31.
20 D. Ben Ali, 'Changement de pacte social et continuité de l'ordre politique au Maroc' in M. Camau (ed.) *Changement Politiques au Maghreb*, Paris: CNRS, 1991, p. 54.
21 Daouad, op. cit., p. 30.
22 Ibid., p. 30.
23 Ibid., p. 32.
24 N. Akesbi, 'Evolution et Perspective de l'Agriculture Marocaine', www.rdh50.ma/fr/pdf/contributions/GT3-3.pdf, p. 98.
25 Haute Commissariat du Plan, 'Horloge de la population: historique de la population du Maroc par milieu de résidence de 1960 à 2004 au milieu de l'année', www.hcp.ma (accessed 1 August 2008); and World Resources Institute, 'Country Profile: Morocco', earthtrends.wri.org/text/agriculture-food/country-profile-126.html (accessed 1 August 2008).
26 Sabagh, op. cit., p. 32.
27 World Resources Institute, op. cit.
28 W.D. Swearingen, 'Morocco's Agricultural Crisis' in W.I. Zartman, 1987, op. cit., p. 160.
29 Ibid.
30 Ibid., p. 162.
31 Kingdom of Morocco, op. cit., p. 15.
32 Swearingen, op. cit., p. 170.
33 The World Bank, 'Cereal Yield', data.worldbank.org/indicator/AG.YLD.CREL.KG/countries/1W-MA?display=graph (accessed 3 September 2015).
34 Ibid., p. 160; Kingdom of Morocco, op. cit., p. 15.
35 www.academia.edu/3842991/Tractor_Industry_Outlook (accessed 3 September 2015); Ministère de l'Economie des Finances. Direction des Etudes et des Prévisions Financières, 'Note de Conjoncture No. 222, Aout 2015', www.finances.gov.ma/Docs/dep f/2015/NC%20222%2024%20ao%C3%BBt%202015.pdf (accessed 3 September 2015), p. 10.
36 Office des Changes, 'Balance Commerciale 2006', p. 167, www.oc.gov.ma/Publications/publications.htm#8.
37 Kingdom of Morocco, op. cit., p. 10.
38 Ben Ali, op. cit., p. 56.
39 A. Rhazaoui, 'Recent Economic Trends: Managing Indebtedness' in W.I. Zartman, 1987, op. cit., p. 145.

40 J.F. Clement, 'Morocco's Bourgeoisie: Monarchy, State, and Owning Class' in *MERIP Report*, September–October 1986, p. 15.
41 Ben Ali, op. cit., p. 57.
42 Ibid.
43 Kingdom of Morocco, op. cit., p. 3.
44 Ibid., p. 14.
45 Clement, op. cit., pp. 16–17.
46 G.P. Deneoux and A. Mahgraoui, 'The Political Economy of Structural Adjustment in Morocco' in A. Layachi (ed.) *Economic Crisis and Political Change in North Africa*, London: Praeger Publishers, 1998, p. 56.
47 Rhazaoui, op. cit., p. 145.
48 T. Desrues and E. Moyano, 'Social Change and Political Transition in Morocco' in *Mediterranean Politics*, Vol. 6, No. 1, Spring 2001, p. 32.
49 Rhazaoui, op. cit., pp. 142, 146.
50 L. Madi, 'L'Alphabétisation et l'Education des Adultes', www.rdh50.ma/fr/pdf/contributions/GT4-9.pdf, p. 311.
51 Ben Ali, op. cit., p. 64.
52 Y.H. Zoubir, 'Western Sahara: Political Economy of a Conflict' in A. Layachi, op. cit., p. 152.
53 Deneoux and Mahgraoui, op. cit., pp. 56–58.
54 G. Joffé, 'The Political Economy of Privatisation in Morocco' in *Moroccan Studies*, Vol. 1, 1991, p. 54.
55 Harrigan and El Said, op. cit., p. 1.
56 Ben Ali, op. cit., pp. 65–66.
57 For details, see Rhys Payne, 'Economic Crisis and Policy Reform in the 1980s' in W. I. Zartman and M. Habeeb (eds) *Polity and Society in Contemporary North Africa*, Boulder, CO: Westview Press, 1993, pp. 148–155.
58 Ibid., p. 155.
59 Harrigan and El Said, op. cit., p. 17.
60 Ibid., p. 15.
61 Ibid., p. 15.
62 Joffé, op. cit., p. 56.
63 Ibid., pp. 60–61.
64 *Le Journal Hebdomadaire*, 11–17 November 2006.
65 See, for example, 'L'Alaouisation de l'Economie' in *Le Journal Hebdomadaire*, 7–13 October 2006, pp. 20–25. For a highly critical account, see Eric Laurent, *Le Roi Prédateur*, Paris: L'Editions du Seuil, 2012.
66 See A. Boukhima, 'Les Telecoms Pris on Otage par l'ONA' in *Economie et Entreprise*, No. 74, September 2005, p. 36.
67 Forbes, 'The World's Richest Monarchs', www.forbes.com, 2010.
68 Cited in M. Catusse, *L'Entrée en Politique des Entrepreneurs au Maroc*, unpublished PhD thesis, Université de Droit, d'Economie, et de Sciences d'Aix-Marseille, Institut d'Etudes Politiques d'Aix-en-Provence, 1999, pp. 113–114, emphasis added.
69 J.P. Bras, 'Les Enjeux Socio-Culturels de la Privatisation au Maroc et en Tunisie' in D. Guerraoui and X. Richet (eds) *Stratégie de Privatisations: Comparaison Maghreb-Europe*, Paris: L'Harmattan, 1995, cited in M. Catusse, op. cit., p. 113.
70 Deneoux and Maghraoui, op. cit., p. 58.
71 Akesbi, op. cit., p. 117.
72 Royal Speech, 15 September 1995, www.mincom.gov.ma (accessed 29 September 2003) (now: www.maroc.ma).
73 G. Deneoux, 'Understanding Morocco's "Sanitation Campaign" (December 1995 to May 1996)' in *The Journal of North African Studies*, Vol. 13, No. 1, Spring 1998, p. 109.
74 Ibid., p. 101.
75 B. Hibou and M. Tozy, 'Une Lecture d'Anthropologie Politique de la Corruption au Maroc' in *Tiers Monde*, Vol. 41, No. 161, 2000, p. 38.

76 Catusse, op. cit., p. 278.
77 *Le Point*, 23 March 1996.
78 Royal speech, www.mincom.gov.ma (now www.maroc.ma).
79 See High Planning Commissioner Ahmed Lahlimi, 'Une Reaction Défaitiste' in *Aujourd'hui Le Maroc*, No. 945, 18 July 2005, www.aujourdhui.ma/couverture-deta ils37786.html.
80 K. Tritki, 'Patrons. La PME dans le Jeu du Pouvoir' in *TelQuel*, No. 191, 17–23 September 2005, www.telquel-online.com/191/eco_sujet_191.shtml.
81 M. Catusse, 'De la Lutte des Classes au Dialogue Social' in *Monde Arabe Maghreb-Machrek*, No. 162, October–December 1998, pp. 20–38.
82 Royal Discourse delivered on 18 May 2005 in Rabat, www.indh.gov.ma/fr/discours.asp.
83 Ibid.
84 www.indh.gov.ma/fr/programme4_2006-2010.asp.
85 Martín, op. cit., p. 434.
86 Royal Discourse delivered on 18 May 2005, www.indh.gov.ma/fr/discours.asp.
87 Observatoire National du Developement Humain (ONDH), *Evaluation des Realisations de la Premiere Phase de l'INDH (2005–2010) et Leurs Effets sur Le Populations Cible*, Rabat: Royaume du Maroc, 2013, www.ondh.ma/sites/default/files/documents/synthese_du_rapport_ondh_2013.pdf.
88 *Le Matin du Sahara et du Maghreb*, 18 July 2008, www.lematin.ma/Actualite/Journal/Article.asp?idr=110&id=95143 (accessed 1 September 2008).
89 Kingdom of Morocco, Ministere de l'Interieur et Ministere des Finances et de la Privatisation, 'Rapport de synthèse – Mission d'audit conjoint IGAR/IGF – Certification des comptes de l'exercise 2006', Rabat, December 2007, www.indh.gov.ma/fr/Rapports_Audits.asp (accessed 5 September 2008).
90 *Le Matin du Sahara et du Maghreb*, 13 August 2008, www.lematin.ma/Actualite/Express/Article.asp?id=96509.
91 *Le Matin du Sahara et du Maghreb*, 17 June 2008, www.lematin.ma/Actualite/Journal/Article.asp?idr=110&id=93231.
92 Office des Changes, 'Balance Commerciale 2001', p. 68, www.oc.gov.ma; Jalal Baazi, 'Échanges commerciaux avec le Maroc: L'Espagne détrône la France' in *Les Inspirations Eco*, 26 July 2015, www.leseco.ma/decryptages/evenements/34296-echanges-comm erciaux-avec-le-maroc-l-espagne-detrone-la-france-2.html.
93 I. Martín, 'The Social Impact of Euro-Mediterranean Free Trade Areas: A First Approach with Special Reference to the Case of Morocco' in *Mediterranean Politics*, Vol. 9, No. 3, Autumn 2004, pp. 433, 437.
94 Ibid., pp. 437–438.
95 Office des Changes, 'Balance Commerciale 2007 – Editions Provisoire', www.oc.gov.ma, pp. 60–63.
96 R.M. Alami, 'Le Secteur Informel au Maroc: 1954–2004', www.rdh50.ma/fr/pdf/contributions/GT3-7.pdf, p. 435.
97 Cited in Harrigan and El Said, op. cit., p. 18.
98 Lahcen Achy, 'Morocco's Experience with Poverty Reduction. Lessons from the Arab World' in *Carnegie Papers*, No. 25, Washington, DC: Carnegie Middle East Center, 2010, p. 15, carnegieendowment.org/files/morocco_poverty1.pdf.
99 Martín, 2004, op. cit., pp. 440–441.
100 *Le Matin du Sahara et du Maghreb*, 2 September 2008, www.lematin.ma/Actualite/Express/Article.asp?id=97511.
101 www.finances.gov.ma/pls/portal/docs/PAGE/PORTAIL_INTERNET_MFP/VIE_PUBLIQUE/…/LF…/desengagement_de_letat.pdf.
102 International Monetary Fund, 'Maroc – Conclusions Préliminaires des Consultations de 2008 au Titre de l'Article IV', 30 May 2008, www.imf.org/external/np/ms/2008/fra/053008f.htm (accessed 15 October 2008).
103 *Le Journal Hebdomadaire*, 28 October–3 November 2006, p. 52.

104 F. Beaugé, 'Le Maroc s'Industrialise et s'Enrichit mais Déficits et Inégalités se Creusent' in *Le Monde*, 10 August 2008, www.lemonde.fr.
105 International Monetary Fund, op. cit.
106 Beaugé, op. cit.
107 F. Ghannam, 'Le Départ Sauve le Budget' in *Aujourd'hui Le Maroc*, 27 October 2005, www.aujourdhui.ma/couverture-details40950.html.
108 Beaugé, op. cit.
109 See Fawaz Yusuf, 'A Structural Change Analysis of EU–Moroccan Trade Liberalisation and Economic Development between 1995 and 2010' in *The Journal of North African Studies*, Vol. 19, No. 3, 2014, p. 428.
110 See, for example, A. Boukhima, 'L'Incitation a l'Investissement: Le Maroc, Dernier de la Classe' in *Economie et Entreprises*, No. 74, September 2005, pp. 68–70.
111 'Morocco Lures Sharia Cash with First Islamic Bank' in *The National*, 9 March 2015, www.thenational.ae/business/banking/morocco-lures-sharia-cash-with-first-islamic-bank.
112 Achy, op. cit., p. 21.
113 N. Akesbi, 'Le Ministre a Dit Tout et Son Contraire' in *Le Journal Hebdomadaire*, 10–16 May 2008, p. 36.

# 5
# STATE LEGITIMACY AND FOREIGN POLICY

Morocco's 2014–15 participation in wars in Yemen and Syria, as well as the invitation to join the Gulf Cooperation Council (GCC) in 2011, may come as a surprise for those who believe that the country's foreign relations mainly focus on Europe. In addition, controversies surrounding a boycott of Swedish goods in retaliation for the country's position towards Western Sahara and Polisario in 2015 may be viewed as countering the country's policy of good neighbourliness, which it had emphasised in its relations with the EU. Finally, a bilateral French–Moroccan dispute over French judicial proceedings against Moroccan officials, accused of CIA-sponsored torture and other human rights violations, illustrates that the country's foreign policy evolved in a complex network of structures, short- and long-term objectives, which regularly shape the country's policy vis-à-vis other states.

Among the most influential structures that have had a long-lasting impact on its foreign policy have been Morocco's internal and external environment, as well as its colonial past with its geographical fragmentation into Spanish and French zones, including an international zone in Tangier. Morocco is one of the few Arab countries in which the monarchy in power today can look back to centuries of rule that included diplomatic ties with world powers. Morocco was among the first to recognise the US Declaration of Independence, and before that the Alawi Sultan Moulay Ismail proposed to the daughter of Louis XIV. In the colonial period, Sultan Mohamed V's support for the allied coalition against Vichy France, as well as his refusal to round up Moroccan Jews as demanded by the French under Nazi occupation, not only questioned its status as a colonised country, but also restored some foreign policy making. Ultimately, the Sultan's push towards independence, his forced abdication in 1953, and the nationalist movement's attempts to re-establish the Sultan's sovereignty, had the effect of making foreign policy a key policy area. With independence, the core question of Moroccan territorial integrity and borders became a key nationalist concern. From a Moroccan perspective, all territory that was unlawfully occupied by colonialists should become a part of the now re-created state.

International and national consensus as to what was to be considered 'Moroccan territory' existed on the Spanish northern zone as well as the international zone of Tangier. In turn, other parts that had historical ties to the Sultan remained disputed. The until now Spanish-held Mediterranean *presidios* Ceuta (Sebta) and Melilla, with their large Muslim populations, had been in Spanish possession since the sixteenth century. The Atlantic town of Sidi Ifni was also disputed between Morocco and Spain until the late 1960s. In turn, Moroccan nationalists' claims to Western Sahara, parts of western Algeria (Tindouf), but also Mauritania and parts of Mali remained contested.

In the light of the above territorial questions, it is the objective of this chapter to illustrate that foreign policy has been intrinsically linked to the country's post-colonial state-building process and pursued two main objectives. The first was establishing Morocco's territorial integrity by focusing on the Western Sahara as the minimum territorial claim after claims to Mauritania and western Algeria were shelved at the end of the 1960s. The second objective was to ensure economic welfare especially of Morocco's elites by linking the economy to its main economic partner, France, the European Community (EC), and more recently the GCC. These two objectives reflected the elite struggle inside the state apparatus between the nationalist movement and the monarchy, and the pursuit of state legitimacy. On one hand, the monarch ensured that the interests of his core power base, agricultural elites, were secured in Morocco's economic and trade policies. On the other, the Western Sahara issue granted him great domestic popularity, especially among nationalists at the height of the Green March in Western Sahara in November 1975, which initiated the 'reintegration' of the 'Southern Provinces' into Morocco.

As much as the Sahara issue has been a political opportunity as it reinforced the King's monopoly over the state apparatus, it has also been a liability. After all, the monarchy's claim to power is based on representing a diversity of tribes and ethnic divisions, including Hassani tribes in Western Sahara. This claim is not only historical, but also religious, based on the King's status as *Amir Al Mu'minin*, i.e. the leader of the Muslim community of believers, in whose name the Friday prayer was called all across Morocco, including Western Sahara and other remote areas prior to colonisation. Hence, a political division of this community of believers puts at risk the monarchy's overall claims to power, as much as this community's protection against divisions remains a core religious obligation of the King. King Hassan's appropriation of this core nationalist claim to the Sahara, most fervently expressed by the Istiqlal Party in the 1950s, consequently made the monarch's success or defeat a core criterion for evaluating his performance. After all, legitimacy has not only been intrinsic, i.e. a combination of past achievements and religious-symbolic references, but also performance related. As a result, the monarchy's and King Hassan's domination of the issue has rendered the monarch's legitimacy increasingly linked to success in Western Sahara, measured in military, political, economic, social, as well as diplomatic terms.

## 5.1 Morocco's domestic, regional and international environment

Morocco's broader foreign policy orientation reflects much of its history and geography, upon which Morocco's identity is constructed. The two most important Medieval empires, the Almoravids (1073–1147) and the Almohads (1147–1276), both came from southern areas of what is today southern Morocco and Western Sahara. Their control stretched through *al Andalus* on the Iberian peninsula, and, in the case of the Almohads, the eastern Maghreb as far as Ifriquia (today's Tunisia). Morocco's traditional ruling *shurfa* class claims ancestry to the Prophet Mohamed, and consequently, along with Islam and the use of Arabic, a significant cultural orientation towards the East is reflected in Morocco's foreign relations. With French colonisation came not only a closer economic and political interaction with Europe and France, but also the import of cultural goods – the most important being the French and Spanish languages. Even if French is not an official language, contemporary Morocco counts with 10 million the sixth largest number of French speakers, after France, Canada, Côte d'Ivoire, Congo and Algeria.[1] Due to this cultural orientation towards Europe, compounded by migratory movements towards France, Belgium, Italy, Germany and more recently Spain, Morocco has invested significant efforts to have close relations with the EU. In 2008, Morocco was the first southern Mediterranean country to obtain the status of an 'advanced' partner after its Association Agreement and FTA with the EU of 1996. This reflects its ambition to create as close a political partnership as possible with the EU, and to capitalise on its political and economic reform programmes that the EU is partially sponsoring.

Hassan II expressed this south–north–east orientation rather poetically in the following words:

> Morocco is like a tree nourished by roots deep in the soil of Africa, which breathes through foliage rustling to the winds of Europe. Yet Morocco's existence is not only vertical. Horizontally, it looks to the East, with which it is bound by ties of religion and culture.[2]

This complex nature of Morocco's foreign policy and identity also reflects the monarchy's own attempts at reconciling partially contradictory political currents among its political elite. One part of its urban elite looked towards European political and economic models such as representation, political party activism and market economies, which the French introduced in 44 years of colonial rule. However, the search for Moroccan national union in its struggle for independence made religion become a dominant feature. The violent independence struggle in neighbouring Algeria (1954–62), as well as Algeria's later adoption of socialist economic features based on achieving complete economic independence, fuelled anti-colonialist and socialist sentiments. In turn, the creation of the state of Israel in 1948, as well as the West's increasing support for the Jewish state, made pan-Arab thinking widespread, and led to the creation of the Liberation Army of the

Maghreb (1948–55).[3] More than anything, conflicts between Moroccan Muslims and Jews and the ensuing mass departure of approximately 270,000 Moroccan Jews[4] to Israel, France and the United States in the first 15 years of independence illustrated this. In the name of pan-Arabism, Morocco also organised the 1958 pan-Maghreb conference in Tangier, even if the concrete goal was supporting the struggle for independence in neighbouring Algeria.

Despite pan-Arab thinking, nationalism remained very strongly embedded and expressed by the Istiqlal Party. Consequently, the power struggle between the nationalist movement and the monarchy, aggravated by an even more fragile political base of Hassan II after Mohamed V's premature death, required that the monarch would not be out-paced by nationalist claims to Mauritania, the Western Algerian region around Tindouf, as well as Western Sahara. Such claims and the problem of colonial borders caused that, regionally, Morocco's environment was characterised by Algerian–Moroccan irredentist claims and rivalry, which reached a climax during the Moroccan–Algerian October 1963 Sand War just one year after Algerian independence. Moroccan claims to the areas of Bechar, Touat and Tindouf in Western Algeria were motivated by the French decision gradually to transfer administrative control over these provinces from Agadir in Morocco to Algiers. The Sultan's pre-colonial indirect control over these provinces as the religious authority added to Moroccan nationalists' belief in the legality of these claims. When the French transferred administrative control of Tindouf as late as 1952 from Agadir to Algiers, it seemed that France was preparing to stay indefinitely in Algeria as it was considering granting independence to Morocco. While Morocco protested and made its intention clear not to recognise this expansion of Algerian territory at the expense of its own, it could also not demarcate the border with France once it reached independence. The reason was that France demanded that Morocco stop its support for Algerian independence. In turn, the provisional government of the Republic of Algeria under Ferhat Abbas declared in July 1961 that it would open talks with Morocco about the demarcation of the border as soon as it obtained independence from France. In hindsight, the dependent character of Morocco's economy and military on France significantly reduced Morocco's bargaining power vis-à-vis the French, who were still hoping to create an autonomous French-controlled region in the Sahara, the Organisation Commune des Régions Sahariennes (OCRS). Consequently, Ferhat Abbas's promise to open talks about the border as soon as it gained its independence may have yielded better territorial gains. In turn, Algeria's 'promise' was motivated by preventing a Moroccan–French deal at its own expense, and was consequently based on the Moroccan promise to 'support the Provisional Government of the Algerian Republic without reservation in its negotiations with France on the basis of respect for the integrity of Algerian territory'.[5] In addition, in the political turmoil of the Algerian struggle for independence, Ferhat Abbas's statements need to be taken with a pinch of salt. After all, he did not represent the real power brokers from within the National Liberation Front (FLN).

Consequently, after independence a series of brief and disappointing diplomatic exchanges between Algeria's first President Ahmed Ben Bella and King Hassan quickly illustrated the mistaken premise of both countries' previous relations. On one hand, Ben Bella seemed disinclined to give up even one inch of territory that the young Algerian nation had fought for so hard – reflecting his own unstable power base that was largely based on General Boumedienne's border army. In turn, Hassan understood Algeria's U-turn as betrayal: after all, from his perspective Algeria had 'promised' to return Moroccan provinces after Morocco had refrained from a separate French–Moroccan border agreement. The fact that Morocco had significantly supported the Algerian revolution both logistically and diplomatically added to King Hassan and many Moroccans' bitterness.[6]

Amidst these political tensions, violence broke out around the border town of Hassi Beida and Tinjoub on 1 October 1963. Previous violent exchanges were blamed on Algeria's National Liberation Army (ALN) forces, Moroccan nationalists in Tindouf, and the FAR, and the link between regional conflict and domestic power struggles became increasingly clear.[7] After all, the revolutionary spirit in neighbouring Algeria was seen as a threat to King Hassan's conservative power base. When King Hassan's main opponent, Mehdi Ben Barka, sought refuge in Algeria, he condemned Moroccan expansionism, illustrating how the domestic political situation and regional rivalry were intertwined. A swift victory over the People's Democratic Republic of Algeria, and a return of Tindouf, would have helped the King to ride on a wave of nationalist sentiment and may have contained the increasing attraction of Moroccans by the Algerian revolution and its rapid redistribution of land left by the French. From an Algerian point of view, concessions to 'feudal' Morocco were not only a problem of Algerian nationalism and its emphasis on territorial integrity, but also of the socialist experiment on which the Algerian leadership under Ahmed Ben Bella had embarked. Comments made by Ahmed Ben Bella to the Egyptian newspaper *Al Ahram* in March 1963 that the Algerian revolution would not stop at its borders certainly alarmed the young monarch in Rabat.[8]

After four weeks, hostilities between Morocco and Algeria ended. When Moroccan troops came close to Tindouf, Algerian troops started shelling the Moroccan town of Figuig towards the north, leading to an impasse: a continuation of the war became too costly given the inability of both parties to defend the long border effectively. The OAU mediated between the two parties and brokered a ceasefire; both countries withdrew to the original demarcation line left by the French and promised to solve the issue by negotiations. Despite future attempts at negotiating the border, the dispute has remained very much alive both among Algeria's political elite and in Morocco. More than just a systemic conflict between revolutionary Algeria and conservative Morocco, with two opposing claims to regional hegemony due to their respective glorious past, both accuse each other of treason and betrayal. Ever since the Sand War, Algeria has viewed Morocco's nationalist elite as aggressive and expansionist, whereas Morocco sees the Algerian elite as untrustworthy and ungrateful.

Within this regional and domestic environment, external links to Europe and the United States served to bolster Morocco's regional position, and to achieve specific economic, military and diplomatic support. Due to the absence of oil and gas resources and its conservative monarchical leadership, Morocco did not embark upon a radical reorientation of its commercial and economic policies and continued to rely heavily on France as its main trading partner. France, in turn, also had an interest in creating a sphere of French influence through preferential trade agreements, cultural, linguistic and educational programmes (*francophonie*). For these strategic reasons, French–Moroccan political conflicts never had a long-lasting impact. Charles de Gaulle's severing of diplomatic links after the disappearance and assassination of Mehdi Ben Barka in Paris in 1965, as well as French criticism of Morocco's tarnished human rights records under François Mitterrand, ended quickly. As with France, Spain's 'rediscovery' of the Southern Mediterranean under the socialist Prime Minister Felipe González created relatively strong cultural, economic and political links with Spain. In 1991, Spain signed its first friendship treaty with Morocco, and started to view its southern flank not only in military terms, but also as a wider zone of interest.[9] Clearly, though, due to the Sahara conflict, conflicting economic interests, drug and migration issues, as well as Moroccan territorial claims to Ceuta and Melilla, these links were subject to political manoeuvrings of both Morocco's and Spain's political class. Morocco recalled its ambassador on multiple occasions when it felt provoked by Spain, most recently in November 2007 after a visit by King Juan Carlos I to Ceuta.

To these bilateral relations must be added the multilateral implications of Spain's admission to the EC in 1986, as well as the Maastricht Treaty of 1992. As trade, fisheries and migration became key concerns of the EU, the EU became Morocco's primary focus, especially as Morocco aimed at securing European capital.[10] Although Germany and Great Britain were only marginally interested in the Southern Mediterranean, an intra-European trade-off between the EU's eastern expansion and southern integration proved advantageous for Morocco. This has been especially the case since the EU attempted to redefine its position in the Middle East as a foreign policy terrain. While the Cold War had only a marginal impact in North Africa, the post-Cold War context opened some opportunities. Morocco transformed itself from a French backyard, or *chasse gardée*, to an 'advanced' partner of the EU, with its own geo-strategic importance for EU foreign policy makers.

US foreign policy makers have traditionally had similar geo-strategic ideas, even if the linguistic connection to France proved very resilient. With increasing US involvement in the Arab–Israeli conflict, Morocco could establish itself as a force of moderation and even encouraged diplomatic contacts between Arabs and Israelis, legitimising its role with reference to Morocco's history that was framed by the alleged peaceful coexistence of Jews and Muslims in Morocco's historical sultanates.[11] The Cold War-driven ambition of Soviet containment, as well as the need to have friendly states from which to launch military operations if necessary, also offered important opportunities. Morocco could present itself as a moderate, pro-

United States, Arab monarchy that could serve as a bulwark against pro-Soviet socialism in Algeria. Even if Algeria was not a Soviet client state, the fact that Algeria bought Soviet arms was exploited by the Moroccan leadership, and used as an argument for preferential military support, shipments and diplomatic support for its Western Sahara policy under the US Carter and Reagan Administrations in the late 1970s and early 1980s. The anti-Soviet argument could be turned upside down from the end of the Cold War and rise of radical Islamism and associated instability. After the Iranian revolution of 1979, Morocco could quite successfully portray itself as a bulwark against Islamic radicalism. Algeria's civil war from 1992 to 1999, the post-9/11 'war on terror', as well as widespread instability after the Arab Spring, all proved formidable political resources to this end. Likewise, sustained cultural links with the United States were to provide a counterbalance to Morocco's French links, as were Morocco's repeated calls on the United States to mediate in diplomatic rows, such as the Leila/Perejil crisis of 2002. In turn, Morocco became a primary recipient of US educational programmes in the Arab world: AMIDEAST, Fulbright scholarships for US and Moroccan citizens, and Peace Corps activities were supplemented by Hassan II's ill-fated promotion of English literature at Moroccan public universities, and Moroccan studies programmes at major US universities.

The result of this complex set of relations has been succinctly analysed by Messari and Willis by employing Steven David's concept of 'omnibalancing'. The concept emphasises how the country's leadership perceived Morocco's domestic, regional and international foreign policy environment, and how these perceived dimensions interrelate. In particular, omnibalancing pays specific attention to Third World leaders' perception of domestic risks, and how the external environment may help to overcome these.[12] Consequently:

> Morocco's alignment with the West, its relationships with Spain, and its open links with Israel can only be explained if mutual considerations and influences from one dimension are taken into consideration. Hence, Morocco's alignment with the West was due to domestic politics and domestic preferences … Spain's relationship with Morocco was mediated by the US more than once … And, whether under correct assumptions or not, one of the reasons why Morocco tried to befriend Israel was to attract US support on the Western Sahara issue. In all three instances, domestic, regional and international factors were played simultaneously in order to obtain some advantage at another level.[13]

While the domestic realm has been marked by the political opposition of the nationalist movement with its particular characteristics as explained in Chapter 3, foreign policy aimed at neutralising all potential opposition. This meant ensuring that the King became the guarantor of Morocco's national integrity as well as the promoter of the country's economic interests as perceived by the country's rural and urban elite. The three key areas of foreign policy – first the Western Sahara and the question of national integrity, second the EU and foreign economic policy, and third the United States and Middle Eastern conflict – directly or indirectly served to increase the King's and the political elite's control of domestic political groups.

## 5.2 The Western Sahara issue

Obtaining international recognition for Morocco's claims to Western Sahara can be safely regarded as Morocco's top foreign policy priority. As with Tindouf, and extravagant claims to Mauritania and parts of Senegal, claims to Western Sahara have been based on the nature of the Sultan's pre-colonial sovereignty, which was only partially territorial and more importantly religious, best reflected in the dichotomy and shifting boundaries of *bled el makhzen* and *bled es siba* before the imposition of colonial rule.[14] In itself, this might not have transformed the issue into Morocco's foreign policy priority, had it not been for the outspoken Istiqlal Party that fed the nationalist fever, which would have threatened the monarchy had it not acquiesced to some of its demands. In the 1950s and 1960s, however, more limited territorial questions, first and foremost Tarfaya and Tindouf, took precedence, as they seemed more urgent and feasible. After all, Western Sahara had been a Spanish colony since 1884 and not directly related to the 1912 Treaty of Fes that established colonial rule over Morocco. In addition, Spain under Franco was an unlikely negotiation partner, as became clear in the 1958 *Opération Ecouvillon* – a joint French–Spanish military operation that defeated the autonomous southern Moroccan Liberation Army. Much to the bitterness of the Sahrawi independence movement, the King appeared to stop open support of the movement in exchange for immediate territorial gains in Tarfaya in 1958 (and Sidi Ifni in 1969) from Spain. It can also be argued that an uncontrollable southern independence army of 'irregulars' was not to the liking of the throne. Its own attempts at establishing authority were already weakened by the Rif uprising in the same year, contributing to monarchical complacency in the 1958 French–Spanish joint operation.[15]

Instead of confrontation, a better strategy seemed to influence the United Nations (UN) process of decolonisation – in 1964 the UN committee on decolonisation recognised the right of the people of Spanish Sahara (as it was called) to self-determination. The potential of oil reserves in the territory, as well as Spanish Sahara's significant phosphate deposits in Bou Craa, added to Moroccan interests, especially that of the OCP. Morocco supported the principle of self-determination as it seemed obvious to the political elite that Sahrawis were as Moroccan as any other ethnic, regional and linguistic group that constituted the country's diversity.

Unwelcome evidence to the contrary came in 1973, when Sahrawi students influenced by Marxist-Leninist ideas founded the independence movement Frente Popular de Liberación de Saguía el Hamra y Río de Oro (Polisario), which openly demanded independence from Spain but *not* integration with Morocco.[16] When Spain conducted a census in a move towards organising a referendum under the auspices of the UN on the question of independence or integration, Morocco, together with Mauritania, which held similar claims to the southern part of Western Sahara, started an intensive diplomatic campaign. Both countries wanted to secure their share of the territory by stopping a Spanish-organised referendum on independence. This became all the more urgent as a 1975 UN fact-finding mission in Western Sahara found overwhelming support for independence, as well as for Polisario as the most legitimate representation of the Sahrawi people.[17] Morocco argued that, in international law, the principle of territorial sovereignty – of which it claimed validity in the dispute – took precedence over the principle of self-determination. In order to gain time and stop the referendum, it requested the UN General Assembly in 1974 to support its request to submit its territorial claims to the International Court of Justice (ICJ) in The Hague. For Morocco, the question was whether or not the legal ties it had with Western Sahara prior to Spanish colonisation of 1884 constituted sovereignty in its territorial sense, and, as the answer to such a question was most likely to be negative, it framed the question in the following words:

> Was Western Sahara (Rio de Oro and Sakiet El Hamra) at the time of colonisation by Spain a territory belonging to no one (*terra nullius*)? What were the legal ties between this territory and the Kingdom of Morocco and the Mauritanian entity?[18]

The aim was twofold: first, to prevent Spain from unilaterally giving independence to Western Sahara; second, to increase Morocco's chances of obtaining UN, and possibly Spanish, recognition of its claims if it chose to increase pressure on the ground. Given the evidence that it submitted, King Hassan believed correctly that the ICJ would agree that there were legal ties between the throne and the tribes of Western Sahara before colonisation.

The ICJ examined the evidence submitted by Morocco and Mauritania, and in its advisory opinion of 16 October 1975 it agreed predictably that legal ties existed, as well as to the fact that Western Sahara was not no man's land before 1884. However, as to the nature of these ties, and hence the dispute, it emphasised that they:

> Do not establish any tie of territorial sovereignty between the territory of Western Sahara and the Kingdom of Morocco or the Mauritanian entity. Thus the Court has not found legal ties of such a nature as might affect the application of General Assembly resolution 1514 (XV) in the decolonisation of Western Sahara and, in particular, of the principle of self-determination through the free and genuine expression of the will of the peoples of the Territory.[19]

For King Hassan, the domestic political situation became of paramount importance: two assassination attempts, in 1971 and 1972, and the consequences of purging the military rendered his coercive rule fragile – the key position of minister of defence was abolished. Politically, a leftist uprising in the countryside in early 1973, as well as an ongoing negotiation process with the nationalist movement, further weakened his hold over the country. However, the Western Sahara did not simply represent an opportunity to divert domestic political attention away from his domestic difficulties to a question of national unity.[20] Rather, the danger was that the military could suddenly act without his agreement and possibly against him, as in previous years. In addition, the nationalist movement would openly hold him responsible should he fail to deliver on the promise of national unification. Morocco's top military commanders still resented that they had been called back from Tindouf after the OAU negotiated a ceasefire agreement between King Hassan and the Algerian government in October 1963.[21] More importantly, perhaps, an (unsuccessful) war with Spain would have had disastrous consequences not only for Morocco's economy, but also for the legitimacy of the King as the guarantor of Morocco's sovereignty. After all, Moulay Abdelaziz's forced abdication in 1908 during the 'Hafidhian revolution' came precisely as a response to Abdelaziz's inability to guarantee Morocco's territorial sovereignty after the 1906 Acts of Algeciras.

King Hassan's November 1975 response to all of these challenges was what is considered in Morocco his master coup: according to Hassan, the ICJ's decision had legitimised Morocco's claims, and now he called upon his people to reclaim the Sahara themselves in a giant 'Green March'. Clearly, a direct military confrontation with Spain would have yielded uncertain results, an important lesson drawn from the previous Algerian–Moroccan Sand War. However a 'peaceful' march of unarmed men and women into the territory, facing the Spanish military and forcing it to withdraw would increase the pressure on the ailing Franco to make pro-Moroccan concessions. It would also increase international, and especially US support by illustrating the mass support that existed inside the country for the cause. Morocco's military would play only a limited role by secretly marching in from the north-east (should there be a military confrontation between Polisario and the Moroccan forces) and following the 'peaceful' march under the guise of logistical support.[22] The future of Western Sahara could then be discussed not within a UN-supervised process of decolonisation that included a referendum and the right to self-determination, but rather as a territorial dispute between two parties: Morocco (and Mauritania) on one hand and Spain on the other. As a result, the day the ICJ advisory opinion was made public on 16 October 1975, King Hassan called on 350,000 volunteers to participate in the march armed only with the Koran – hence the name Green March, referring to the symbolic colour of Islam. The march started on 6 November from the southern city of Agadir, to approach the border with Western Sahara on 9 November, when the King called the demonstrators back. The Spanish government had contacted the monarchy to discuss an agreement and it had called on its troops to withdraw in order to avoid any bloodshed. Although Spain, especially its colonial administrators and the foreign ministry, remained committed to the Sahrawis' right to self-determination, it was unable to confront Morocco given its domestic political turmoil.[23] Franco had effectively disappeared from the political scene on 29 October 1975 when Prince Juan Carlos I took over due to the *caudillo*'s illness, which led to his death on 20 November.

In the ensuing hastily written Tripartite Agreement of November 1975 after the Green March, Spain gave Morocco and Mauritania administrative control over the territory – not sovereignty – and Moroccan and Mauritanian troops moved in quickly to control their respective shares of the territory. Given the domestic context in Spain as well as the overwhelming support inside Morocco for Hassan's Sahara policy, in addition to US support for Morocco and doubts over Polisario's ideological alignment,[24] this might have been the end of a short, intensive diplomatic struggle. Morocco obtained the northern two thirds and Mauritania the southern third. In 1976 Morocco quickly organised a traditional *bay'a* between selected tribal sheikhs in the regional capital Layoune, claiming that this was an exercise of self-determination that granted legitimacy to Moroccan claims.

However, Sahrawi nationalist feelings had significantly strengthened in the previous decade, and Polisario received increasing support from Algeria and Libya in its fight for independence, no longer from Spain but from Morocco and its ally Mauritania. From the first day of Moroccan nominal control over the territory, Moroccan and Mauritanian troops encountered stiff resistance. As a sign of widespread Sahrawi support for independence, almost half the Sahrawi population went into exile to Tindouf in Algeria,[25] from where Polisario launched its political and military campaign. Polisario's military campaign was initially very successful, as its fighters could use their knowledge of the desert terrain to launch quick attacks, while they could take advantage of Algerian territory as safe havens from the Royal Armed Forces. Except for a brief encounter in 1976, Algerian forces did not directly engage in the conflict, but its logistical and diplomatic support was crucial for Polisario's early successes. In turn, King Hassan's fear of military coups had centralised the command lines, so that its troops on the ground were unable to move quickly or to obtain support from nearby troops.[26]

## *The struggle for recognition*

When Moroccan troops went into the territory, Polisario resistance led to a 15-year armed struggle and a diplomatic effort for international recognition that has not yet ended. No country has recognised Morocco's sovereignty over Western Sahara, even if some Western countries, especially France and the United States, have been quite sympathetic to Moroccan claims. In turn, Polisario's military and diplomatic efforts were initially very successful, even if these efforts ultimately depended on Algerian protection and the financial and diplomatic resources that Algeria was willing to invest in what is a highly ideological issue in Algerian politics – the right to self-determination. By 1983, 53 countries had recognised the state in exile declared by Polisario, the Saharan Arab Democratic Republic (SADR).[27]

In turn, Morocco had to make sure that it obtained sufficient arms supplies from the United States, as well as other military aid, to control the territory effectively.

While the Carter Administration was initially reluctant given the more general hesitation and limitation posed by Congress on sending arms into conflict zones, the Reagan Administration was more cooperative. King Hassan successfully argued that, as Algeria was using Soviet arms, Morocco was effectively fighting the Soviet Union. The need to sustain US support also made Morocco adopt a more moderate position in the Arab League concerning Egypt's expulsion, by refusing to join the 'steadfastness group' composed of Syria, Algeria, Libya and the Palestine Liberation Organization (PLO). This moderation, however, could not be at the expense of Gulf and especially Saudi aid, which started to support Morocco with sums that reached US$3 billion dollars from 1979 to 1987.[28] Hence, although the King supported talks over confrontation in the Arab–Israeli conflict, he insisted on Palestinians' right to self-determination. Consequently, Morocco built with the help of US advisers and Saudi aid a defensive ring of sand berms that from the early 1980s started to cover more than two thirds of Western Sahara and secured Moroccan military superiority.

While all of this secured US military support and ultimately Morocco's military success, the diplomatic struggle was more difficult, especially on the African continent. This was mainly due to the OAU's broad acceptance of Sahrawis' right to self-determination as well as the principle of inheritance of colonial borders as founding principles not only of the OAU but of African states in general. It was therefore particularly difficult for Moroccan diplomacy to convince the OAU that the 1976 *bay'a* of selected tribal sheikhs constituted an exercise in the right to self-determination, especially as the majority tribal group of Western Sahara, the *Rgibat*, joined the ranks of Polisario. In addition, Morocco could not convince the OAU that Polisario was not representative of the Sahrawi people, and even when it finally agreed to hold a referendum at the June 1981 Nairobi conference of the OAU, it could not prevent the SADR from obtaining a majority of African states' support to become a member of the OAU at the organisation's 1982 Addis Ababa summit. The crux of the matter was that Morocco considered Polisario a creation of Algeria, and it considered that, due to Algeria's support for Polisario, it was ultimately Algeria with which Morocco had to negotiate, not with its 'creation', Polisario. Clearly for Morocco, accepting direct talks with Polisario meant to imply that it was Polisario that was representative of the Sahrawi people, a claim that Morocco denied, as it contradicted its own claims ultimately to represent the interests of all Moroccans, including Sahrawis. With the acceptance of SADR membership in the OAU, the organisation's attempts at brokering an acceptable solution ended: Morocco no longer considered the OAU to be neutral and King Hassan suspended Morocco's membership of the organisation.[29]

## From referendum towards autonomy

On 26 June 1981, King Hassan accepted in Nairobi to hold a 'controlled referendum whose modalities should give justice to ... the committee of wise men [of the OAU] and to Morocco's conviction regarding the legitimacy of its rights'.[30]

He emphasised on Moroccan national TV in the weeks preceding his trip to Nairobi that:

> This Sahara is ours. We are not prepared to give it up, and though we are in favour of an agreement that can put an end to the conflict, we cannot allow any such agreement to be made at the expense of an integral part of our national territory ... We will not renounce a single grain of this Moroccan Sahara for which so many of us have sacrificed our blood and which has cost us so much money.[31]

Ten years later, in 1991, a UN-brokered ceasefire came into effect. In the same year, Morocco allowed the UN Mission for a Referendum in Western Sahara (MINURSO) into the territory to organise a referendum based on UN Security Council resolution 690. Due to the sand berms, Morocco had achieved complete military control in Western Sahara and it also occupied the southern third of the territory. Mauritania renounced its claims in 1979 following a military coup. From this position of relative strength, as well as two traditional pro-Moroccan powers as permanent members of the Security Council – France and the United States – Hassan II believed he could influence the UN referendum process to ensure a positive outcome. Similarly, Polisario's position was relatively strong despite its military setbacks. It had become a member of the OAU, and by the late 1980s more than 70 members of the UN had recognised its state in exile, the SADR. In 1988 King Hassan even met with top Polisario officials to engage in direct talks, even if from his perspective he was talking to 'Moroccan subjects'.

The UN referendum process under MINURSO was also made possible by significantly improved Moroccan–Algerian relations under Algerian President Chadli Benjedid. After the Algerian–Moroccan border was demarcated in the early 1970s, Morocco finally ratified the agreement in 1989. The northern border between Oujda and Tlemcen was opened after years of closure, which led to intensive cross-border trade and economic opportunities. The political events after Algeria's October 1988 riots promised the advent of political pluralism and with it the opening of a new chapter in bilateral relations. Consequently, Morocco believed that Algeria would cease its support for Polisario. Given Algeria's domestic context, overall positive Moroccan–Algerian relations appeared to be more important than an independent Sahrawi state. The 1989 Treaty of Marrakech that founded the Arab Maghreb Union (UMA) between Libya, Mauritania, Tunisia, Algeria and Morocco seemed to confirm this idea. Article 15 stipulated that no member state should allow on its territory activities of groups that might threaten the territorial integrity of another state. As Polisario operated out of Tindouf in Algeria, for Morocco this seemed to promise the end of Algerian support. Ironically, Article 17 of the treaty also allowed other African or Arab states to join in the future.[32] From an Algerian point of view, this made Morocco appear willing to accept the outcome of a referendum process, as there clearly was just one possible other Maghreb state that could join the Arab *Maghreb* Union, the SADR.

As the 1990s showed, however, the willingness to make symbolic concessions did not extend to realities on the ground. Although both Morocco and Polisario agreed that only Sahrawis, not the thousands of Moroccans who had moved to the Sahara after 1975, were allowed to vote on independence or integration, the voter identification process was contested and repeatedly delayed. The 74,000 Sahrawis registered by the Spanish Census of 1974 proved only partially useful, as not all Sahrawis who now lived in southern Morocco were included. Nomadic lifestyles as well as refugees from hostilities in previous years had led to significant cross-border movement. As a result, it was agreed that voters should include children of a man who was born in Western Sahara, as well as people who could prove that they had lived in the territory for six consecutive years, or 12 years intermittently, prior to 1974. Due to the difficulty of producing administrative evidence, an 'expert witness system' was put in place. Tribal sheikhs could give oral testimony that would recognise a potential voter. The Moroccan government would collect and present applications from Western Sahara and Morocco, and Polisario would collect and present applications from about 92,000 Tindouf refugees, who were to be validated by MINURSO officials.[33] In the process, Morocco presented 176,533 voters where only oral testimonies existed, of whom only a fraction were accepted by MINURSO officials. The 'expert witness system' was too politicised and lost credibility, as applicants often did not speak the local Arabic dialect, nor did they have any knowledge of tribal or regional characteristics that could be expected from 'real' Sahrawis. This led to Moroccan frustration and an impasse over the voter-identification process. It appeared that Morocco was trying to inflate the numbers of pro-Moroccan voters, causing likewise frustration among MINURSO officials. In turn, Polisario had a keen interest in not changing the agreed referendum option as it believed that it could win a UN vote if only the UN would exert meaningful pressure on Morocco to accept MINURSO decisions. However, the permanent members of the UN Security Council did not respond to such requests. Due to the threat of French and US veto, the conflict was never put under Chapter VII of the UN Charter, which might have resulted in international sanctions or the use of force to implement a referendum or its outcomes. Ironically, the absence of hostilities on the ground and the well-observed ceasefire since 1991 meant that Moroccan policies were not seen as a threat to international peace and security. The gridlock between Polisario and Morocco was compounded as Algerian as well as other countries' diplomatic support for Polisario continued, the most significant new recognition of SADR coming from South Africa in 2004. In the meantime, no other solution seemed in sight that would fulfil both the nationalist aspirations of Sahrawis including their meaningful right to self-determination and Moroccan claims.

As a result, despite UN efforts from 1991 to 2001, the Western Sahara conflict remained unresolved. With the costs of UN peacekeeping constantly increasing, UN Secretary-General Kofi Annan nominated former US Secretary of State James Baker as his personal envoy to consider other options than the stalled referendum process. Taking into account the often repeated affirmation by Hassan II that everything was negotiable except for the currency and the flag – i.e. the primary symbols of Moroccan sovereignty – there seemed to be at least some scope for a negotiated settlement that did not include a referendum with its 'winner takes all' implication. In fact, according to former UN Under-Secretary for Peace Operations Marrack Goulding, the high-profile nomination of James Baker as Annan's personal envoy in 1997 was intended to achieve 'enhanced autonomy within the Kingdom of Morocco'.[34]

## Policy changes under Mohamed VI

Domestic political changes under Mohamed VI, while insisting on the Moroccan character of the Sahara, appeared to facilitate a possible negotiated settlement. The particularly bad human rights record in the Sahara significantly improved with the dismissal of Driss Basri from the Ministry of the Interior in November 1999, shortly after Basri's heavy-handed suppression of Sahrawi demonstrators in the regional capital Layoune. Morocco also rediscovered local Sahrawi culture and language as part of Morocco's linguistic and cultural diversity. Hence, a Sahrawi TV station has been allowed to operate, and Moroccan official channels tentatively promote other expressions of Sahrawi cultural identity, despite its political sensitivity.

Amidst this policy of appeasement on the ground, Morocco promised it would propose 'extended autonomy' under Moroccan sovereignty with the aim of dismissing the 'unrealistic' referendum option altogether. In order to increase the credibility of this policy, the kingdom included more Sahrawis in its foreign policy making by reinvigorating a Council for Sahrawi Affairs, CORCAS. This came after both Morocco and Polisario rejected 2001–03 UN proposals for a five-year interim autonomy with a concluding referendum. In April 2007, after two years of behind-the-scenes consultations and extensive international diplomatic activities in favour of such an autonomy proposal, Morocco presented to the UN Secretary-General Ban Ki-moon a five-page document entitled 'Moroccan Initiative for Negotiating an Autonomy Statute for the Sahara Region'.[35] It outlined the organisation of a Saharan government that was responsible for day-to-day affairs including education and taxation, while the central monarchical state would continue to have control over security, religious and external affairs. After the deadlock over the referendum process, Morocco needed to ensure that a dialogue with Polisario under the auspices of the UN was maintained, as well as the MINURSO peace-keeping force. Increasing tourism but also worker remittances have amplified the necessity for Morocco to maintain its reputation as a stable country. In addition, Morocco attempted to influence the UN-sponsored negotiation process and discuss autonomy with Polisario, not the referendum option.

Morocco's initiative had the desired effect. The UN called for direct negotiations between Polisario and Morocco, and the United States stepped up its traditional support for Morocco. On 10 April 2007, the US Under-Secretary of State for Political Affairs Nicolas Burns called the plan 'serious' and 'credible'[36] one day *before* the plan was submitted to UN Secretary-General Ban Ki-moon. Not surprisingly, the words 'serious' and 'credible' to characterise Morocco's initiative also made it to the UN Security Council resolution 1754 of 30 April 2007. In June 2008, the United States adopted an even stronger position by suggesting in the words of the White House Press Secretary Dana Perino that 'autonomy under Moroccan sovereignty is the only feasible solution for the Western Sahara dispute'. In April 2008, after four rounds of failed negotiations between Polisario and the Kingdom of Morocco in Manhasset, New York, the formal negotiations ceased. Reporting to the UN Security Council, the UN secretary-general's personal envoy, Peter Van Walsum, concluded that 'an independent Western Sahara is not an attainable goal',[37] a conclusion that his successor, Christopher Ross, has so far failed to refute.

As a result, even if Morocco's autonomy proposal seemed to have softened the deadlock over the referendum process by giving way to negotiations, the positions hardened after four rounds of failed negotiations. While Morocco tried to ensure that Polisario no longer negotiated the process of self-determination, but rather autonomy, Polisario rejected this suggestion with a counter-proposal based on the referendum process. Even if the United States has sided more strongly with Morocco after a very well-organised public pressure campaign based on US fears of Al Qaeda and other Islamist groups operating out of an uncontrolled zone,[38] this has not changed the fundamentals of the conflict. On one hand, a well-organised and internationally supported independence movement continues to struggle for the right to self-determination, a right endorsed by the UN Security Council as well as by the ICJ on many occasions. On the other, Morocco has expanded its territory by military means and, while the nature of its claims have an historical basis, it has not lived up to its commitment to organise a referendum that would be an internationally recognised act of self-determination. Consequently, the deadlock over the Western Sahara continues as long as both sides believe in a 'winner takes all' solution, a position that Morocco unsuccessfully tried to sweeten by proposing 'autonomy' that would, in the end, only cement its own military victory, as well as by engaging in a regionalisation process that gives more authority to local councils.

## 5.3 The EU and foreign economic policy

While the Western Sahara conflict has been of primary importance for Morocco's state- and nation-building process, Morocco had to ensure that its economic ties with the EC (from 1992 the EU) remained intact. As discussed in the previous two chapters, the political ascendance of the rural bourgeoisie in post-independence Morocco meant that Morocco started to rely heavily on an export-oriented agricultural policy. Above all, this class's economic supremacy depended on the agricultural market of the EC. To this end, Morocco needed to maintain its privileged relations with France which also remained the country's most important ally inside the EC.

Political controversies, however, occurred regularly. Ben Barka's 1965 kidnapping in Paris by the Moroccan secret services led President Charles de Gaulle to cut diplomatic ties with Morocco in 1966. In the late 1980s, President François Mitterrand's increasing focus on human rights issues, and his wife's NGO France Solidarité's help to both Sahrawi and Moroccan political prisoners, also caused severe diplomatic rows. Still, migrant labour in France, as well as cultural links to France through organisations such as L'Institut Français, remained crucial assets for positive bilateral relations, and Morocco aimed at keeping French residents in Morocco (about 100,000) with its comparatively liberal residency and property laws outside agriculture. Ultimately, strong links with French companies through trade and investments were continuously maintained, from Vivendi Universal's share in Maroc Telecom to French arms supplies and credit facilities.

With increasing European integration from the late 1970s culminating in the Single European Act (1986) and the Treaty of Maastricht (1992), Europe also increased its protectionist policies. Due to its extensive CAP, the EU became self-sufficient in agriculture and a net exporter. From the early 1980s, this affected Morocco's textile and food processing industries, while the 1986 accession of Spain and Portugal to the EC diminished the quotas allocated to Morocco's agriculture. As Morocco had a comparative advantage in all these areas, it became clear that economic and trade integration and policies vis-à-vis external commercial partners had a negative impact on Morocco's development prospects. The basic power asymmetry was compounded by asymmetric trade relations: Morocco exports more than 70 per cent of all its exports to the EU,[39] while the EU exports only a small percentage of its overall exports to Morocco. Hence there has been little that Morocco could do about increasing protectionist measures, even if it managed to obtain financial aid that aimed at alleviating some of these negative consequences.

With Spain's accession to the EC in 1986, fisheries agreements became one issue with which Morocco tried to obtain financial advantages as the EC financial aid protocols remained modest ($268 million from 1979 to 1987).[40] Since independence, the Spanish fleet in Andalusia has been fishing extensively in Moroccan waters in exchange for financial compensation. Consequently, employment among Andalusian fishermen became dependent on Morocco granting access to its rich fishing resources, especially off the coast of Western Sahara – a fact that Morocco could use to exert pressure on Europe. As Morocco's economy was already so dependent on Europe as well as linked through labour movements and fishing resources, King Hassan applied for EC membership in 1987 to cement Morocco's European orientation. The application was rejected as Morocco was not considered European.

Difficulties with Europe were not only related to EU protectionism. By the early 1990s, France's but also Spain's public opinion had become more critical towards Morocco's bad human rights record, especially in Western Sahara. At the Franco-African summit in 1990, France's President Mitterrand linked French development assistance to progress towards freedom. Although France never applied conditionality to the Maghreb for reasons related to history and its 'special relationship',[41] the EU started to include a 'Human Rights and Democracy Clause' in all its treaties with non-EU members. This originally targeted Eastern European countries that sought EU membership, and resulted from the EU's strategic concern with stabilising former communist countries.[42] The European Parliament in particular became receptive to ideas of linking foreign aid with the promotion of human rights and democracy, and when Morocco's fourth financial protocol was to be passed by the European Parliament in 1992, it vetoed the financial aid programme. Despite all its diplomatic manoeuvring, Morocco could no longer downplay its human rights violations. In his doctoral thesis, the then Crown Prince Mohamed criticised EU interference with reference to the principle of self-determination:

> The principle of self-determination, by which people freely pursue their economic, social, and economic development, as well as choose their political system, was violated by the attitude of the European Parliament.[43]

The kingdom's increasing economic dependence on European markets, as analysed in Chapter 4, backfired and the EU continued with pressure in the realm of democratisation. First, however, the fourth financial protocol was quickly ratified by the European Parliament after Morocco cancelled its fisheries agreement. Morocco benefited from thousands of Spanish fishermen who mounted a pressure campaign on Brussels, as without a fisheries agreement they remained unemployed. Still, the subsequent 1996 Association Agreement, which accorded Morocco privileged access to the EU's agricultural and textile markets, was linked to the Euro-Mediterranean Partnership (EMP), which included assistance to civil society, human rights protection and, ultimately, democratisation. While the EU used the rhetoric of partnership to achieve cross-Mediterranean consensus, and refrained from imposing itself, the unequal trade relationship as well as partial financial dependency provided Morocco with enough pressure to become a 'model' partner of the EU. Funds allocated to Morocco through the EU's *mésures d'ajustement* (MEDA) programme almost tripled compared with the previous financial protocols, to about €88 million per year in direct assistance. Under the first assistance programme, MEDA I (1996–99), the Commission allocated €352 million to Morocco, while MEDA II funds (2000–06) were €615 million.[44] In addition to substantial loans from the European Investment Bank of approximately the same value,[45] Morocco became the primary recipient of EU aid in the region, which also included assistance to promote human rights and civil society. While Morocco's input in how these funds were allocated was limited under both MEDA I and II,[46] the EU increased partner countries' input in its European Neighbourhood Policy. As pointed out in the previous chapter, Morocco continued to decrease tariffs with the EU, and in 2006 it renewed its fisheries agreement after a five-year pause. Politically, it displayed an ambitious reform programme that culminated in the IER (2005–06), which publicly examined human rights violations under Hassan II and allowed victims to talk about their experiences on Moroccan public

TV. Not surprisingly, Morocco obtained as the first Mediterranean country 'advanced status' with the EU, after it had been a major supporter of the French proposal to create a union for the Mediterranean.

In order to understand all of these efforts to anchor itself firmly in the European orbit, it is important to remember that Morocco constantly seeks diplomatic support as it faces its regional competitor, Algeria, and a potential escalation of violence with Polisario. Morocco is willing to compromise on many issues with the EU, not only because it has no choice due to a structural trade imbalance, but also because the EU secures Morocco's financial, military and energy needs. In addition, even if a closer association with the EU has led to short-term financial losses due to the reduction in customs duties, as pointed out in Chapter 4, it may yield long-term benefits. In the long run Morocco hopes to see, if not an end to the EU's CAP with its restrictive implications for Moroccan agricultural exports, then at least an increase in its quota. In addition, remittances from Morocco's more than 2 million migrants in the EU are, together with tourism, the most important source of foreign exchange, and seasonal work in Spain remains an important source of revenue for thousands of families in northern Morocco. Politically, strong relations with the EU also help mediate recurrent conflicts between Morocco and Spain.

Spain's pro-Sahrawi public opinion, fisheries agreements, migration movements, Moroccan cannabis production, as well as the two Spanish enclaves of Ceuta and Melilla on the African continent, led to repeated and intensive diplomatic disputes with Spain under José-María Aznar (prime minister, 1996–2004). Morocco repeatedly understands pro-Sahrawi public opinion as reflecting Spain's official government attitude. In turn, the Spanish conservative party reflects a more anti-Moroccan public opinion, which in the past accused Morocco of not curbing illegal migration or drug trafficking for its beneficial economic and political effects in Morocco itself. After all, the northern Berber-speaking Rif region, from which many young Moroccans have tried to cross the Straits of Gibraltar, is economically deprived and an historical source of political opposition to centralised rule from Rabat. Partly fed by historical animosity, these rows culminated in the 2002 military standoff over the Moroccan-claimed Leila (Perejil) islet. While the Perejil/Leila crisis was mediated by the United States, it is clear that the preferential status sought by Morocco has also helped to limit the potential for violence between both countries.

## *Morocco's migration policy and the EU*

With two Spanish enclaves on the African continent surrounded by Moroccan territory, Morocco has become over the past ten years not just a country of emigration, but also a transit point for many sub-Saharan African youth who attempt to cross the border into Spanish Ceuta or Melilla.

With as many as three six-metre-high fences topped with barbed wire, deadly border incidents frequently raise ethical questions about the policies on both sides of the fence. In 2005, a border shooting by both Spanish and Moroccan guards left 15 dead among the migrants. Many more have suffered severe injuries or died since. Reports emerged that Morocco transported migrants back into the Algerian desert, leaving them to their own devices and sometimes death. Apart from such tragic events, Morocco has regularly flown migrants back to their countries of origin in chartered flights, not only adding to its financial difficulties but also increasing the number of those who are hiding inside the country and seeking an illegal way to cross into Europe. An estimated 30,000–40,000 irregular migrants live in Morocco, often after having studied at Moroccan universities, yet without Morocco granting these individuals work permits that would facilitate their integration into the workforce. Near the borders to Ceuta and Melilla makeshift camps have been set up, from where hundreds of individuals have regularly attempted to break through the fences into Spanish territory. Heavy-handed police raids on many of these camps have been severely criticised by the Moroccan Anti-Racist Defence and Support Group of Foreigners and Migrants.[47]

Given this impasse, Morocco recently adopted a new policy reflecting an African, Moroccan and European concerted effort to alleviate the crisis, called the Rabat Process.[48] First, it agreed to sign the UN Protocol to Prevent, Suppress and Punish Trafficking in Persons, and in 2013 it concluded a political agreement in which it accepted the readmission of individuals under the so-called Mobility Partnership.[49] Second, Morocco started processing asylum claims itself, a task that until then the UN High Commissioner for Refugees had performed. Third, in 2014, the state engaged in a large regularisation campaign, through which 17,916 migrants were offered legal status and residency. Fourth, access to the labour market and effective social integration were promised by the King in a landmark speech on 6 November 2013 about migrant rights, reflecting the new constitution's Article 30 by which foreign residents enjoy equal rights to Moroccan nationals. Finally, it increased its efforts at the borders with Ceuta and Melilla, not just by collaborating with Spanish border guards, but also by more comprehensively raiding the clandestine camps from where migrants have planned their risky and desperate attempts to scale the fences.

Whilst on one hand the new policy clearly aimed to show Morocco's emphasis on human rights and a break with its abusive past, it was also able to portray itself more clearly as a reliable partner in the EU's and Spain's struggle with clandestine migration from Morocco. It thereby limited an important push factor for migration towards the EU and Spain, i.e. the lack of any rights enjoyed by the sub-Saharans inside Morocco itself, whilst also trying to diminish the pull factors that have made Morocco one of the preferred transit countries, i.e. the lack of effective collaboration with the Spanish authorities. Furthermore, Morocco mobilised more resources to clamp down on the makeshift camps near the borders with Melilla and Ceuta, whilst also collaborating with the Spanish authorities to prevent the massive attempts to jump the fences and, if unsuccessful, to receive back migrants who were caught in between the fences by one of Spain's border control guards. Through the Mobility Partnership with the EU, Morocco gained access to funds in the area of €26 million, which the EU earmarked in 2014 for its 10th Development Fund to support migration policies in North and West Africa. In exchange, the EU furthermore agreed to soften its visa requirements for Moroccan nationals.[50]

## 5.4 The United States and the Middle East conflict

As Morocco's trade relations with the United States remain marginal, the primary aim of its foreign policy towards the United States is to obtain diplomatic and military support for its Western Sahara policy and potentially trade diversification. Morocco has traditionally viewed the United States in friendly terms. In the post-World War II environment, it perceived the United States as anti-colonialist and as a player that pushed for the principle of self-determination, which also helped Morocco obtain its independence. The role played by the United States in ending the Suez Crisis in 1956 supported this view. This positive relationship was helped by the historical nicety that Morocco was the first country to recognise the independence of the United States, and that Morocco has the longest lasting uninterrupted friendship agreement with the United States, dating from 1787. In addition, economic affinities between the ruling elite and Western capitalism immediately after independence influenced Morocco's decision to become anchored into the Western camp after a short honeymoon with the non-alignment movement, and even with the Soviet Union under the socialist Ibrahim government (1959–60). After all, the monarchy valued private ownership as much as Morocco's landed elite and urban bourgeoisie, and the reproduction of this stratum's wealth depended on its business links with the former colonial power. Quite naturally, Morocco's traditional *'ulema* rejected the atheist components associated with the Soviet Union and communism.[51] As a result, during the Cold War, Morocco became linked to the capitalist West, even if the Cold War logic of West vs. East alliances was of limited significance in North Africa. Yet, Morocco's relations with the United States were also affected by US electoral outcomes. The United States backed Morocco during the Green March, and even seemed to have pressured Spain into the Tripartite Agreement under the Republican Administration of Gerald Ford.[52] Yet, the subsequent Democratic Carter Administration was more critical of Moroccan claims. Initially, the Carter Administration even blocked weapons deliveries to Morocco, as they were used in the Sahara. In addition, the Carter Administration also remained unreceptive to King Hassan's argument that, as Polisario was using Soviet weapons provided by Algeria, Morocco was actually fighting the Soviet Union.[53] Still, after the fall of the Shah in 1979, the Carter Administration resumed weapons deliveries, which increased further when the Soviet argument fell on the more receptive ears of the Republican Reagan Administration. According to former US Ambassador to Algeria Richard Parker, 'the United States was going to show that it stood by its friends, even though it had reservations about how the arms package was going to be used'.[54] Military aid increased during the 1980s, and in Western Sahara, US military advisers were crucial in helping Morocco build the defensive berm in the 1980s that enabled Moroccan troops to gain the upper hand in its war against Polisario. In turn, starting in 1982 Morocco became a strategic partner for US Rapid Deployment Forces, when Morocco allowed US troops to use its airfield infrastructure.[55]

Partly to increase the importance of Morocco for US policies in the Middle East, Hassan II also pushed Morocco towards playing a mediating role in the Arab–Israeli conflict. This stood in contrast to its prior military involvement in the October 1973 war, when Moroccan troops fought together with Syria in the Golan Heights. The most important example of this mediation was Morocco's role in encouraging talks between Egypt and Israel that led to the 1978 Camp David Accords. Prior to the accords, King Hassan met with Israeli leaders such as Yitzhak Rabin and Moshe Dayan,[56] often using Moroccan Jews as intermediaries. Morocco never renounced citizenship status for its Jews who migrated to Israel. This overall moderate approach, however, was risky, as any controversial position on the Arab–Israeli conflict threatened Arab support for its Western Sahara policy. After all, Morocco's refusal to be part of the 'Steadfastness Front' against Israel and Egypt after Camp David in 1978 led to Syria's and Libya's recognition of the SADR. Throughout the 1980s, the kingdom depended especially on Saudi financial help, which was used to offset the economic repercussions of the Sahara conflict. Consequently, King Hassan remained a primary supporter of the Palestinian cause, for example by rallying support for the recognition of the PLO as the representative of the Palestinian people at the Arab League's 1974 summit in Rabat. After Camp David, Morocco half-heartedly followed the Arab League in its decision to expel Egypt from the pan-Arab organisation, even though it had sponsored Egyptian–Israeli talks that had led to the peace accords and to Sadat's historical visit to the Knesset in 1977. The difficulty was to strike a balance between the need to promote non-violence and dialogue, and the need to join the Arab consensus.

To find a way out of this difficulty, King Hassan increasingly emphasised his religious status. In 1979, King Hassan sponsored the creation of the Al Quds (Jerusalem) Committee of the Organisation of the Islamic Conference (now Organisation of Islamic Cooperation), which he chaired until his death in 1999. In this capacity, Hassan II was able to host a series of meetings on questions of inter-faith dialogue, which included meeting the Pope as well as high-level Jewish and Israeli dignitaries throughout the 1980s. His efforts at promoting peace in the Middle East led to the adoption of the Fahd peace plan at the 1982 Arab League summit in Fes, and King Hassan also coordinated a response to the 1982 Israeli invasion of Lebanon. As Morocco became more involved in the Middle East, King Hassan legitimised Morocco's role in fostering peace with reference to his religious status and, above all, Morocco's historical Andalusian heritage. He thereby successfully reinvented Morocco's past and justified Morocco's role by an idealisation of a peaceful coexistence of Muslims and Jews in pre-colonial Morocco and *al Andalus*. The fact that Morocco was home to the largest Jewish community in the Arab world before the mass exodus of the 1960s legitimised Hassan II's vision of a particular Semitic brotherhood.[57] Short of visiting Israel itself, King Hassan regarded 'the continuation of normal relations with the US as contingent upon rapprochement with Israel', as Abadi succinctly put it.[58]

Consequently, when the Cold War ended in 1990–91, Morocco's geo-political importance was not confined to its pro-Western status, but was also based on King Hassan's moderate position and his being, along with King Hussein of Jordan, a preferred interlocutor among Israelis, Palestinians and Americans. However, Hassan II was careful not to violate Arab consensus, and Morocco continuously called for an independent Palestinian state within its pre-1967 borders.[59] When the 1993 Oslo Agreement initiated the 1993–2000 peace process, Morocco did not normalise its relations with Israel, and it did not sign a peace treaty as did Jordan. Complete peace with and diplomatic recognition of Israel could only be established in exchange for an acceptable agreement between Israelis and Palestinians, i.e. a viable Palestinian state with Jerusalem as its capital. However, Morocco still seized the opportunity and it opened an economic liaison office in both Gaza and Tel Aviv, which temporarily ended its diplomatic boycott. To further boost its role as a pragmatic peace maker, Hassan II together with his Jewish adviser, André Azoulay, sponsored the first Arab–Israeli economic forum, held in Casablanca in 1994, which was co-chaired by US President Bill Clinton and Russian President Boris Yeltzin. However, with the second Intifada and the breakdown of the peace process in 2000, Morocco closed its liaison office.

While Morocco's Middle East policy was related to its need to secure US military and diplomatic aid in Western Sahara, additional policies aimed at reinforcing its alliance with the United States and Gulf monarchies. In 1991, Morocco supported the US-led coalition against Iraq's occupation of Kuwait despite strong domestic opposition, and it even sent combat troops to its main Middle Eastern ally, Saudi Arabia. Throughout the 1990s, Morocco was able to capitalise on the rise of Islamist movements, especially in Algeria, Sudan, Lebanon and Egypt. US apprehension of seeing a rise in hostile, anti-US Islamist governments rendered the Moroccan monarchy a likely candidate for continuing support. Morocco's domestic reconciliation process, which culminated in both the appointment of the Youssoufi government of 1998, as well as in the IER in 2005, also had the effect of promoting Morocco as a model of Arab democracy. After 9/11 and the Bush Administration's increased focus on democracy issues in the Arab world, together with the Middle East Partnership Initiative (MEPI), this became even more valuable.

Despite Morocco's critical position concerning the US invasion of Iraq, as well as its criticism of Israeli military action against Palestinians during the second Intifida, Morocco allowed the United States to play an increasing role in domestic political issues, which led to contradictory consequences. In 2006, a controversial liberticidal law that aimed at regulating survey work was shelved after the intervention of the US Embassy. In turn, the United States was also able to use Moroccan prisons in order to interrogate some of its prisoners using techniques that are illegal on US territory.[60] In addition, in 2004 the Moroccan government signed an

FTA with the United States, the second FTA that the United States had signed with an Arab state. It was the first in a series of FTAs (Oman and Bahrain followed) that became the economic underpinning of the Bush Administration's Middle East policy. The United States became more active in the Sahara dispute. In 2006, it brokered an agreement between Morocco and Polisario for the release of some 400 Moroccan prisoners of war who were still kept in Tindouf. In addition, while the United States has been critical of Moroccan delaying tactics about the implementation of the referendum in Western Sahara throughout the 1990s, it appreciated Morocco's 2007 autonomy plan and US President George W. Bush wrote in a letter to King Mohamed VI that 'substantial autonomy under Moroccan sovereignty is the only possible solution to the dispute over the Sahara and an independent state on that territory is not a realistic option'.[61]

While US President Barack Obama appears more cautious in extending US support and prefers the UN to settle the dispute with a view to alleviating the suffering of the Sahrawi people in another letter to King Mohamed VI,[62] the fact that 172 members of Congress supported Moroccan diplomatic efforts illustrates that Morocco succeeded in convincing the United States that an independent state in Western Sahara would be a security risk in the Maghreb due to alleged Al Qaeda and other terrorist links.[63] The US–Moroccan strategic partnership was compounded by a multi-billion-dollar arms deal of F-16 fighter planes. After Morocco's 2004 admission as a major non-NATO (North Atlantic Treaty Organization) ally, this ensured that Morocco enjoyed strategic parity with Algeria.

## 5.5 Moroccan foreign policy after the Arab Spring

When the Arab Spring rocked the Arab world and the King issued a constitutional project that resulted in a new Islamist PJD government, Morocco could count on multiple sources of support for its revamped democratic façade that could stand as a model for 'democratic' evolution and stability. In a speech to the Moroccan parliament in April 2013, French President François Hollande declared that 'every day, your country takes decisive steps towards democracy', praising the new constitution's emphasis on minority and women's rights. Given the French involvement in Mali and rising security concerns with respect to Islamic militant groups operating from the Sahel area in the aftermath of the 2011 disintegration of the Libyan state, France reiterated its support for Morocco's Western Sahara policy and autonomy proposals.[64] Together with Morocco's increasing cooperation with the EU concerning migration, as explained above, the country's strategic value has been further increased from French and European perspectives.

Similarly, support for stable government in North Africa has been crucial for the conservative governments in the Gulf. The more the three countries of Saudi Arabia, Qatar and the United Arab Emirates embarked on a new interventionist policy in key Arab countries such as Egypt, Libya, Syria, Iraq and Yemen, the more it also needed support for these policies from Arab allies. Driven by the historical alliance between Morocco and Saudi Arabia, part of which was the participation of Moroccan forces in the defence of Saudi Arabia during Operation Desert Storm in 1991, Moroccan forces have further participated in Saudi-led military efforts against ISIS as well as in the Saudi-led alliance against Houthi rebel groups in Yemen. While the GCC offer of membership to Morocco and Jordan was not seriously followed up by Morocco or the GCC, given the geographical realities, meetings between King Mohamed and various GCC heads of state became frequent, especially as Morocco could attract considerable Gulf interest as a preferred tourist destination, especially among Gulf royal families. The current relationship between the countries could furthermore easily develop into investment opportunities, such as the Rabat waterfront project, which is a landmark $2 billion investment by Dubai Holding.

In spite of such opportunities, a key challenge arose with the election of the Islamist-dominated PJD government under Abelilah Benkirane, with respect to Morocco's relationship with Egypt. After all, the Moroccan PJD party shared key affinities with the Muslim Brotherhood and the elected President Mohamed Morsi. This was all the more critical in the first PJD government when the Ministry of Foreign Affairs was headed by PJD politician Saad Eddine Othmani. When Morsi was removed from power, the head of the Istiqlal Party, which had left the coalition government, called for Benkirane to step down 'like his Brotherhood brother Mohamed Morsi'.[65] However, as discussed in Chapter 3, the monarchy never left the partisan foreign minister in charge of foreign relations and instead relegated important functions to the royal cabinet, as well as the two advisers to Saad Eddine Othmani. The King has managed the key strategic orientation of the state with respect to regional and international politics himself, allowing partisan politicians to fulfil only a ceremonial function.

## 5.6 Summary

Moroccan foreign policy remains primarily driven by its ambition to obtain international, i.e. UN recognition for its sovereignty over Western Sahara. The issue has its origins in the complexity of defining what sovereignty means in the post-colonial context. While this is a necessary condition that helps explain the issue's importance, it is not sufficient. Equally important explanatory variables have been the pressure that nationalist parties could mount in the 1970s, as well as the internal political fragility following the 1971–72 coup attempts. Consequently, Morocco has not only invested financial and military sources into success, but has also sacrificed relations with Algeria as well as the African Union (the successor organisation to the OAU) over their support of the Sahrawis' right to self-determination.

As illustrated in this chapter, other foreign policy areas, notably towards the Arab–Israeli conflict, have also been conditioned by the primary objective of obtaining diplomatic advantages in its struggle over the Sahara. This was particularly true for US support, as Morocco's strategic position in North-West Africa and its status as a former French colony made it only marginally important for US policy makers. In turn, Morocco's relations with the EU, while threatened by

Moroccan–Spanish nationalist rivalry and territorial claims, were secured by France's ambition to preserve as much of a special relationship with its former French colonies in the Maghreb as possible. In spite of this, Morocco's margins for manoeuvre remained fairly limited, given its *de facto* dependency on trade relations with the EU. Consequently, Morocco's relations with the EU required concessions from Morocco in the area of human rights in the early 1990s, but as pointed out in Chapter 3, this also corresponded to domestic requirements. Both Hassan II and Mohamed VI were able to strengthen their rule domestically with an increased state-led discourse on human rights. From this resulted Morocco's forthcoming attitude towards political reforms all through the 1990s and 2000s, culminating in the 2011 constitutional reform. Interestingly, the United States' increasing focus on democratisation issues with the Bush Administration's MEPI programme, which continued under the Obama Administration as part of its policy to combat Middle Eastern terrorism, strengthened Morocco's positive image, as it had already engaged in a multitude of reforms in its partnership with the EU. This is despite the fact that the state-led discourse on political reform has successfully excluded the question of democracy. The Bush Administration's aspirations to sign FTAs with Middle Eastern states and its desire to have terrorism suspects interrogated outside US territory were successfully traded for open support for Morocco's reforms and, especially, its 2007 autonomy proposal for the Western Sahara.

Accelerated instability in much of the Middle East since the 2011 uprisings, especially in countries that have experienced revolts against their autocratic rulers, such as Egypt, Libya and Syria, have further strengthened the foreign support that the Moroccan regime enjoys. Morocco has not only proven to be a bulwark against radical Islamism, as it had been in the 1990s, but also against deep-rooted and chronic political instability, which characterised many of its neighbours. It has furthermore been able to capitalise on being able to help the EU to limit the migration flows to Ceuta and Melilla, whilst also supporting, diplomatically and militarily, its Gulf partners, which in turn provide financial assistance and support to Morocco's primary foreign policy priority – its claim to Western Sahara.

After so much effort and with all the support that Morocco has been able to generate, its willingness to make meaningful concessions to Sahrawis remains very limited. In addition to its military superiority on the ground, this unwillingness is likely to continue as the contemporary regional context ensures that its main international partners will avoid risking any political instability in one of the rare Arab countries that appear stable and continue to evolve positively. Although the UN has often been blamed for accepting stalemate and, in the case of Ban Ki-moon's special envoy to Western Sahara, Peter Van Walsum, pro-Moroccan partiality, it has been Morocco's allies inside the UN Security Council that have blocked any meaningful pressure that might resolve the conflict.

## Notes

1 *Le Soir*, 16 October 2008.

2 Hassan II, *The Challenge*, London: Macmillan, 1978, p. 169, cited in M.J. Willis and N. Messari, 'Analyzing Moroccan Foreign Policy and Relations with Europe' in G. Nonneman (ed.) *Analyzing Middle East Foreign Policies and the Relationship with Europe*, Abingdon, Oxon.: Routledge, 2005, p. 60.
3 See D. Djerbal (ed.), *L'Armée de Libération du Maghreb 1948–1955*, Algiers: Fondation Mohamed Boudiaf, 2004.
4 B. Maddy-Weitzman, 'Israel and Morocco: A Special Relationship' in *The Maghreb Review*, Vol. 21, No. 1–2, 1996, p. 37.
5 T. Hodges, *Western Sahara: The Roots of a Desert War*, Westport: Lawrence Hill, 1983, p. 92.
6 J. Damis, 'The Western Sahara Conflict as a Source of Regional Conflict in North Africa' in Halim Barakat (ed.) *Contemporary North Africa: Issues of Development and Integration*, Kent: Croom Helm, 1985, pp. 140–141; Hodges, op. cit., p. 93.
7 For an Algerian account, see M. Bennoune and A. El-Kenz, *Le Hasard et l'Histoire. Entretiens avec Belaid Abdesselam, Tome I*, Algiers: ENAG Editions, 1990, pp. 197–206.
8 Hodges, op. cit., p. 93.
9 R. Gillespie, *Spain and the Mediterranean*, Basingstoke: Macmillan, 2000, pp. 42–77.
10 See G. White, *A Comparative Political Economy of Tunisia and Morocco*, Albany, NY: State University of New York Press, 2001, pp. 145–171.
11 See Hassan II, *La Memoire d'un Roi. Entretiens avec Eric Laurent*, Paris: Librairie Plon, 1993, pp. 256–257.
12 S.R. David, 'Explaining Third World Alignment' in *World Politics*, Vol. 43, No. 2, January 1991, pp. 238–242.
13 Willis and Messari, op. cit., p. 44.
14 A. Maghraoui, 'Ambiguities of Sovereignty: Morocco, The Hague and the Western Sahara Dispute' in *Mediterranean Politics*, Vol. 8, No. 1, Spring 2003, pp. 113–126.
15 Hodges, op. cit., p. 88.
16 J. Damis, 'King Hassan and the Western Sahara' in *The Maghreb Review*, Vol. 25, No. 1–2, 2000, pp. 13–20.
17 T. Shelley, *Endgame in the Western Sahara. What Future for Africa's Last Colony*? London and New York: Zed Books, 2004, p. 171.
18 International Court of Justice, 'WESTERN SAHARA – Advisory Opinion of 16 October 1975', www.icj-cij.org/docket/index.php?sum=323&code=sa&p1=3&p2=4&case=61&k=69&p3=5 (accessed 20 June 2007).
19 Ibid.
20 Hodges, op. cit., pp. 174–188.
21 Damis, 1985, op. cit., p. 141.
22 J. Mundy, 'Thirty Years of Conflict: How the US and Morocco Seized the Spanish Sahara' in *Le Monde Diplomatique*, January 2006, English edition, mondediplo.com/2006/01/12asahara (accessed 10 October 2007).
23 Ibid.
24 Ibid.
25 Ibid.
26 Damis, 2000, op. cit., p. 21.
27 Hodges, op. cit., p. 307.
28 M. Alaoui, *La Cooperation entre l'Union Europeenne et les Pays du Maghreb*, Paris: Editions Nathan, 1994, p. 55.
29 On the details, see Tony Hodges, op. cit., pp. 307–320.
30 Ibid., p. 311.
31 Ibid., pp. 311–312.
32 'Traité instituant l'Union du Maghreb Arabe', www.maghrebarabe.org/images/traite_de_marrakech.pdf (accessed 10 October 2008).
33 C. Dunbar, 'The Saharan Stasis: Status and Future Prospects of the Western Sahara Conflict' in *Middle East Journal*, Vol. 54, No. 4, Fall 2000, pp. 528–529.
34 Cited in Shelley, op. cit., p. 142.
35 www.maec.gov.ma/Initiative/Docs/Initiative%20ang.pdf (accessed 8 September 2008).

36 www.maec.gov.ma/fr/default.asp (accessed 8 September 2008).
37 White House Press Secretary Dana Perino, cited in a press release by Moroccan American Center for Policy to Reuters, www.reuters.com/article/pressRelease/idUS246402+28-Aug-2008+PRN20080828 (accessed 2 October 2008).
38 S. Zunes, 'The Future of Western Sahara' in *Foreign Policy in Focus*, 20 July 2007, www.globalpolicy.org/security/issues/wsahara/2007/0720future.htm (accessed 8 October 2008).
39 See Table 4.6.
40 Alaoui, op. cit., p. 55.
41 J.F. Daguzan, 'France, Democratization and North Africa' in *Democratization*, Vol. 9, No. 1, Spring 2002, pp. 135–136.
42 R. Youngs, *The European Union and the Promotion of Democracy*, Oxford: Oxford University Press, 2001, pp. 34–35.
43 Alaoui, op. cit., p. 45.
44 www.delmar.ec.europa.eu/fr/meda2006/sommaire.htm (accessed 10 October 2008).
45 J. Damis, 'Morocco's 1995 Association Agreement with the European Union' in *The Journal of North African Studies*, Vol. 3, No. 4, Winter 1998, p. 105.
46 See P. Holden, 'Partnership Lost? The EU's Mediterranean Aid Programmes' in *Mediterranean Politics*, Vol. 10, No. 1, March 2005, pp. 26–33.
47 Katharina Natter, 'Almost Home? Morocco's Incomplete Migration Reforms' in *World Politics Review*, 15 May 2015, www.worldpoliticsreview.com/articles/15691/almost-home-morocco-s-incomplete-migration-reforms (accessed 18 October 2015).
48 Jaafar Debbarh, *La Nouvelle Politique d'Immigration et d'Asile du Royaume du Maroc*, Rabat: Royaume du Maroc, 2014, www.processusderabat.net/web/uploads/SOM-Rabat/La-nouvelle-politique-d-immigration-et-d-asile-du-Maroc-%28partie-1%29.pdf (accessed 5 October 2015).
49 Migration Policy Center, 'Migration Profile Morocco', Florence: European University Institute, 2013, www.migrationpolicycentre.eu/docs/migration_profiles/Morocco.pdf (accessed 18 October 2015).
50 European Commission, Press Release, 'The European Union's Cooperation with Africa on Migration', Brussels, 22 April 2015, europa.eu/rapid/press-release_MEMO-15-4832_en.htm (accessed 18 October 2015).
51 Willis and Messari, op. cit., pp. 56–57.
52 Mundy, op. cit.
53 J. Damis, 'The Western Sahara Dispute as a Source of Regional Conflict in North Africa' in Halim Barakat (ed.) *Contemporary North Africa: Issues of Development and Integration*, Kent: Croom Helm, 1985, p. 147.
54 R.B. Parker, *Regional Tensions and Strategic Concerns*, New York: Praeger, 1987, p. 160.
55 See Congress of the United States, Congressional Budget Office, 'The US-Moroccan Agreement and its Implication for U.S. Rapid Deployment Forces', March 1983, www.cbo.gov/doc.cfm?index=5062 (accessed 10 October 2008).
56 See King Hassan, 1993, op. cit., pp. 259–272.
57 Maddy-Weitzman, op. cit., p. 37.
58 J. Abadi, 'The Road to Israeli-Moroccan Rapprochement' in *The Journal of North African Studies*, Vol. 5, No. 1, Spring 2000, p. 32.
59 N. Messari, 'Moroccan and US Approaches in the Middle East' in D. Ouaouicha, M. Willis and J. Kalpakian (eds) *Moroccan-American Relations in the New Millennium*, Ifrane: AUI Press, 2003.
60 A.W. McCoy, 'Invisible in Plain Sight: CIA Torture Techniques Go Mainstream' in *Amnesty International Magazine*, 2008, www.amnestyusa.org/amnesty-magazine/amnesty-magazine/page.do?id=1105051 (accessed 2 December 2008).
61 'Obama Seeks Moroccan Help, Cut then Undercuts Rabat' in *Defense and Foreign Affairs Strategic Policy*, Vol. 37, No. 7, 2009, p. 20.
62 Ibid.
63 Zunes, op. cit.

64 'Hollande Hails Morocco's Path Towards Democracy' on France 24, 4 April 2013, www.france24.com/en/20130404-morocco-hollande-praise-steps-democracy (accessed 17 October 2015).
65 Mohammed Masbah, 'What Will Egypt Mean for Morocco' in *Carnegie Endowment for International Peace*, 29 August 2013, carnegieendowment.org/sada/?fa=52780 (accessed 23 October 2015).

# 6

# CONCLUSION

With the constitutional reform and the appointment of the PJD-led government, it appears that the monarchy has entered a period in its political development in which no major changes to its system of governance can be expected. While both the appointment and the constitutional reform appeared to have been resisted by the monarch towards the end of the 2000s, the disappearance of Zine Eddine Ben Ali, Muammar Gadhafi and Hosni Mubarak significantly weakened the monarch's control over domestic political processes. The 20 February Movement's ability to mobilise tens of thousands of Moroccans in the streets in the first half of 2011 all too clearly illustrated this shifting balance of power. The state's response in turn marked an attempt to re-balance the system and to re-strengthen the role of the monarch.

In spite of this re-balancing through constitutional reform and a new set of governmental appointments, the state-led reformist discourse appears unable to address some of the fundamental dilemmas. First, significant challenges have emerged to the monarchy's policy of building alliances based on immediate domestic imperatives. They arose in response to a number of problems including the economy and the monarchy's half-hearted educational reforms of the 1970s and 1980s, which were themselves responses to the two coup attempts of 1971 and 1972, and the monarchy's subsequent short-lived alliance with the nationalist Istiqlal Party. Political gridlock emerged between the older and perhaps fatally co-opted political parties – seen by many as lacking credibility – and the rising, vigorous, potentially anti-systemic Islamist movements. While the gridlock seems stable at first sight, a period of open conflict may follow should some of the Islamist organisations disintegrate. After the death of *Al 'Adl wal Ihssane* spiritual leader Abdessalam Yassine, this may occur if Nadia Yassine, his daughter, is unable to contain the radical Islamic wing inside Morocco's political landscape. This risk may be fuelled by returning militant youth from the battlefields in Iraq and Syria. In the case of the PJD, this risk is even more acute, given the reduction in credibility that has come with the recognition of the monarchy's constitutional order and its participation in government, coupled with a moralising public discourse in which Islamist government ministers participate. The frequent involvement of young Moroccans in terrorist attacks both inside and outside the country indicates the dangers inherent in political disintegration and the absence of credible political channels.

Second, while Morocco has successfully maintained its claims to Western Sahara in its foreign policy, a political solution to the conflict that satisfies all parties involved seems as far away as ever. Here, the maximalist position it took during a period of nationalist outbidding has made it difficult to engage in a meaningful compromise. So far, none of Morocco's proposals for the Western Sahara represents a real step towards finding a solution. The risk of renewed violence continues in spite of the high price that Morocco has paid. Economically, bilateral difficulties with Algeria have weighed heavily on its eastern region; politically, its alignment with the United States remains domestically highly contested.

Third, the last 15 years have seen the increasing importance of two external sources of revenue: tourism and workers' remittances. Both have stimulated economic growth, yet they have had little impact on Morocco's agricultural economy and rural development. As a result, the consequences of a global economic recession, increasing unemployment in countries where Moroccan migrants predominantly live, or a downturn in international tourism would be cataclysmic to Morocco's economy. Long-term changes in patterns of remittances paid by Moroccans living in Europe, a likely possibility as the community is composed increasingly of third-generation immigrants, is an equally potent risk factor. Regardless of this dependency, it is worth recalling that the Moroccan economy is marked by profound divisions and, ironically, Morocco's poor, both in the cities and in rural areas, may be only marginally affected due to their distance from, and the differentiated impact of, international capital flows. Instead, as already happened in the 1980s, Morocco's fluid middle classes may take the crunch. This will certainly sharpen the economic conflicts that are already very visible in many towns, especially at the periphery.

While it is important to emphasise these structural problems, it is equally important to stress the state's ongoing capacity to adapt to domestic and regional changes. Morocco under Hassan II and Mohamed VI took advantage of the diplomatic and financial resources that arose from the country's strategic location at the most western point of the Arab world. As illustrated in this book, many of the strategies of state and nation building were traditional in origin. They have been adapted to a modern setting in which the state controlled the monopoly over the use of coercion, and established territorial claims based on nationalist ideologies and economic development. The state's attempts at creating an allied class on the basis of economic opportunities, however, have intrinsically changed the structure of Moroccan society. Effectively, class identities have increasingly replaced ethnic, tribal and linguistic ones. The politics of inclusion has therefore created a class-based political system based on horizontal stratification. While the country illustrates signs of open class conflict, it is tempered by the traditional and religious cloak that surrounds state power. In addition, this class conflict is fragmented by a strong rural–urban divide; it is marked by the co-optation of traditionally leftist political parties and the corresponding rise of Islamist ideology. Far from undermining the state, it has further empowered the monarchical institution, especially its traditional role of arbiter, and it has also allowed for the development of a plurality of entrenched interests that defend the status quo. For Morocco's bourgeoisie, the development of a nationalist political project with liberal overtones and a liberal economic ideology with protectionist features has emerged as the ideological surrogate to the traditional ideology that was the foundation of Morocco's monarchical state.

Consequently, with the development of entrenched groups and political ideologies that focus both on Islam and on a version of enlightened authoritarianism as sources of state legitimacy, Mohamed VI could capitalise by emphasising differences between his rule and that of his father. Especially towards the question of human rights abuses and the years of lead, culminating in the IER and a new constitution, his rule has so far emphasised more liberal aspects of monarchical rule. However, as few of the political and economic questions of exclusion are addressed by any of the political and economic reforms, these liberal aspects of monarchical rule are as much under threat as the regime's focus on history and Islam as modes of legitimacy. After all, religious ideologies and a traditional myth of contestation embodied in *bled es siba* and *bled el makhzen* undermine the ideological hegemony of liberalism and traditional rule. This is evidenced by the unprecedented rise of religious and violent dissenters.

It needs to be pointed out, though, that, as much as profound challenges have arisen from the state's mode of governance, regional conflicts and the country's international economic integration, the continuing uncertainty thereby produced plays back into the hands of the country's supreme political institution. After all, the same personalised leadership qualities that Anderson emphasises in the early period of state and nation building may be equally important in dealing with challenges that arise in later stages.[1] For this reason, any future reform of the state will remain centred on the monarchy as, quite simply, it remains the ultimate vehicle through which a plurality of class interests and ideologies can seek inclusion. This illustrates that all these challenges to both tradition and modernity tend to reinforce existing power structures, even if they are anti-systemic. In terms of the existing class structure, the question remains, though, how far income disparities and unequal access to social mobility can be pushed without large-scale, organised resistance occurring. From this perspective, the end of emigration as a safety valve since the early 1990s may very well create unmanageable instability in Morocco.

## Note

1  L. Anderson, 'Dynasts and Nationalists: Why Monarchies Survive' in J. Kostiner (ed.) *Middle East Monarchies. The Challenge of Modernity*, Boulder: Lynne Rienner, 2000, pp. 53–70.

# GLOSSARY

**'abudiyya**   traditional notion of obedience
**Al 'Adl wal Ihssane**   Justice and Benevolence
**Al Islah wal Tajdid**   Moroccan Islamic movement, transl. Reform and Renewal
**'alim**   (plural, 'ulema) religious scholar
**Amazigh**   Berber
**Amir Al Mu'minin**   Commander of the Faithful
**baltagiyya**   thugs
**baraka**   blessing
**bay'a**   act of allegiance
**bled el makhzen**   land of makhzen
**bled es siba**   land of tribal rebellion
**caids**   local government representative
**colons**   colonial settlers
**dahir**   decree
**dar al mulk**   lit: house of authority
**dar el makhzen**   lit: house of the makhzen
**fatiha**   first chapter of the Quran
**fatwa**   religious opinion
**fitna**   civil strife, unrest
**habous**   Islamic property legislation
**harka**   pre-colonial military campaign against rebellious tribes conducted by the sultan
**Hizb al 'Adala wal Tamniyya**   Justice and Development Party
**istiqlal**   independence
**jahiliyya**   age of ignorance prior to Islam
**jama'a**   tribal assembly
**jellaba**   traditional Moroccan garment

**koutla dimukratiyya** democratic bloc
**koutla wataniyya** National Bloc
**madrasa** (religious) school
**makhzen** monarchical authority and pre-colonial state
**marabout** traditional Muslim leader, especially in West Africa and the Maghreb
**melk** traditional private ownership over land
**mellah** traditional Jewish neighbourhood
**moudawana** family code
**mouqqadem** low-level functionary of the Ministry of the Interior
**qabila** tribe
**qawma** uprising
**Sahrawi** people living in Western Sahara
**salafiyya** Islamic revivalism
**shari'a** Islamic law
**sherifian status** of lineage from the Prophet Mohamed
**shura** Islamic concept of political participation based on advice
**shurfa** (plural, ashraf) descending from the Prophet Mohamed
**siba** tribal rebellion
**sufism** non-orthodox religious learning widespread in North Africa
**Sura** chapter of the Quran
**tahara** purity
**Tamazight** Berber language
**tariqa** brotherhood, widespread in North Africa
**Tertib** traditional tax
**thawra** revolution
**'umma** Muslim community
**'urf** tribal customary law
**wali** regional governor
**wazir** minister
**zawiyya** (plural, zuwaya) religious brotherhoods, intertwined with tariqa, widespread in North Africa

# BIBLIOGRAPHY

### Books and articles

Abadi, J., 'The Road to Israeli-Moroccan Rapprochement' in *The Journal of North African Studies*, Vol. 5, No. 1, Spring 2000: 27–54.

Ahmad, E. and S. Schaar, 'Human Rights in Morocco and Tunisia: A Critique of State Department Findings' in *MERIP Report*, No. 67, 1978: 15–17.

Al Ahnaf, M., 'Maroc. Le Code du Statut Personnel' in *Monde Arabe Maghreb-Machrek*, No. 145, July–September 1994, No. 145: 3–26.

Alaoui, M.A., *Maroc: Du Traité de Fes à la Libération 1912–1956*, Rabat: La Porte, 1994a.

Alaoui, M., *La Coopération entre l'Union Européenne et les Pays du Maghreb*, Paris: Editions Nathan, 1994b.

Alaoui, M.A., *Le Maroc Face aux Convoitises Européenne 1830–1912*, Salé: Beni Snassen, 2001.

Anderson, L., 'Dynasts and Nationalists: Why Monarchies Survive' in J. Kostiner (ed.) *Middle East Monarchies. The Challenge of Modernity*, Boulder, CO: Lynne Rienner, 2000: 53–70.

Association des Familles des Victimes des Evenements de Skhirat, *Le Massacre de Skhirat 10 juillet 1971 'crime contre l'humanité'*, Rabat: Editions A.F.V.E.S, 2002: 1–13.

Basri, D. (ed.), *Le Maroc et Les Droits de l'Homme: Position, Réalisations et Perspectives*, Paris: L'Harmattan, 1994.

Bayart, J.-F., *L'Etat en Afrique. La Politique du Ventre*, Paris: Fayard, 1989.

Bazzaz, S., 'Reading Reform Beyond the State: Salwat al-Anfas, Islamic Revival and Moroccan National History' in *The Journal of North African Studies*, Vol. 13, No. 1, March 2008: 1–13.

Belouchi, B., *Portraits d'Hommes Politiques du Maroc*, Casablanca: Afrique-Orient, 2002.

Ben Ali, D., 'Changement de Pacte Social et Continuité de l'Ordre Politique au Maroc' in M. Camau (ed.) *Changement Politiques au Maghreb*, Paris: CNRS, 1991: 51–72.

Benhaddou, A., *Maroc: Les Elites du Royaume. Essai sur l'Organisation du Pouvoir au Maroc*, Paris: L'Harmattan, 1997.

Bennani-Chraibi, M., *Soumis et Rebelles. Les Jeunes au Maroc*, Casablanca: Le Fennec, 1995.

Bennouna, M., *Heros sans Gloire. Echec d'une révolution*, Paris: Tarik Editions, 2002.

Bennoune, M. and A. El-Kenz, *Le Hasard et l'Histoire. Entretiens avec Belaid Abdesselam, Tome I*, Algiers: ENAG Editions, 1990.

Bensaid, D., 'L'Etudiant et l'Institution' in R. Bourqia, M. El Harras and D. Bensaid (eds) *Jeunesse Estudiantine Marocaine*, Series Essais et Etudes No. 14, Rabat: Faculté des Lettres et des Sciences Humaines, Université Mohamed V, 1995: 13–39.

Bouaziz, M., *Aux Origins de la Koutla Démocratique*, Casablanca: Editions de la Faculté des Lettres Aïn-Chock, 1997.

Bouzidi, M. (pseudonym Ben Kaddour, A.), 'The Neo-Makhzen and the Berbers' in E. Gellner and C. Micaud (eds) *Arabs and Berbers*, London: Gerard Duckworth, 1972: 259–267.

Bras, J.P., 'Les Enjeux Socio-Culturels de la Privatization au Maroc et en Tunisie' in D. Guerraoui and X. Richet (eds) *Stratégie de Privatisations: Comparaison Maghreb-Europe*, Paris: L'Harmattan, 1995.

Buehler, M., 'Labour Demands, Regime Concessions: Moroccan Unions and the Arab Uprising' in *British Journal of Middle Eastern Studies*, 2014, DOI: 10.1080/13530194.2015.973189.

Burke III, E., *Prelude to Protectorate in Morocco*, Chicago, IL: The University of Chicago Press, 1976.

Camau, M., *Pouvoirs et Institutions au Maghreb*, Tunis: Cérès Productions, 1978.

Catusse, M., 'De la Lutte des Classes au Dialogue Social' in *Monde Arabe Maghreb-Machrek*, No. 162, Oct.–Dec. 1998: 18–38.

Catusse, M., *L'Entrée en Politique des Entrepreneurs au Maroc*, unpublished PhD thesis, Université de Droit, d'Economie, et de Sciences d'Aix-Marseille, Institut d'Etudes Politiques d'Aix-en-Provence, 1999.

Chafik, M., 'Le Manifeste Berbere', unpublished manifesto, 2000.

Charrad, M.M., *States and Women's Rights: The Making of Postcolonial Tunisia, Algeria, and Morocco*, Berkeley, CA: University of California Press, 2001.

Claisse A., 'Makhzen Traditions and Administrative Channels' in I.W. Zartman (ed.) *The Political Economy of Morocco*, London and New York: Praeger Publishers, 1987: 34–56.

Clement, J.F., 'Morocco's Bourgeoisie: Monarchy, State, and Owning Class' in *MERIP Reports*, No. 142, Sept.–Oct. 1986: 13–17.

Clement, J.F. and J. Paul, 'Trade Unions and Moroccan Politics' in *MERIP Reports*, No. 127, Oct. 1984: 22–24.

Combs-Schilling, M.E., 'Performing Monarchy, Staging Nation' in R. Bourqia and S. Gilson Miller (eds) *In the Shadow of the Sultan. Culture, Power, and Politics in Morocco*, Cambridge, MA: Harvard University Press, 1999: 176–214.

Daguzan, J.F., 'France, Democratization and North Africa' in *Democratization*, Vol. 9, No. 1, Spring 2002: 135–148.

Damis, J., 'The Western Sahara Dispute as a Source of Regional Conflict in North Africa' in Halim Barakat (ed.) *Contemporary North Africa: Issues of Development and Integration*, Kent: Croom Helm, 1985: 138–154.

Damis, J., 'The impact of the Western Sahara Dispute on Moroccan Foreign and Domestic Policy' in I.W. Zartman, *The Political Economy of Morocco*, New York: Praeger, 1987: 188–211.

Damis, J., 'Morocco's 1995 Association Agreement with the European Union' in *The Journal of North African Studies*, Vol. 3, No. 4, Winter 1998: 91–112.

Damis, J., 'King Hassan and the Western Sahara' in *The Maghreb Review*, Vol. 25, No. 1–2, 2000: 13–30.

Daouad, Z., 'Agrarian Capitalism and the Moroccan Crisis' in *MERIP Reports*, No. 99, September 1981: 27–29.

Daouad, Z., *Les Années Lamalif*, Casablanca: Tarik Editions, 2007.

David, S.R., 'Explaining Third World Alignment' in *World Politics*, Vol. 43, No. 2, Jan. 1991: 233–256.

Deeb, M.J., 'Islam and the State in Algeria and Morocco: A Dialectical Model' in J. Ruedy (ed.) *Islamism and Secularism in North Africa*, London: Macmillan, 1996: 275–288.

Deneoux, G.P. and L. Gateaux, 'L'Essor des Associations au Maroc. A la Recherche de la Citoyenneté?' in *Monde Arabe Maghreb-Machrek*, No. 150, October–December 1995: 19–39.

Deneoux, G.P., L. Gateaux and A. Maghraoui, 'King Hassan's Strategy of Political Dualism' in *Middle East Policy*, Vol. 5, No. 4, January 1998: 104–127.

Deneoux, G.P. and L. Gateaux, 'Understanding Morocco's "Sanitation Campaign" (December 1995 to May 1996)' in *The Journal of North African Studies*, Vol. 3, No. 1, Spring 1998: 101–131.

Deneoux, G.P., L. Gateaux and A. Maghraoui, 'The Political Economy of Structural Adjustment in Morocco' in A. Layachi (ed.) *Economic Crisis and Political Change in North Africa*, London: Praeger Publishers, 1998: 55–88.

Deneoux, G.P., L. Gateaux and H.R. Desfosses, 'Rethinking the Moroccan Parliament: The Kingdom's Legislative Development Imperative' in *The Journal of North African Studies*, Vol. 12, No. 1, March 2007: 79–108.

Desrues, T. and E. Moyano, 'Social Change and Political Transition in Morocco' in *Mediterranean Politics*, Vol. 6, No. 1, Spring 2001: 21–47.

Djerbal, D. (ed.), *L'Armée de Libération du Maghreb 1948–1955*, Algiers: Fondation Mohamed Boudiaf, 2004.

Dunbar, C., 'The Saharan Stasis: Status and Future Prospects of the Western Sahara Conflict' in *Middle East Journal*, Vol. 54, No. 4, Fall 2000: 522–545.

Eibl, Ferdinand, 'The Party of Authenticity and Modernity (PAM). Trajectory of a Political Deus Ex Machine', *The Journal of North African Studies*, Vol. 17, No. 1, 2012: 45–66.

Eickelman, D.F., 'Religion in Polity and Society' in I.W. Zartman (ed.) *The Political Economy of Morocco*, London and New York: Praeger Publishers, 1987: 84–97.

Eickelman, D.F., 'Re-imagining Religion and Politics: Moroccan Elections in the 1990s' in J. Ruedy (ed.) *Islamism and Secularism in North Africa*, London: Macmillan, 1996: 253–274.

El Mansour, M., 'Salafis and Modernists in the Moroccan Nationalist Movement' in J. Ruedy (ed.) *Islamism and Secularism in North Africa*, London and Houndsmill, Basingstoke: Macmillan, 1996: 53–72.

El Mossadeq, R., 'Political Parties and Power Sharing' in I.W. Zartman (ed.) *The Political Economy of Morocco*, London and New York: Praeger Publishers, 1987: 59–83.

El Mossadeq, R., *Les Labyrinthes de l'Alternance. Rupture ou Continuité?* Casablanca: Souchepress, 1998.

Entelis, J.P., *Culture and Counterculture in Moroccan Politics*, Lanham, MD: University Press of America, 1996.

Entelis, J.P., 'Political Islam in the Maghreb. The Non-Violent Dimension' in J.P. Entelis (ed.) *Islam, Democracy and the State in North Africa*, Bloomington, IN and Indianapolis, IN: Indiana University Press, 1997: 43–74.

Entelis, J.P., 'Democratic Desires and the Authoritarian Temptation in the Central Maghreb' in Y.H. Zoubir and H. Amirah-Fernandez, *North Africa. Politics, Region, and the Limits of Transformation*, Abingdon and New York: Routledge, 2008: 9–30.

Gallison, R., 'Illusion révolutionnaire et contre-révolution monarchique' in M. Bennouna, *Heros sans Gloire. Echec d'une Révolution*, Paris: Tarik Editions, 2002.

Garon, L., *Dangerous Alliances: Civil Society, the Media and Democratic Transition in North Africa*, London and New York: Zed Books, 2003.

Gaudio, A., *Allal El Fassi ou L'Histoire de l'Istiqlal*, Paris: Alain Moreau, 1972.

Gellner, E., 'Tribalism and Social Change in North Africa' in W.H. Lewis (ed.) *French Speaking Africa: The Search for Identity*, New York: Walker, 1965: 107–118.

Gellner, E., 'Patterns of Tribal Rebellion in Morocco' in P.J. Vatitiokis, *Revolution in the Middle East and other Case Studies*, London: Allen and Unwin, 1972: 120–145.

Gershovich, M., *French Military Rule in Morocco*, London: Frank Cass, 2000.
Gillespie, R., *Spain and the Mediterranean*, Basingstoke: MacMillan, 2000.
Halstead, J.P., *Rebirth of a Nation. The Origins and Rise of Moroccan Nationalism. 1912–1944*, Cambridge, MA: Harvard University Press, 1969.
Hammoudi, A., *Master and Disciple. The Cultural Foundations of Moroccan Authoritarianism*, London and Chicago, IL: The University of Chicago Press, 1997.
Hammoudi, A., 'The Reinvention of Dar al-mulk. The Moroccan Political System and its Legitimation' in R. Bourqia and S. Gilson Miller (eds) *In the Shadow of the Sultan. Culture, Power and Politics in Morocco*, Cambridge, MA: Harvard University Press, 1999: 129–175.
Hart, D.M., 'Scratch a Moroccan, Find a Berber' in D.M. Hart, *Tribe and Society in Rural Morocco*, London: Frank Cass Publishers, 2000: 23–26.
Hart, D.M., 'Moroccan Dynastic *Shurfa*'-hood in Two Historical Contexts: Idrisid Cult and 'Alawid Power' in *The Journal of North African Studies*, Vol. 6, No. 2, Summer 2001: 81–94.
Hassan II, *Le Defis*, Paris: Albin Michel, 1976.
Hassan II, *The Challenge: The Memoirs of King Hassan II of Morocco*, London: Macmillan, 1978.
Hassan II, *La Memoire d'un Roi. Entretiens avec Eric Laurent*, Paris: Librairie Plon, 1993.
Hegasy, S., *Staat, Öffentlichkeit und Zivilgesellschaft*, Hamburg: Deutsches Orient Institut, 1997.
Hermassi, E., *Leadership and National Development in North Africa*, Berkeley, CA and London: University of California Press, 1972.
Hibou, B. and M. Tozy, 'Une lecture d'Anthopologie Politique de la Corruption au Maroc' in *Tiers Monde*, Vol. 41, No. 161, 2000: 23–48.
Hodges, T., *Western Sahara: The Roots of a Desert War*, Westport: Lawrence Hill, 1983.
Holden, P., 'Partnership Lost? The EU's Mediterranean Aid Programmes' in *Mediterranean Politics*, Vol. 10, No. 1, March 2005: 19–39.
Howe, M., *Morocco. The Islamist Awakening and Other Challenges*, Oxford: Oxford University Press, 2005.
Hughes, S.O., *Morocco Under King Hassan*, Reading: Ithaca, NY, 2001.
Human Rights Advisory Council, *10 Years in the Service of Human Rights. The Royal High Instructions, Legislative and Statutory Texts, Advisory Opinions*, Rabat: Kingdom of Morocco, 2001.
Huntington, S., *Political Order in Changing Societies*, New Haven, CT: Yale University Press, 1968.
Joffé, G., 'The Political Economy of Privatisation in Morocco' in *Moroccan Studies*, Vol. 1, 1991.
Joffé, G., 'Elections and Reform in Morocco' in Richard Gillespie (ed.) *Mediterranean Politics*, Vol. I, London: Pinter Publishers, 1994.
Kably, M., 'Legitimacy of State Power and Socio-Religious Variations in Medieval Morocco' in R. Bourqia and S. Gilson Miller (eds) *In the Shadow of the Sultan. Culture, Power, and Politics in Morocco*, Cambridge, MA: Harvard Center for Middle Eastern Studies, 1999: 17–29.
Karem, M., 'La Notion des Droits de l'Homme au Maghreb. Essai sur une Nouvelle Culture Politique', Thèse de Doctorat, Université de Droits, d'Economie et de Science Politique d'Aix-Marseille, 1991.
Kingdom of Morocco, *50 Ans de Développement Humain & Perspectives 2025*, Rabat: Kingdom of Morocco, 2007.
Korany, B., 'Monarchical Islam with a Democratic Veneer: Morocco' in B. Korany, R. Brynen and P. Noble (eds) *Political Liberalization and Democratization in the Arab World*, Vol. 2, Boulder, CO: Lynne Rienner, 1998: 157–184.

Lahbabi, M., *Le Gouvernement Marocain à l'Aube du 20ème siècle*, Rabat: Editions Techniques Nord-Africaines, 1958.
Laroui, A., *Idéologie Arabe Contemporaine*, Paris: La Decouverte, 1983.
Laskier, M., *The Alliance Israelite Universelle and the Jewish Communities of Morocco, 1862–1962*, Albany, NY: State University of New York Press, 1983.
Laurent, E., *Le Roi Prédateur*, Paris: L'Editions du Seuil, 2012.
Leveau, R., 'Islam et contrôle politique au Maroc' in E. Gellner and J.-C. Vatin, *Islam et Politique au Maghreb*, Paris: CNRS, 1981: 271–280.
Leveau, R., *Le Fellah Marocain: Défenseur du Trône*, Paris: Fondation Nationale de Sciences Politiques, 1985.
Leveau, R., 'Morocco at the Crossroads' in *Mediterranean Politics*, Vol. 2, No. 2, Autumn 1997: 95–113.
Maddy-Weitzman, B., 'Israel and Morocco: A Special Relationship' in *The Maghreb Review* Vol. 21, No. 1–2, 1996: 36–48.
Maddy-Weitzman, B., 'Contested Identities: Berbers, "Berberism" and the State in North Africa' in *The Journal of North African Studies*, Vol. 6, No. 3, Autumn 2000: 23–47.
Maddy-Weitzman, B., 'Women, Islam, and the Moroccan State: The Struggle over the Personal Status Law' in *Middle East Journal*, Vol. 59, No. 3, Summer 2005: 393–410.
Maddy-Weitzman, B. and Daniel Zisenwine, 'Patronage and Democratic Citizenship in Morocco' in Nils Butenschon and Roel Meijer (eds) *Arab Citizenship in the New Political Era*, Leiden: Brill, forthcoming.
Maghraoui, A., 'Ambiguities of Sovereignty: Morocco, The Hague and the Western Sahara Dispute' in *Mediterranean Politics*, Vol. 8, No. 1, Spring 2003: 113–126.
Maghraoui, A., 'Depoliticization in Morocco' in *Journal of Democracy*, Vol. 13, No. 4, October 2002: 24–32.
Maghraoui, D., 'Moroccan Soldiers: Between Selective Memory and Collective Memory' in *Arab Studies Quarterly*, Vol. 20, No. 2, 1998: 21–41.
Martín, I., 'The Social Impact of Euro-Mediterranean Free Trade Areas: A First Approach with Special Reference to the Case of Morocco' in *Mediterranean Politics*, Vol. 9, No. 3, Autumn 2004: 422–458.
Martín, I., 'Morocco Wakes Up to Human Development' in *Mediterranean Politics*, Vol. 11, No. 3, November 2006: 433–439.
Marzouki, A., *Tazmamart, Cellule 10*, Paris: Paris-Méditerranée and Tarik, 2000.
Maxwell, G., *Lords of the Atlas*, London: Cassel and Co, 2000.
Messari, N., 'Moroccan and US Approaches in the Middle East' in D. Ouaouicha, M. Willis and J. Kalpakian (eds) *Moroccan-American Relations in the New Millennium*, Ifrane: AUI Press, 2003: 99–108.
Mohamed VI, *Discours de Sa Majesté le Roi Mohammed VI Que Dieu l'Assiste à l'Occasion de l'Ouverture de la Deuxième Année Legislative de la VIIe Legislature*, Rabat: Kingdom of Morocco, October 2003.
Munson Jr, H., *Religion and Power in Morocco*, New Haven, CT and London: Yale University Press, 1993.
Norton, A.R., *Civil Society in the Middle East*, Vol. I, Leiden: E.J. Brill, 1995.
OMDH and Article 19, *Liberté de la Presse et de l'Information au Maroc*, Rabat: OMDH, 1995.
Parker, R.B., *Regional Tensions and Strategic Concerns*, New York: Praeger, 1987.
Payne, R., 'Economic Crisis and Policy Reform in the 1980s' in W.I. Zartman and M. Habeeb (eds) *Polity and Society in Contemporary North Africa*, Boulder, CO: Westview Press, 1993: 139–167.
Pennel, C.R., *Morocco Since 1830. A History*, London: Hurst and Company, 2000.
Perrault, G., *Notre Ami Le Roi*, Paris: Gallimard, 1990.

Pruzan-Jørgensen, Julie E., 'Analyzing Authoritarian Regime Legitimation: Findings from Morocco' in *Middle East Critique*, Vol. 19, No. 3, 2010: 269–286.
Raiss, M., *De Skhirat à Tazmamart. Retour du Bout de l'Enfer*, Casablanca: Afrique Orient, 2002.
Rhazaoui, A., 'Recent Economic Trends: Managing Indebtedness' in William I. Zartman, *The Political Economy of Morocco*, New York: Praeger, 1987: 141–158.
Rousset, M., 'Changements Institutionnels et Equilibre des Forces Politiques au Maroc: Un Essai d'Interprétation' in J. Leca, *Développement Politique au Maghreb*, Paris: Centre National de la Recherche Scientifique, 1979: 181–191.
Saaf, A., *La Transition au Maroc. L'Invitation*, Casablanca: Eddif Editions, 2001.
Sabagh, G., 'The Challenge of Population Growth in Morocco' in *Middle East Report*, March–April 1993.
Salahdine, M., *Maroc: Tribus, Makhzen et Colons. Essai d'Histoire Economique et Sociale*, Paris: L'Harmattan, 1986.
Santucci, J.C., 'Les Elections Législatives Marocaines de Juin 1977' in J. Leca, *Développement Politique au Maghreb*, Paris: Centre National de la Recherche Scientifique, 1979: 215–242.
Santucci, J.C., *Les Partis Politiques Marocains à l'Epreuve du Pouvoir*, Publications de la Revue Marocaine d'Administration Locale et de Développement, No. 24, 2001.
Sater, J.N., 'The Dynamics of State and Civil Society in Morocco' in *The Journal of North African Studies*, Vol. 7, No. 3, Autumn 2002: 101–118.
Sater, J.N., 'Changing Politics from Below? Women Parliamentarians in Morocco' in *Journal of Democratization*, Vol. 14, No. 4, August 2007a: 723–742.
Sater, J.N., *Civil Society and Political Change in Morocco*, Abingdon and New York: Routledge, 2007b.
Sater, J.N., 'Elections and Authoritarian Rule in Morocco' in *Middle East Journal*, Vol. 63, No. 3, Summer 2009: 381–400.
Sater, J.N., 'New Wine in Old Bottles: Political Parties Under Mohammed VI' in Bruce Maddy-Weitzman and Daniel Zisenwine, *Contemporary Morocco: State, Politics and Society under Mohammed VI*, Abingdon and New York: Routledge, 2013: 9–23.
Sater, J.N., 'Patronage and Democratic Citizenship in Morocco' in Nils Butenschon and Roel Meijer (eds) *Citizenship in the Middle East. History, Theory and Practice*, Leiden: Brill, forthcoming.
Schroeter, D.J., 'Royal Power and the Economy in Precolonial Morocco: Jews and the Legitimation of Foreign Trade' in R. Bourqia and S. Gilson Miller (eds) *In the Shadow of the Sultan. Culture, Power and Politics in Morocco*, Cambridge, MA: Harvard University Press, 1999: 74–102.
Shahin, E.E., 'Secularism and Nationalism: The Political Discourse of Abd al-Salam Yassin' in J. Ruedy (ed.) *Islamism and Secularism in North Africa*, London: Macmillan, 1996: 167–186.
Shelley, T., *Endgame in the Western Sahara. What Future for Africa's Last Colony?* London and New York: Zed Books, 2004.
Stillmann, N.A., *The Jews of Arab Lands*, Philadelphia, PA: The Jewish Publication Society of America, 1979.
Storm, L., *Democratization in Morocco. The Political Elite and Struggles for Power in the Post-Independence State*, Abingdon, Oxon and New York: Routledge, 2007.
Swearingen, W.D., 'Morocco's Agricultural Crisis' in I.W. Zartman, *The Political Economy of Morocco*, New York: Praeger, 1987: 159–172.
Tozy, M., *Champ et contre champ politico-religieux au Maroc*, unpublished PhD thesis, Université de Droit, d'Economie et des Sciences d'Aix-Marseille, 1984.

Tozy, M., 'Représentation/Intercession. Les Enjeux de Pouvoir dans les "champs politiques désamorcés" au Maroc' in *Annuaire de l'Afrique du Nord*, Vol. 28, CNRS, 1989: 153–168.
Tozy, M., 'Islam and the State' in I.W. Zartman and W.M. Habeeb (eds) *Polity and Society in Contemporary North Africa*, Boulder, CO: Westview Press, 1993: 102–122.
Tozy, M., *Monarchie et Islam Politique au Maroc*, second edition, Paris: Presses de la Fondation Nationale des Sciences Politiques, 1999a.
Tozy, M., 'Reformes politiques et transition démocratique' in *Monde Arabe Maghreb-Machrek*, No. 164, April–June 1999b: 67–84.
Tozy, M., 'L'Islamisme à l'Epreuve du Politique' in *Confluences Méditerranée*, No. 31, Autumn 1999c: 91–105.
Tuquoi, J.-P., *Le Dernier Roi. Crépuscule d'une Dynastie*, Paris: Editions Grasset & Fasquelle, 2001.
US State Department, *Morocco Human Rights Practices for the Year 1994*, Washington, DC, February 1994.
Vermeren, P., *Histoire du Maroc Depuis l'Independence*, Paris: La Decouverte, 2002a.
Vermeren, P., *Ecole, Elite et Pouvoir au Maroc et en Tunisie au XXe siècle*, Rabat: Alizés, 2002b.
Waltz, S.E., *Human Rights and Reform. Changing the Face of North African Politics*, London and Berkeley, CA: University of California Press, 1995.
Waltz, S.E., 'Interpreting Political Reform in Morocco' in R. Bourqia and S. Gilson Miller (eds) *In the Shadow of the Sultan. Culture, Power, and Politics in Morocco*, Cambridge, MA: Harvard University Press, 1999: 282–306.
Waterbury, J., *The Commander of the Faithful. The Moroccan Political Elite – A Study in Segmented Politics*, London: Weidenfeld and Nicolson, 1970.
Waterbury, J., 'Democracy Without Democrats. The Potential for Political Liberalization in the Middle East' in G. Salamé (ed.) *Democracy Without Democrats. The Renewal of Politics in the Muslim World*, London and New York: I.B. Tauris, 1994: 23–47.
Weber, M., *Economy and Society*, Totawa, NJ: Bedminster, 1968.
White, G., *A Comparative Political Economy of Tunisia and Morocco*, Albany, NY: State University of New York Press, 2001.
Willis, M.J., 'Between Alternance and the Makhzen: Al Tawhid wa Al Islah's Entry into Moroccan Politics' in *The Journal of North African Studies*, Vol. 4, No. 3, Autumn 1999: 45–80.
Willis, M.J., 'Political Parties in the Maghrib: The Illusion of Significance' in *The Journal of North African Studies*, Vol. 7, No. 2, Summer 2002: 1–22.
Willis, M.J., 'Morocco's Islamists and the Legislative Elections of 2002' in *Mediterranean Politics*, Vol. 9, No. 1, 2004: 53–81.
Willis, M.J. and N. Messari, 'Analyzing Moroccan Foreign Policy and Relations with Europe' in G. Nonneman (ed.) *Analyzing Middle East Foreign Policies and the Relationship with Europe*, Abingdon: Routledge, 2005: 152–172.
The World Bank, *World Development Indicators*, Washington, DC: International Bank for Reconstruction and Development, 2005.
Yassine, A., *Islamiser La Modernité*, Al Ofok, 1998.
Youngs, R., *The European Union and the Promotion of Democracy*, Oxford: Oxford University Press, 2001.
Zartman, I.W., 'Farming and Land Ownership in Morocco' in *Land Economics*, Vol. 39, No. 2, May 1963: 187–198.
Zartman, I.W., *Man, State and Society in the Contemporary Maghreb*, London and New York: Praeger Publishers, 1973.
Zartman, I.W., 'King Hassan's New Morocco' in I.W. Zartman (ed.) *The Political Economy of Morocco*, London and New York: Praeger Publishers, 1987: 1–33.

Zoubir, Y.H., 'Reactions in the Maghreb to the Gulf Crisis and War' in *Arab Studies Quarterly*, Vol. 15, No. 1, Winter 1993: 83–103.

Zoubir, Y.H., 'Western Sahara: Political Economy of a Conflict' in A. Layachi, *Economic Crisis and Political Change in North Africa*, Westport, CT: Praeger, 1998: 149–164.

## Online documents and articles

Achy, L., 'Morocco's Experience with Poverty Reduction. Lessons from the Arab World', *Carnegie Papers*, No. 25, Washington, DC: Carnegie Middle East Center, 2010, carnegieendowment.org/files/morocco_poverty1.pdf.

Akesbi, N., 'Evolution et perspective de l'agriculture marocaine', www.rdh50.ma/fr/pdf/contributions/GT3-3.pdf (accessed 3 June 2008).

Alami, R.M., 'Le Secteur Informel au Maroc: 1954–2004', www.rdh50.ma/fr/pdf/contributions/GT3-7.pdf (accessed 15 April 2008).

Amnesty International, 'Torture in the "Anti-terrorism" Campaign – The Case of Témara Detention Centre', www.amnesty.org/en/library/asset/MDE29/004/2004/en/dom-MDE290042004en.pdf (accessed 8 April 2008).

Baazi, Jalal, 'Échanges commerciaux avec le Maroc: L'Espagne détrône la France' in *Les Inspirations Eco*, 26 July 2015, www.leseco.ma.

Beaugé, F., 'Le Maroc s'Industrialise et s'Enrichit mais Déficits et Inégalités se Creusent' in *Le Monde*, 10 August 2008, www.lemonde.fr.

Benchemsi, A., 'CIH: jusqu'où ira le scandale?' in *Jeune Afrique*, 13 February 2001, www.jeuneafrique.com/jeune_afrique/article_jeune_afrique.asp?art_cle=LIN13023cihjueladna0 (accessed 12 June 2008).

Congress of the United States, Congressional Budget Office, 'The US-Moroccan Agreement and its Implication for U.S. Rapid Deployment Forces', March 1983, www.cbo.gov/doc.cfm?index=5062 (accessed 10 October 2008).

Debbarh, J., *La Nouvelle Politique d'Immigration et d'Asile du Royaume du Maroc*, Rabat: Royaume du Maroc, 2014, www.processusderabat.net/web/uploads/SOM-Rabat/La-nouvelle-politique-d-immigration-et-d-asile-du-Maroc-%28partie-1%29.pdf (accessed 5 October 2015).

Delegation of the European Commission in Morocco, 'Bulletin d'Information 183 Oct–Dec 2006', www.delmar.ec.europa.eu/fr/meda2006/sommaire.htm (accessed on 10 October 2008).

Desrues, Thierry and Irene Fernández Molina, 'L'expérience gouvernementale du Parti de la Justice et du Développement: les islamistes au pouvoir?' in *Année du Maghreb*, Vol. IX, 2013: 345–365, anneemaghreb.revues.org/1954 (accessed 15 August 2015).

European Commission, 'The European Union's Cooperation with Africa on Migration', press release, Brussels, 22 April 2015, europa.eu/rapid/press-release_MEMO-15-4832_en.htm (accessed 18 October 2015).

Forbes, 'The World's Richest Monarchs', 2010, www.forbes.com.

France 24, 'Hollande Hails Morocco's Path Towards Democracy', 4 April 2013, www.france24.com/en/20130404-morocco-hollande-praise-steps-democracy (accessed 17 October 2015).

Ghannam, F., 'Le Départ Sauve Le Budget' in *Aujourd'hui Le Maroc*, 27 October 2005, www.aujourdhui.ma/couverture-details40950.html.

*The Guardian*, '52 in Court over Suicide Bombings', 22 July 2003, www.guardian.co.uk/world/2003/jul/22/alqaida.terrorism (accessed 10 April 2008).

Harrigan, J. and H. El Said, 'Economic Reform, Social Welfare, Civil Society and Islamists in Morocco', iicas.ucsd.edu/research/projects/dwds/papers/El-Said_Social%20Capital%20in%20Morocco.pdf (accessed 12 May 2008).

Hassan II, 'Royal Speech Delivered on 15 September 1995', 1995, www.mincom.gov.ma (now: www.maroc.ma) (accessed 29 September 2003).

Haute Commissariat Du Plan, 'Horloge de la population: Historique de la Population du Maroc par Milieu de Résidence de 1960 à 2004 au Milieu de l'Année', www.hcp.ma/frm Ind.aspx?id=0404000000&vara=10 (accessed 1 August 2008).

Instance Equité et Réconciliation, 'Synthèse du rapport final', www.ier.ma/article.php3?id_a rticle=1496 (accessed 5 April 2008).

International Court of Justice, 'Western Sahara – Advisory Opinion of 16 October 1975', 1975, www.icj-cij.org/docket/index.php?sum=323&code=sa&p1=3&p2=4&case=61&k=69&p3=5 (accessed 20 June 2007).

International Monetary Fund, 'Maroc – Conclusions Préliminaires des Consultations de 2008 au Titre de l'Article IV', 30 May 2008, www.imf.org/external/np/ms/2008/fra/053008f.htm (accessed 15 October 2008).

Kingdom of Morocco, 'Elections Legislatives 2007', 2007, www.elections.gov.ma (accessed 10 November 2007).

Kingdom of Morocco, Ministry of Interior and Ministry of Finance and Privatization, 'Rapport de Synthèse – Mission d'audit conjoint IGAR/IGF – Certification des comptes de l'exercise 2006', Rabat, December 2007, www.indh.gov.ma/fr/Rapports_Audits.asp (accessed 5 September 2008).

Kingdom of Morocco, 'Moroccan Initiative for Negotiating an Autonomy Statute for the Sahara Region', www.maec.gov.ma/Initiative/Docs/Initiative%20ang.pdf (accessed 8 September 2008).

Lahlimi, A., 'Une Reaction Défaitiste' in *Aujourd'hui Le Maroc*, No. 945, 18 July 2005, www.aujourdhui.ma/couverture-details37786.html.

La République Française, 'Traité pour l'organisation du Protectorat français dans l'Empire Chérifien', 30 March 1912, www.ambafrance-ma.org/EfMaroc/cea/hg/dosh1.pdf (accessed 12 March 2007).

Le Matin du Sahara et du Maghreb, 'Affaire Rosamor', 2 September 2008, www.lematin.ma/Actualite/Express/Article.asp?id=97511 (accessed 2 September 2008).

Le Matin du Sahara et du Maghreb, 'Le rapport du PNUD sur le développement humain au Maroc pèche par la mauvaise foi', 17 June 2008, www.lematin.ma/Actualite/Journal/Article.asp?idr=110&id=93231.

Le Matin du Sahara et du Maghreb, 'Les limites de l'approche du Pnud', 13 August 2008, www.lematin.ma/Actualite/Express/Article.asp?id=96509.

Le Matin du Sahara et du Maghreb, 'S.M. le Roi reçoit Abbas El Fassi et Rachid Belmokhtar Le Premier ministre a présenté au Souverain le bilan de l'INDH', 18 July 2008, www.lematin.ma/Actualite/Journal/Article.asp?idr=110&id=95143 (accessed 1 September 2008).

Madi, L., 'L'Alphabétisation et l'Education des Adultes', www.rdh50.ma/fr/pdf/contribu tions/GT4-9.pdf (accessed 3 June 2008).

Maghreb Arab Union, 'Traité instituant l'Union du Maghreb Arabe', www.maghrebarabe.org/images/traite_de_marrakech.pdf (accessed 10 October 2008).

Masbah, Mohammed, 'What Will Egypt Mean for Morocco' in *Carnegie Endowment for International Peace*, 29 August 2013, carnegieendowment.org/sada/?fa=52780 (accessed 23 October 2015).

McCoy, A.W., 'Invisible in Plain Sight: CIA Torture Techniques Go Mainstream', *Amnesty International Magazine*, 2008, www.amnestyusa.org/amnesty-magazine/amnesty-maga zine/page.do?id=1105051 (accessed 2 December 2008).

Migration Policy Centre, *Migration Profile Morocco*, Florence: European University Institute, 2013, www.migrationpolicycentre.eu/docs/migration_profiles/Morocco.pdf (accessed 18 October 2015).

Mohamed VI, 'Royal Discourse Delivered on 18 May 2005', 2005, www.indh.gov.ma/fr/discours.asp.

Moroccan American Center for Policy, 'Polisario Obstructs UN Negotiations for Peaceful Resolution of Western Sahara Conflict', press release to Reuters, www.reuters.com/article/pressRelease/idUS246402+28-Aug-2008+PRN20080828 (accessed 2 October 2008).

Mundy, J., 'Thirty Years of Conflict: How the US and Morocco Seized the Spanish Sahara' in *Le Monde Diplomatique*, January 2006, English edition, mondediplo.com/2006/01/12asahara (accessed 10 October 2007).

*The National*, 'Morocco Lures Sharia Cash with First Islamic Bank', 9 March 2015, www.thenational.ae/business/banking/morocco-lures-sharia-cash-with-first-islamic-bank.

National Audit Office, *Financial Management in the European Union*, London: The Stationery Office, 2008, www.nao.org.uk/publications/nao_reports/chronindex.asp?type=vfm.

Natter, Katharina, 'Almost Home? Morocco's Incomplete Migration Reforms' in *World Politics Review*, 15 May 2015, www.worldpoliticsreview.com/articles/15691/almost-home-morocco-s-incomplete-migration-reforms (accessed 18 October 2015).

Observatoire National du Développement Humain (ONDH), *Evaluation des Realisations de la Premiere Phase de l'INDH (2005–2010) et Leurs Effets sur le Populations Cible*, Rabat: Royaume du Maroc, 2013, www.ondh.ma/sites/default/files/documents/synthese_du_rapport_ondh_2013.pdf.

Office de Changes, 'Balance Commerciale 2000–2008', 2008, www.oc.gov.ma.

OMDH, 'Communiqué au Sujet de la Commission d'Enquête sur le CIH', Rabat, 27 January 2001, www.omdh.org/newomdh/def.asp?codelangue=23&info=784 (accessed 8 April 2008).

Sater, James N., 'Morocco's "Arab" Spring' in Middle East Institute, Viewpoint Series, Revolutions and Political Transformations in the Middle East, October 2011, www.mei.edu/LinkClick.aspx?fileticket=QnpP0vmNOX8%3d&tabid=541.

Shalhoub, I., *Comparative Report on the State of the Judiciary in Egypt, Jordan, Lebanon and Morocco*, Washington, DC: IFES, May 2007, www.eldis.org/assets/Docs/33831.html (accessed 5 April 2008).

Silverstein, Paul, 'Weighing Morocco's New Constitution' in *Middle East Report*, No. 260, 5 July 2011, www.merip.org/mero/mero070511 (accessed 10 June 2012).

Transparency Maroc, 'Royal Power and Judicial Independence in Morocco' in *Transparency International: Global Corruption Report 2007. Part Two – Country Reports on Judicial Corruption*, www.transparency.org/content/download/18702/255302 (accessed 12 June 2008).

Tritki, K., 'Patrons. La PME dans le Jeu du Pouvoir' in *TelQuel*, No. 191, 17–23 September 2005, www.telquel-online.com/191/eco_sujet_191.shtml.

United Nations Development Programme, *Human Development Report 2014*, 2014, hdr.undp.org/sites/default/files/hdr14-summary-en.pdf.

The World Resources Institute, 'Country Profile: Morocco', earthtrends.wri.org/text/agriculture-food/country-profile-126.html (accessed 1 August 2008).

Zunes, S., 'The Future of Western Sahara' in *Foreign Policy in Focus*, 20 July 2007, www.globalpolicy.org/security/issues/wsahara/2007/0720future.htm (accessed 8 October 2008).

## Newspapers and magazines

*Economie et Entreprise*, Casablanca
*L'Economiste*, Casablanca
*L'Opinion*, Rabat
*La Vie Economique*, Casablanca
*Le Courrier International*, Paris

*Le Journal Hebdomadaire*, Casablanca
*Le Monde*, Paris
*Le Point*, Paris
*Le Soir*, Brussels
*Libération*, Rabat
*TelQuel*, Casablanca

## Websites

Ministry of Finance, www.finances.gov.ma.
Mohamed VI, Royal Speeches, www.maroc.ma.
National Initiative for *Hum Dev*, www.indh.gov.ma.

# INDEX

Abdelaziz, Moulay 4, 20–1
Acts of Algeciras 4, 20–1,159
Addi Ou Bihi 30
advanced status 168
Aherdane, Mahjoubi 8, 32, 34, 75, 77–8
Al 'Adl Wal Ihssane 60, 64–5, 75, 81, 83, 179
Al Islah Wal Tajdid 60, 64, 81–2
Algiers, occupation of 18–19
*Alliance Israélite Universelle* 23,
Alternance 68, 70–4, 78, 81, 83, 85, 103, 132
Amazigh rights 75, 77–8, 80, 81, 89, 93–4
*Amir Al Mu'minin* 3, 6, 34, 43, 53, 62, 98, 151
Amnesty International 57, 69
Arab Maghreb Union 162
Arabisation 45, 48, 61, 66, 77
Arab Spring 1, 14, 37–8, 90, 97–100, 102, 103, 113, 142, 156, 173
Atlantic Charter 7, 22, 27
Authenticity and Modernity Party 9, 10, 90, 102, 104

*baraka* 6, 44, 52
Barcelona Process 128, 138
Basri, Driss 60, 69, 70, 73–4, 83, 87, 132, 164
*bay'a,* 4, 6, 30, 39, 57, 160–1
Ben Arafa, Mohamed 28–9
Ben Barka, Mehdi 7–8, 11, 30, 31–3, 40–2, 45, 52, 57, 154–5, 166
Benjelloun, Omar 19, 48, 63,

Berber Manifesto 94
Bouabid, Abderrahim 7, 31–3, 41, 45, 47–50, 58–9

Camp David 171
CAP *see* Common Agriculture Policy
Casablanca riots 42, 159
CGEM *see* Confédération Générale des Entreprises du Maroc
Charter of Agadir 78, 80
Cold War 14, 155–6, 170, 172
Commander of the Faithful *see Amir al Mu'minin*
Common Agriculture Policy 142, 166, 168
Confédération Générale des Entreprises du Maroc 86, 132–4, 141
constitution 56–7, 61, 68–74, 77, 80–1, 90, 94–5; 2011 reform of 96–104.
CORCAS *see* Royal Advisory Council for Saharan Affairs

Dlimi, Ahmed 59
Driss Benzekri 95

El Fassi, Allal 7–8, 10, 26, 31–2, 38–9, 44, 47, 52, 59, 61
El Glaoui, Thami 22, 28
El Himma, Fouad 9, 84, 90, 96–7
EMP *see* Euro-Mediterranean Partnership
ENP *see* European Neighbourhood Policy
Euro-Mediterranean Partnership 167
European Neighbourhood Policy 167

family code 76–7, 79, 89, 93–4, 96
February 20 Movement 90, 97, 99, 102, 131, 179
Free Trade Agreement 91, 134, 137
FTA *see* Free Trade Agreement

GCC *see* Gulf Cooperation Council
Green March 96,103, 124, 151, 159–60, 170
Gulf Cooperation Council 150–1, 174

Hafidh, Moulay 4–5, 20–2, 28
Hafidhian revolution 20, 159
human development index 137
human rights 37, 45, 48, 57–8, 69, 75–81, 85, 87, 89, 90, 93, 95, 126, 150, 155, 164, 166–7, 169, 175, 181

ICJ *see* International Court of Justice
Idriss, Moulay 3, 61
IER *see* Justice and Reconciliation Commission
Ilal Amam 48–9, 63, 66, 76, 95
IMF *see* International Monetary Fond
Import Substitution Industrialisation 114, 120, 122, 144
Independence Manifesto 7, 26
INDH *see* National Initiative for Human Development
International Court of Justice 158–9, 165,
International Monetary Fund 58–9, 123–5
IRCAM *see* Royal Institute for Amazigh Culture
ISI *see* Import Substitution Industrialisation
Islamic State in Iraq and Syria 92, 174
ISIS *see* Islamic State in Iraq and Syria
Istiqlal Party 7–9, 26–7, 29–34, 38–41, 43, 45–52, 58–9, 31, 70–76, 86–7, 96, 100–101, 104, 150, 124, 151, 153, 157, 174, 179

jews, 19–20, 24, 150, 153, 155, 171
Justice and Development Party 1, 10–11, 81–83, 86–90, 92, 96, 99–103, 173–174, 179
Justice and Reconciliation Commission 89

Kalima 75
King's Dilemma 3
Koutla 43–44, 50, 52, 57, 70–74

Lamalif 75
League of Moroccan *'Ulama* 7, 39, 53–54, 84
Lyautey, Hubert 5, 22, 24

*makhzen* 4, 6, 8, 10, 17–20, 22, 25–26, 43, 57, 61–62, 84, 120, 157, 181
migration 68, 119, 155, 168–170, 173, 175
military coups 37, 43, 160
MINURSO *see* United Nations Mission for a Referendum in Western Sahara
*mise à niveau* 128, 138–139
Mobility Partnership 169
Mohamed V 3, 6–8, 17, 26–31, 33–34, 38, 40, 54, 67, 85, 116, 120, 150, 153
Moroccan Communist Party 27, 39, 46
Moroccanisation 11, 45–47, 115, 121–122, 130, 144
*Moudawana see* family code
Movement of All Democrats 90, 97
MP *see* Popular Movement

National Independence Party 27
National Initiative for Human Development 95, 113, 134–138
National Union of Popular Forces 32–33, 39–41, 43–47, 52, 58, 63
Nationalist movement 2–3, 5, 7–8, 14, 20, 24–25, 27–29, 39–41, 43–46, 48, 51–52, 74, 77–78, 116, 150–151, 153, 156, 159

OCP *see* Office Chérifien des Phosphates
Office Chérifien des Phosphates 86
Omnium Nord Africain 10, 121, 130–131, 133
ONA *see* Omnium Nord Africain
Opération Ecouvillon 157
Oufkir, Mohamed 42, 44–45, 49

PAM *see* Authenticity and Modernity Party
parliament 2–3, 7, 41–43, 50, 55, 57, 59–60, 70–75, 83–84, 86, 88–90, 92–93, 96, 98, 100, 126, 132, 167, 173
Party of Progress and Socialism 9, 46–47
phosphates 23, 86, 123, 137, 139, 141
PJD *see* Justice and Development Party
Plan d'Action pour l'Intégration de la Femme au développement 80, 83, 93
Polisario 50, 58, 150, 157–165, 168, 170–171, 173
Popular Movement 8–9, 31–32, 34, 49, 74–75, 77–78, 82, 87, 100, 116, 133
PPS *see* Party of Progress and Socialism
privatisation 10, 85, 116, 124–125, 128, 130–132, 134, 138, 141, 143
protectorate 5, 7, 21–26, 30, 66, 115

Qarawiyyin University 26, 54, 61, 66

Royal Advisory Council for Saharan Affairs 85
Royal Institute for Amazigh Culture 85
rural exodus 42, 49, 54, 67–68, 77, 114, 119, 127, 133, 135, 144

SADR *see* Saharan Arab Democratic Republic
Saharan Arab Democratic Republic 160–163, 171
*salafiyya* 5, 21–23, 25–26, 51, 91
Sand War 55, 153–154, 159
Shabiba Islamiyya 48, 60, 63
*shari'a* 24–25, 53, 77, 79, 82, 93
*shurfa* 17–18, 43, 53, 78, 152
*siba* 4, 20, 24, 61–62, 157, 181
Socialist Union of Popular Forces 9, 45, 47–51, 57–59, 69–76, 86–87, 96, 100–101, 124
Structural Adjustment 63, 120, 123–124, 134

*tahara* 6, 53
Tanger-Med 14, 134, 143
*tariqa* 22, 28, 51, 61, 64

Tazmamart 69
Tindouf 32, 151, 153–154, 157, 159–160, 162–163, 173
Tripartite Agreement 160, 170

UMA *see* Arab Maghreb Union
United Nations Mission for a Referendum in Western Sahara 162–164
USFP *see* Socialist Union of Popular Forces

Washington Consensus 125
Western Sahara, 3, 6, 14, 32, 43, 45–50, 55, 57–59, 68, 70, 85, 98, 101, 103, 113, 123, 142, 150–153, 156–163, 165–166, 170–175, 180
women's rights 75–80, 83, 85, 93–95, 173
World Bank 10, 80, 93, 114, 117, 120, 122–127, 132, 135, 141
World Trade Organization 125, 143
WTO *see* World Trade Organization

Yassine, Abdessalam 54, 57, 62, 64–65, 69–70, 81, 83, 95, 179
Years of Lead, 18, 95, 99, 181

*zawiyya* 4, 51, 63

# eBooks from Taylor & Francis

Helping you to choose the right eBooks for your Library

Add to your library's digital collection today with Taylor & Francis eBooks. We have over 50,000 eBooks in the Humanities, Social Sciences, Behavioural Sciences, Built Environment and Law, from leading imprints, including Routledge, Focal Press and Psychology Press.

**Choose from a range of subject packages or create your own!**

Benefits for you
- Free MARC records
- COUNTER-compliant usage statistics
- Flexible purchase and pricing options
- 70% approx of our eBooks are now DRM-free.

Benefits for your user
- Off-site, anytime access via Athens or referring URL
- Print or copy pages or chapters
- Full content search
- Bookmark, highlight and annotate text
- Access to thousands of pages of quality research at the click of a button.

**Free Trials Available**

We offer free trials to qualifying academic, corporate and government customers.

## eCollections

Choose from 20 different subject eCollections, including:

- Asian Studies
- Economics
- Health Studies
- Law
- Middle East Studies

## eFocus

We have 16 cutting-edge interdisciplinary collections, including:

- Development Studies
- The Environment
- Islam
- Korea
- Urban Studies

For more information, pricing enquiries or to order a free trial, please contact your local sales team:

UK/Rest of World: **online.sales@tandf.co.uk**
USA/Canada/Latin America: **e-reference@taylorandfrancis.com**
East/Southeast Asia: **martin.jack@tandf.com.sg**
India: **journalsales@tandfindia.com**

**www.tandfebooks.com**